Learning Strategies in
Second Language Acquisition

THE CAMBRIDGE APPLIED LINGUISTICS SERIES

Series editors: Michael H. Long and Jack C. Richards

This new series presents the findings of recent work in applied linguistics which are of direct relevance to language teaching and learning and of particular interest to applied linguists, researchers, language teachers, and teacher trainers.

In this series:

Interactive Approaches to Second Language Reading *edited by Patricia L. Carrell, Joanne Devine, and David E. Eskey*

Second Language Classrooms – Research on teaching and learning *by Craig Chaudron*

Language Learning and Deafness *edited by Michael Strong*

The Learner-Centred Curriculum *by David Nunan*

The Second Language Curriculum *edited by Robert Keith Johnson*

Language Transfer – Cross-linguistic influence in language learning *by Terence Odlin*

Linguistic Perspectives on Second Language Acquisition *edited by Susan M. Gass and Jaquelyn Schacter*

Learning Strategies in Second Language Acquisition *by J. Michael O'Malley and Anna Uhl Chamot*

The Development of Second Language Proficiency *edited by Birgit Harley, Patrick Allen, Jim Cummins and Merrill Swain*

Second Language Writing – Research insights for the classroom *edited by Barbara Kroll*

Genre Analysis – English in academic and research settings *by John M. Swales*

Evaluating Second Language Education *edited by J. Charles Alderson and Alan Beretta*

Perspectives on Pedagogical Grammar *edited by Terence Odlin*

Academic Listening *edited by John Flowerdew*

Power and Inequality in Language Education *edited by James W. Tollefson*

Learning Strategies in Second Language Acquisition

J. Michael O'Malley
Georgetown University

Anna Uhl Chamot
Georgetown University

CAMBRIDGE
UNIVERSITY PRESS

Published by the Press Syndicate of the University of Cambridge
The Pitt Building, Trumpington Street, Cambridge CB2 1RP
40 West 20th Street, New York, NY 10011-4211, USA
10 Stamford Road, Oakleigh, Melbourne 3166, Australia

© Cambridge University Press 1990

First published 1990
Fourth printing 1995

Library of Congress Cataloging-in-Publication Data
O'Malley, J. Michael.
Learning strategies in second language acquisition / J. Michael
O'Malley, Anna Uhl Chamot.
p.   cm. – (The Cambridge applied linguistics series)
Bibliography: p.
Includes index.
ISBN 0-521-35286-X (hardback) – ISBN 0-521-35837-X (paperback)
1. Second language acquisition.   1. Chamot, Anna Uhl.   II. Title.
III. Series.
P118.2.043   1990
418'.007–dc20   89-9770
                                                                              CIP

British Library Cataloging in Publication Data
O'Malley, J. Michael
Learning strategies in second language acquisition.–
– (The Cambridge applied linguistics series)
1. Foreign language skills. Acquisition
1. Title   II. Chamot, Anna Uhl
401'.9

ISBN 0-521-35837-X paperback

Transferred to digital printing 2002

Contents

Series editors' preface   viii
Preface   ix

1 **Introduction**   1
    Background   3
        Research on learning strategies   3
        Theoretical background in second language acquisition   8
    Overview of the book   13

2 **A cognitive theory of learning**   16
    Background   16
    Language as a cognitive skill   19
        Representation in memory   20
        Stages of skill acquisition   25
        Complements to the stage-related theory of learning   27
        Language comprehension   33
        Language production   37
    Learning strategies as cognitive skills   42
        Definition and classification   43
        Strategies as cognitive processes   47
    Conclusions   54

3 **How cognitive theory applies to second language acquisition**   56
    Background   57
    Relationship of cognitive theory to specific constructs   68
        Declarative knowledge   68
        Procedural knowledge   73
        Stages of skill acquisition   77
    Conclusions   83

4 **Learning strategies: methods and research**   85
    A framework for data collection on learning strategies   86
        Objective of data collection   86
        Language task   88

Temporal relationship   90
Informant training   91
Elicitation procedures   92
Individual versus group data collection   95
Multiple data collection procedures   95
Issues in the use of self-report data   96
Review of research on applications of learning strategies   98
Definition and classification   99
Descriptions of strategy applications   104
Validation of strategy effectiveness   107
Conclusions   112

5 **Strategies used by second language learners**   114
Study 1: learning strategies used by beginning and intermediate ESL students   114
Study 2: learning strategies used by foreign language students   123
Study 3: listening comprehension strategies used by ESL students   128
Study 4: longitudinal study of learning strategies used by foreign language students for different language tasks   133
Summary   143
Metacognitive and cognitive strategies   144
Declarative versus procedural knowledge   145
Stages of skill acquisition   147
Experts versus novices   149
Conclusions   150

6 **Instruction in learning strategies**   151
Issues in instruction   152
Separate versus integrated instruction   152
Direct versus embedded instruction   153
Instructional implementation   154
Student characteristics   160
Review of representative studies   165
Instruction in learning strategies for second language acquisition   165
Learning strategy instruction in first language contexts   167
Study 1: learning strategy instruction with students of English as a second language   170
Study 2: learning strategies taught by foreign language instructors   175
Conclusions   184

7 **Learning strategies: models and materials**   187
Instructional models in first language contexts: strategic
teaching   187
Instructional models in second language contexts: the Cognitive
Academic Language Learning Approach   190
　　Theoretical framework of CALLA   191
　　The components of CALLA   193
　　CALLA lesson plan model   201
Second language learning strategy training materials   204
　　Learning strategy materials for adult language learners   204
　　Learning strategy materials for content-based ESL   210
Conclusions   212

8 **Summary and conclusions**   214
Theoretical developments   214
Research   220
　　Definitional/classification studies   220
　　Strategy description   222
　　Validation studies   224

Glossary   229
References   235
Author index   249
Subject index   253

Series editors' preface

Second language teaching in recent years has moved away from the quest for the perfect teaching method, focusing instead on how successful teachers and learners actually achieve their goals. In the case of teachers, this has led to classroom-centered research on the linguistic, discoursal, and interactional structure of teaching events. In the case of learners, it has led to the study of (1) how learners approach learning, both in and out of classrooms, and (2) the kinds of strategies and cognitive processing they use in second language acquisition.

This latter perspective — learning strategies — is the subject of this important book. J. Michael O'Malley and Anna Uhl Chamot survey the role of cognitive processes in second language learning, reviewing the literature on cognitive processes and language learning, and reporting on large-scale empirical investigations of their own. In the process, the authors offer a highly readable account of the nature and significance of learning strategies, and demonstrate how the research findings on learner strategies can be used as a basis for planning more effective instructional practices. This new title in the Cambridge Applied Linguistics Series hence adds another dimension to what we know about second language acquisition. It also shows how the field of second language teaching can benefit from a greater consideration of the role of cognitive strategies in both the comprehension and learning of second and foreign languages.

Michael H. Long
Jack C. Richards

Preface

In writing this book, we have had a number of goals in mind. Our primary goal is to respond to a need for information on how instruction in second language acquisition can be integrated with recent knowledge from cognitive theory and research on learning strategies. A second goal is to address the need for a synthesis of research and theory in cognition with research and current views of second language acquisition. And a third goal is to respond to the need among second language teachers for guidance on how to present instruction that capitalizes on the knowledge and skills students bring to classrooms and encourages the development of new and more effective strategies for learning.

We have sensed a strong division between linguistic theory and cognitive psychology that originates in part in differing aims and methods but is also related to the rejection of behaviorism by linguists. Whereas cognitive psychology also rejected behaviorism, it has been influenced heavily by linguistics. However, the communication has not occurred in both directions. Very few ideas from cognitive psychology appear to have been adopted in second language acquisition research and theory. As much as the original schism between behaviorism and linguistics may have been necessary, we would like to contribute toward bridging the gap and show how recent thinking in cognitive psychology can be useful for applications in second language acquisition.

We have also sensed that deliberate cognitive processing is ignored, if not disparaged, under prevailing views in second language instruction. The rationale seems to be that true "acquisition" of a second language is said to occur without awareness, that conscious mediation is thought to slow processes that otherwise might occur automatically, and that acquisition in classrooms occurs most effectively when teachers concentrate on making input comprehensible. We wish to show that this notion is only partially accurate, tends to be misleading as stated, and leads to inappropriate consequences for instruction, such as the limited view that a teacher's primary role is to provide comprehensible input. We would prefer to replace it with the view that language learning involves many conscious decisions at both the cognitive and metacognitive levels, which parallel cognitive processes in learning other complex cognitive skills. We would like to see more individuals adopt the view that teachers can encourage and assist students in using effective strategies for learning and can extend and challenge the student's mastery of the language by introducing academic language embedded in substantive content.

Finally, we have sensed that instructional approaches in second language acquisition are rarely based on sound theory and research on how individuals learn. We wish to encourage stronger linkages between theory and practice by illustrating how an instructional model can originate in theory and research and move toward classroom practices that are useful, understandable, and effective for teachers and for students.

This book builds on our previous work on an instructional approach for students with limited English proficiency. The approach is based on cognitive theory and integrates academic language development, content area instruction, and instruction in the application of learning strategies to facilitate the acquisition of both content and language. The approach is referred to as the Cognitive Academic Language Learning Approach (CALLA) and is introduced here in Chapter 6. This book examines the linkages among theory, research, and practice underlying CALLA more closely than in our previous work, which tended to isolate theory, research, or practice in separate publications. The instructional materials we have already published in social studies and mathematics use content-based ESL in a communication-based approach that incorporates learning strategies, academic language development, cooperative learning, and other principles that are characteristic of CALLA. The present book has helped us clarify the thinking underlying both the CALLA model and the development of materials; we believe it will lead to further refinements in our attempts to develop future research and to expand upon and implement the instructional approach.

The intended audience for this book includes applied linguists, educational researchers, teacher trainers, course designers, and language teachers who wish to apply research findings on learning strategies in second language acquisition to their classrooms and help students become more effective and independent learners. These individuals may have interests in English as a second language, bilingual education, or foreign language instruction. Those with interests in second language acquisition in general may include academic researchers or professors, current teachers, teachers-in-training, and curriculum designers. The book may find use in undergraduate and graduate programs, in in-service training programs, or as a text or reference in courses on research and theory. We would be particularly pleased if the book were used by

1 CALLA is a registered trademark of Second Language Learning, Inc.

graduate students interested in selecting a topic for dissertation research in any of these areas.

We have had the opportunity to describe many of the ideas presented in this book at teacher training workshops, in university in-service training courses, and at professional conferences. We wish to acknowledge all of the teachers, teacher trainers, researchers, and other individuals who participated in those activities for challenging us to refine our thinking and to express the concepts with greater clarity. We have also had the opportunity to publish some of the research, theory, and instructional applications in professional journals and have profited greatly from comments by anonymous reviewers. We wish to acknowledge the contributions of Carol Walker of the Catholic University of America, who was co-author on one of these publications, is responsible for introducing us to John Anderson's work, and wrote portions of a government report from which we extrapolated pieces contained in Chapter 2. We are also thankful for the contributions of our other co-authors and fellow researchers on some of those studies, including Maria Impink-Hernandez, Lisa Küpper, Rocco Russo, and Gloria Stewner-Manzanares. We especially wish to express our gratitude for the support of Jack Richards and Michael Long, the editors of the Cambridge Applied Linguistic Series, for comments by Barry McLaughlin of the University of California at Santa Cruz, and for the continuing support and encouragement offered by Ellen Shaw, ESL editor at Cambridge University Press. The book is a finer product for all that they have contributed.

The learning strategies research with ESL students and some of the theoretical work reported in this book was supported by the U.S. Army Research Institute for the Behavioral and Social Sciences in Alexandria, Virginia, under Contracts MDA 903–82–C–0169 and MDA 803–85–0200. We benefitted greatly from the contributions of project officers and other individuals at ARI, including Richard Kern, Harry O'Neil, Mark Sabol, Zita Simutis, and Rick Yekovich. The research with foreign language students reported in this book was supported under grant number 017BH60005 from the U.S. Department of Education. The project officers for this work were Robert Dennis and José Martinez. Naturally, the views and opinions expressed in this book are those of the authors and should not be construed to represent official positions or policy of either the Department of the Army or the Department of Education, unless so stated.

Last, but most important, we each wish to express our appreciation for the support provided by our respective families throughout the writing of this book. That support is the key to maintaining a balance between professional and family involvement, which enabled this work to be completed.

1 Introduction

This book is concerned with "learning strategies," the special thoughts or behaviors that individuals use to help them comprehend, learn, or retain new information. It focuses on the application of learning strategies to second language acquisition by students learning English as a second language as well as by students learning foreign languages. The book addresses the need for an integrated treatment of learning strategies in second language acquisition that is based on theory and research. The theory used here describes how second languages are learned and what role learning strategies play in the language acquisition process. The theory is also used to organize the presentation of research results, examine the findings, and integrate the results with other studies.

The research and theory described in this book are based on a cognitive information processing view of human thought and action. Two fundamental principles underlying this theory are: (a) that behavior can best be explained by reference to how individuals perceive and interpret their experiences, and (b) that the way in which individuals think and reason has parallels with the manner in which computers process information (Shuell 1986). In cognitive theory, individuals are said to "process" information, and the thoughts involved in this cognitive activity are referred to as "mental processes." Learning strategies are special ways of processing information that enhance comprehension, learning, or retention of the information.

This volume presents the view that language is a complex cognitive skill that can be described within the context of cognitive theory. A theory of second language acquisition, to be successful, must be able to describe how knowledge about language is stored in memory and how the process of second language acquisition ultimately results in automatic language comprehension and production. In addition, to be credible, the theory must explain a wide variety of language constructs that have been discussed in the first and second language acquisition literature. For our purposes, we add the further constraint that the theory be able to describe what learning strategies are, how information about learning strategies is stored in memory, how strat-

1

egies are learned and may become automatic, and why they influence learning in a positive manner.

At the onset of our research on learning strategies in 1981, there was no theory to guide our studies and few empirical investigations into the nature of learning strategies and their influence on second language acquisition. What did exist were a few descriptive studies of strategies used by effective second language learners and, quite significantly, over ten years of extensive research in psychology on the influence of learning strategies on reading comprehension and problem solving. The two bodies of research, one in second language acquisition and the other in cognitive psychology, had proceeded fully independent of each other with little cross-referencing of concepts and approaches across topic areas. Furthermore, the methodologies in the studies were different, the ones in second language acquisition being descriptive, and the ones in psychology being experimental and oriented toward training learners to acquire strategies. What these bodies of research had in common was an interest in the mental processes of experts compared with novices, and an undeniable paucity of theory to describe what strategies were or how they influenced learning. The lack of theory to explain learning strategies was compounded in second language acquisition studies by the lack of a comprehensive theory to explain how individuals learn the structures and functions associated with second language use. Only recently have papers appeared in which learning strategies are integrated within cognitive theory (e.g., Rabinowitz and Chi 1987; Garner 1986; Mayer 1988), but when we began our research there was a vacuum with respect to the integration of strategic processing in theories of second language acquisition. We hope to address and at least partially resolve this issue in the later chapters.

The notion that special learner techniques or strategies might assist second language acquisition is actually quite new, having emerged in the research literature just over ten years ago. The suggestion that the "good language learner" might be doing something special or different that we could all learn from was introduced at about the same time in work by Rubin (1975) and by Stern (1975). This notion contrasts sharply with the idea that some people just have an "ear" for language or that some individuals have an inherent ability for language learning. This early work anticipated what cognitive psychologists were realizing independently, that competent individuals are effective because of special ways of processing information. There was also the suggestion that these strategies are not the preserve of highly capable individuals, but could be learned by others who had not discovered them on their own.

Background

In this section we introduce some of the early studies on learning strategies in second language acquisition and cognitive psychology in order to establish a framework for describing the research presented in later chapters. These studies provided the empirical background for the initial investigations we developed. In later chapters we expand upon this selective review to present a more detailed examination of research and to analyze some of the more recent findings concerning learning strategies, leading up to a detailed description of our own work. This section continues with an introduction to relevant theoretical positions on language competence and second language acquisition that were current when we began our studies. We expand upon this description in far greater detail in subsequent chapters, and indicate implications for instructional practice.

Research on learning strategies

The literature on learning strategies in second language acquisition emerged from a concern for identifying the characteristics of effective learners. Research efforts concentrating on the "good language learner" (Naiman et al. 1978; Rubin 1975) had identified strategies reported by students or observed in language learning situations that appear to contribute to learning. These efforts demonstrated that students do apply learning strategies while learning a second language and that these strategies can be described and classified. For example, Rubin (1981) proposed a classification scheme that subsumes learning strategies under two primary groupings and a number of subgroups, as illustrated in Table 1.1.

Rubin's first primary category, consisting of strategies that directly affect learning, includes clarification/verification, monitoring, memorization, guessing/inductive reasoning, deductive reasoning, and practice. The second primary category, consisting of strategies that contribute indirectly to learning, includes creating practice opportunities and using production tricks such as communication strategies. Rubin based her strategies on fairly extensive data collection in varied settings, which included about fifty hours of classroom observation, observation of a small group of students working on a strip story, analysis of self-reports from "a few students" instructed to write down what they did to learn a second language, and analysis of daily journal entries of two students who were directed to report on strategies after having been given strategy examples. The classroom observations proved to be the least useful of these methods for identifying strategies.

TABLE 1.1. CLASSIFICATIONS OF LEARNING STRATEGIES IN SECOND LANGUAGE ACQUISITION

Author	Primary strategy classification	Representative secondary strategies	Representative examples
Rubin (1981)	Strategies that directly affect learning	Clarification/verification	Asks for an example of how to use a word or expression, repeats words to confirm understanding
		Monitoring	Corrects errors in own/other's pronunciation, vocabulary, spelling, grammar, style
		Memorization	Takes note of new items, pronounces out loud, finds a mnemonic, writes items repeatedly
		Guessing/inductive inferencing	Guesses meaning from key words, structures, pictures, context, etc.
		Deductive reasoning	Compares native/other language to target language Groups words Looks for rules of co-occurrence Experiments with new sounds
		Practice	Repeats sentences until pronounced easily Listens carefully and tries to imitate
	Processes that contribute indirectly to learning	Creates opportunities for practice	Creates situation with native speaker Initiates conversation with fellow students Spends time in language lab, listening to TV, etc.
		Production tricks	Uses circumlocutions, synonyms, or cognates Uses formulaic interaction Contextualizes to clarify meaning

Naiman et al. (1978)	Active task approach	Responds positively to learning opportunity or seeks and exploits learning environments	Student acknowledges need for a structured learning environment and takes a course prior to immersing him/herself in target language
			Reads additional items
			Listens to tapes
		Adds related language learning activities to regular classroom program	Writes down words to memorize
			Looks at speakers' mouth and repeats
			Reads alone to hear sounds
		Practices	Uses cognates
			Using what is already known
			Uses rules to generate possibilities
	Realization of language as a system	Analyzes individual problems	Relates new dictionary words to others in same category
		Makes L1/L2 comparisons	
		Analyzes target language to make inferences	
		Makes use of fact that language is a system	
	Realization of language as a means of communication and interaction	Emphasizes fluency over accuracy	Does not hesitate to speak
			Uses circumlocutions
		Seeks communicative situations with L2 speakers	Communicates whenever possible
			Establishes close personal contact with L2 native speakers
			Writes to pen pals
	Management of affective demands	Finds sociocultural meanings	Memorizes courtesies and phrases
		Copes with affective demands in learning	Overcomes inhibition to speak
			Is able to laugh at own mistakes
			Is prepared for difficulties
	Monitoring L2 performance	Constantly revises L2 system by testing inferences and asking L2 native speakers for feedback	Generates sentences and looks for reactions
			Looks for ways to improve so as not to repeat mistakes

An alternative classification scheme proposed by Naiman et al. (1978), also shown in Table 1.1, contains five broad categories of learning strategies and a number of secondary categories. The primary strategies were found to be common to all good language learners interviewed, whereas the secondary strategies were represented only in some of the good learners. The primary classification includes an active task approach, realization of language as a system, realization of language as a means of communication and interaction, management of affective demands, and monitoring of second language performance. Naiman et al. based this classification scheme on interviews with thirty-four good language learners and an initial strategy scheme suggested earlier by Stern (1975). Naiman et al. also identified what they referred to as "techniques" for second language learning, which differed from strategies in their scheme by being focused on specific aspects of language learning. The techniques, with selected examples of each, are as follows:

Sound acquisition
repeating aloud after a teacher, a native speaker, or a tape;
listening carefully; and
talking aloud, including role playing.

Grammar
following rules given in texts;
inferring grammar rules from texts;
comparing L1 and L2; and
memorizing structures and using them often.

Vocabulary
making up charts and memorizing them;
learning words in context;
learning words that are associated;
using new words in phrases;
using a dictionary when necessary; and carrying a notebook to note new items.

Listening comprehension
listening to the radio, records, TV, movies, tapes, etc.; and
exposing oneself to different accents and registers.

Learning to talk
not being afraid to make mistakes;
making contact with native speakers;
asking for corrections; and
memorizing dialogues.

Learning to write
having pen pals;
writing frequently; and
frequent reading of what you expect to write.

Learning to read
reading something every day;
reading things that are familiar;

reading texts at the beginner's level; and
looking for meaning from context without consulting a dictionary.

Among the various techniques Naiman's group identified, those associated with vocabulary learning were used most frequently. This is significant because it suggests that learners either have difficulty in identifying what techniques they use to learn other tasks or have few strategic processes for doing so. More recently, Oxford (1985) has compiled an extensive list of strategies identified in these studies and in our early studies that will be described in this book (e.g., O'Malley, Chamot, Stewner-Manzanares, Küpper, and Russo 1985a). However, Oxford's approach was not available when we began our work.

As can be seen from an inspection of the strategies in Table 1.1 and from the Naiman group's techniques, a number of highly useful deliberate approaches to learning a second language have been identified. Most of these emerged from interviews or, with Rubin, from interviews and diaries. The Rubin and Naiman et al. classification schemes are substantially different, however, and do not have any grounding in theories of second language acquisition or cognition. Consequently, it is difficult to winnow out from the extensive listing of strategies and techniques which ones are fundamental for learning, which ones might be most useful to other learners, and which should be combined with others to maximize learning effectiveness.

Research on training second language learners to use learning strategies has been limited almost exclusively to applications with vocabulary tasks. Dramatic improvements in vocabulary learning tasks presented in one-on-one training have been reported in these studies. The typical approach in this research has been either to encourage students to develop their own associations for linking a vocabulary word with its equivalent in the second language (Cohen and Aphek 1980, 1981) or to train students to use specific types of linking associations to cue the target word, such as the keyword method (e.g., Atkinson and Raugh 1975; Levin 1981; Pressley et al. 1980; Pressley et al. 1981). The strategy training in these vocabulary studies was given individually or was provided to groups by an experimenter using special audio equipment for each subject. There were no instances in which training in learning strategies in second language acquisition was performed in a natural classroom instructional setting or by the teacher of the students who served as subjects.

In cognitive psychology, studies of learning strategies with first language learners have concentrated on determining the effects of strategy training on different kinds of tasks and learners. Findings from these studies generally indicated that strategy training is effective in improving the performance of students on a wide range of reading comprehension and problem-solving tasks (e.g., Brown et al. 1983; Chipman, Segal,

and Glaser 1985; Dansereau 1985; Segal, Chipman, and Glaser 1985).
One of the more important outcomes of these psychological studies was
the formulation of learning strategies in an information-processing theoretical model. This model contains an executive, or metacognitive,
function in addition to an operative, or cognitive-processing, function.
Metacognitive strategies involve thinking about the learning process,
planning for learning, monitoring of comprehension or production while
it is taking place, and self-evaluation after the learning activity has been
completed. *Cognitive strategies* are more directly related to individual
learning tasks and entail direct manipulation or transformation of the
learning materials (Brown and Palincsar 1982). A third type of learning
strategy identified in the literature on cognitive psychology concerns the
influence of social and affective processes on learning. Examples of *so-
cial/affective strategies* are cooperative learning, which involves peer
interaction to achieve a common goal in learning (e.g., Dansereau et al.
1983; Slavin 1980), and asking questions for clarification. Affective
strategies are represented in the exercise of "self-talk," the redirecting
of negative thoughts about one's capability to perform a task with as-
surances that the task performance is within reach. Cooperative strategies have been shown to enhance learning on a variety of reading
comprehension tasks (Dansereau et al. 1983).

Research in metacognitive and cognitive learning strategies suggests
that transfer of strategy training to new tasks can be maximized by
pairing metacognitive strategies with appropriate cognitive strategies
(Brown et al. 1983). Students without metacognitive approaches are
essentially learners without direction or opportunity to plan their learning, monitor their progress, or review their accomplishments and future
learning directions. As will be seen in later chapters, the issue of transfer
is far from being resolved.

Theoretical background in second language acquisition

There has been no comprehensive analysis describing the influence of
cognition in second language acquisition. Nevertheless, at the time of
our initial investigations, a number of theorists had articulated positions
that included a cognitive component in second language processes. Theoretical efforts that can assist in identifying the role of cognition in
second language acquisition had emerged in two general areas: the attempt to describe language proficiency or language competence, and the
attempt to explain influences on second language acquisition. In each
of these areas, cognition had been described and defined but, as will be
seen, was not discussed in sufficient detail to delineate the role of cognition or strategic processing in second language acquisition.

Language proficiency has been described by Cummins (1984) in terms of two continua that concern task difficulty and the context in which language occurs. Difficulty may vary from cognitively undemanding tasks, such as learning definitions or reading road signs, to cognitively demanding tasks, such as reading or making an oral presentation on an academic topic. The context for language use may vary from contexts that are embedded, or enriched with linguistic or paralinguistic cues for meaning, to contexts that are reduced, or absent of such additional cues to meaning. Academic tasks, for example, tend to be cognitively demanding and usually require language in which contextual cues for meaning are reduced. Tasks outside the classroom, on the other hand, are often undemanding cognitively and are characterized by language that either has rich contextual clues or is formulaic and therefore easy to comprehend or produce. The task difficulty dimension, although based on the cognitive demands of the task, has not been used by Cummins to describe the potential role of strategic cognitive processes in enhancing learning or task performance.

The fundamental concept of language competence expressed by Cummins was extended by Tikunoff (1985) in a model intended to elaborate on the description of student functional proficiency in academic settings. To Cummins's (1984) notion of academic language proficiency, Tikunoff added three intersecting concepts: interactional, academic, and participative competence. For example, successful participation in a classroom setting requires that a student: (1) observe classroom social rules of discourse, (2) function at increasingly complex cognitive levels, and (3) be competent in the procedural rules of the class. As Cummins did with language competence, Tikunoff included a cognitive component but did not elaborate on the significance of strategic behavior for enhancing student comprehension or learning.

Other models of language competence also contained cognitive components but left the role of learning strategies ambiguous. Canale and Swain (1980) proposed a theoretical framework in which communicative competence has three major components. The first is grammatical competence, which includes vocabulary and pronunciation as well as grammatical structures and word forms. The second is sociolinguistic competence, which is made up of sociocultural rules for using language appropriately and discourse rules for linking parts of a language text coherently and cohesively. The third component of the Canale and Swain model is strategic competence, which consists of

verbal and non-verbal communication strategies that may be called into action to compensate for breakdowns in communication due to performance variables or to insufficient competence. (p. 30)

In this model, the strategic component refers to communication strategies, which can be differentiated from learning strategies by the intent of the strategy use. That is, learning strategies have learning as a goal, and communication strategies are directed toward maintaining communication (Tarone 1981).

The second area in which studies have assisted in identifying the role of cognition in second language acquisition was the theoretical efforts to identify important influences on second language acquisition. These efforts varied considerably in their attention to cognitive and strategic processing. One of the theorists who included an articulated cognitive component, Bialystok (1978), identified four categories of learning strategies in her model of second language learning: inferencing, monitoring, formal practicing, and functional practicing. In this model, learning strategies are defined as "optimal means for exploiting available information to improve competence in a second language" (p. 71). The type of strategy used by the learner depends on the type of knowledge required for a given task. Bialystok discussed three types of knowledge: explicit linguistic knowledge, implicit linguistic knowledge, and general knowledge of the world. She hypothesized that inferencing may be used with implicit linguistic knowledge and knowledge of the world. Monitoring, formal practicing (such as verbal drills found in a second language class), and functional practicing (such as completing a transaction at a store) contribute both to explicit and implicit linguistic knowledge. That is, strategies introduced explicitly in a formal setting can contribute to implicit linguistic knowledge and therefore to students' ability to comprehend and produce spontaneous language.

Bialystok's model can be contrasted to Krashen's Monitor Model (1982), which does not allow for contributions of explicit linguistic knowledge (learning) to implicit linguistic knowledge (acquisition). The Monitor Model includes two types of language processes: "acquisition" and "learning." "Acquisition" is described by Krashen as occurring in spontaneous language contexts, is subconscious, and leads to conversational fluency. "Learning," on the other hand, is equated with conscious knowledge of the rules of language derived from formal and traditional instruction in grammar. The "monitor" is a conscious process in which the learner applies grammatical rules to language production (either oral or written), which means that the monitor is a highly deliberate form of processing. In Krashen's view, "learning" does not lead to "acquisition," because the sole function of learning is to act as a monitor or editor of the learner's output. Therefore, the inescapable conclusion of this model is that conscious use of learning strategies will make little contribution to the development of language competence.

A comprehensive effort to integrate linguistic with affective and cognitive components of learning by Wong Fillmore and Swain reserved an important role for learning strategies in the cognitive component (Wong Fillmore 1985; Wong Fillmore and Swain 1984). Learning strategies were said to be the principal influence on the rate and level of second language acquisition for children, whereas inherent developmental and experiential factors were considered to be primarily responsible for first language acquisition. The types of strategies described by Wong Fillmore (1985) appear to be more global than those usually described in cognitive psychology, and include knowledge and mental skills as well as strategic processes. Wong Fillmore (1985) suggests that strategies include

> associative skills, memory, social knowledge, inferential skills ... analytical skills ... pattern recognition, induction, categorization, generalization, inference, and the like. (p. 37)

Wong Fillmore noted that differences in the rate and level of second language learning are due to the involvement of general cognitive processes, especially those that are important in language learning. In contrast, the consistency of first language acquisition across individuals is purportedly linked to inherent language acquisition mechanisms. The role that the strategies play with regard to the other model components or to mental processes in second language learning was not identified.

Movement toward a more cognitive view of second language acquisition was evident in the information processing approach suggested by McLaughlin, Rossman, and McLeod (1983). The learner is viewed as an active organizer of incoming information, with processing limitations and capabilities. While motivation is considered to be an important element in language learning, the learner's cognitive system is central to processing. The learner is able to store and retrieve information depending on the degree to which the information was processed. Evidence for aspects of the information processing model comes from studies of language processing and memory. One implication of information processing for second language acquisition is that learners actively impose cognitive schemata on incoming data in an effort to organize the information. McLaughlin et al. (1983) drew on cognitive theory in suggesting that learners may achieve automaticity in second language acquisition by using either a top-down approach (or knowledge-governed system), which makes use of internal schemata, or a bottom-up approach (or an input-governed system), which makes use of external input. In either case, cognition is involved, but the degree of cognitive involvement is set by the interaction between the requirements of the task and the knowledge and mental processes used by the learner.

More recently, Spolsky (1985) proposed a model of second language acquisition based on preference rules in which cognitive processes play an important role. In his view, three types of conditions apply to second language learning: necessary conditions, gradient conditions, and typicality conditions. A *necessary condition* is one that is required for learning to occur. Examples of necessary conditions in second language acquisition are target language input, motivation, and practice opportunities. The *gradient condition* is one in which the more frequently the condition occurs, the more likely learning is to take place. Examples of a gradient condition might be the greater or lesser degree to which a learner actively seeks out interactions with native speakers of the target language, or the greater or lesser degree to which a learner can fine tune a learning strategy to a specific task. The third type of condition is one that typically, but not necessarily, assists learning. An example of a *typicality condition* might be that of risk taking; thus, outgoing personalities tend to be good language learners as a rule, although in some cases quiet and reflective persons can be equally or more effective learners (Saville-Troike 1984).

Spolsky's model of second language acquisition contains two clusters of interrelated conditions representing these three types. The first cluster contains social context conditions, such as the learning setting and opportunities. The second cluster consists of learner factors, such as capability, prior knowledge, and motivation. The learner makes use of these latter conditions to interact with the social context of learning, and this interaction leads to the amount of language learning that takes place. Thus, this model accounts for variability in second language learning outcomes through differing degrees of (or preferences for) application of gradient and typicality conditions. In Spolsky's model, learning strategies, while not specifically identified as such, would be part of the capabilities and prior learning experiences that the learner brings to the task.

A precise description of the role of strategic processing in second language learning was missing from these theories of second language proficiency and acquisition. Although some of the theories proposed a cognitive component, and some indicated that cognitive processes influence proficiency or the rate and level of acquisition, the manner in which the influence of cognitive processes is exerted with respect to other mental processes or with respect to language tasks had not been described. Further, although information processing theory had been used to classify strategies into metacognitive and cognitive categories, agreement on the assignment of individual strategies to these two broad groupings had been difficult to achieve (Brown et al. 1983), and neither the theory nor the research had been extended to second language acquisition.

There was a need for clarification of the role of learning strategies in second language acquisition from both an empirical and a theoretical standpoint. One step that would help to clarify the definition and assignment of discrete strategies to a classification scheme would be to describe the correspondence between mental processes that have been identified in cognitive theory and strategic processes described in the learning strategies literature. Another step that would help in understanding the role of strategic processing in second language acquisition would be to use empirical data from language learners who are asked to describe what they do to assist second language comprehension and learning. This kind of information must be collected using different kinds of data collection procedures and different kinds of language tasks at different stages of second language acquisition. Another step that was needed was the extension of strategy training studies in which the influence of strategy use on language outcomes is determined. In planning the studies that are reported in Chapters 5 and 6, all of these issues, as well as research needs, played a prominent role.

Overview of the book

This background review sets the stage for introducing additional theory and research related to learning strategies and second language acquisition. Chapter 2 of this book presents a theoretical analysis of the role of cognition in learning. It introduces an information processing theory of memory based on the work of selected cognitive researchers, particularly John Anderson. The theory stresses the active nature of mental processes during learning and describes the types of information stored in long-term, as distinguished from short-term, memory. Information in long-term memory consists of declarative knowledge, or the facts we know, and procedural knowledge, or the complex cognitive skills and other processes we know how to perform. Language is stored much like any other complex cognitive skill but, like other procedural information, is learned differently from factual information. As will be seen, this difference has important implications for learning and instruction. We review some potential limitations of the theory and analyze the extent to which they present problems in the second language acquisition area. The cognitive theory is also used to examine language comprehension processes and language production. Finally, the theory is used as the foundation for relating learning strategies to cognitive processes and to show the influence of strategic processing on learning.

In Chapter 3, the review of cognitive theory in second language acquisition presented in Chapter 2 is updated with new research and theory. As will be seen, there has been additional discussion by some of the same theorists, while the views of others have either shifted or have become less important in view of more recent developments. We also analyze new contributions by researchers and theorists whose work was unknown to us earlier. The core of the chapter is our use of the cognitive theory introduced in Chapter 2 to describe many of the phenomena and constructs regularly discussed in the second language literature. One test of the theory is its success in portraying disparate concepts within a single theoretical framework. We believe that the theory stands up to this integrative test remarkably well considering that it was not intended originally to describe second language acquisition.

Chapter 4 presents descriptive research that is designed to identify and classify learning strategies. The data collection procedures used to identify learning strategies are reviewed, including interviews, observations, questionnaires, and "think-aloud" procedures. We review the rationale for using different data collection procedures and indicate the strengths and weaknesses of each. Some attention is devoted to the criticisms of self-report measures of strategic processing, and we analyze the adequacy of those criticisms. This chapter also reviews the early literature on learning strategies in both second language acquisition and cognitive psychology, including the early work in the second language area by Naiman et al. (1978) and Rubin (1975, 1981), as well as more recent work by Wenden (1983) and others.

In Chapter 5, we highlight and describe in detail the studies we have performed in both English as a second language and the foreign language areas, illustrating the use of different types of data collection methodologies, which include retrospective interviews and think-aloud procedures. One of the studies examines strategies used with a variety of language learning tasks that are characteristic of ESL classrooms, one focuses on listening comprehension, and others concentrate on the varied language tasks that are found in foreign language classrooms.

The focus of Chapter 6 is on studies in which second language students have been trained to use learning strategies. The chapter begins with an analysis of the training variables that influence the way in which strategy instruction for second language acquisition is presented. For example, one of the major issues is whether strategy training should be presented separately from or incorporated with course content. Another issue is the extent to which the strategies should be explicitly identified or should be embedded in the materials for a course. The chapter continues with an analysis of recent studies drawn from the psychological literature as well as those from the second language acquisition literature. Again, we highlight the studies we have conducted ourselves, one in an ESL setting and one in a foreign language instructional environment. In each of the two training studies we conducted, students were taught in the natural language learning environment of the classroom rather than trained in a laboratory. In the foreign language study, the trainer was the regular classroom teacher. The training approaches used in the studies are analyzed, with implications drawn for transfer of strategy training with both foreign language and ESL students.

Chapter 7 describes instructional models in which learning strategies play an important role. When we began our early studies, there were no formal instructional models containing learning strategies, although some instructional approaches and materials did exist. We describe a number of recent models designed for native English speakers and their potential applications to second language acquisition. We then describe our own content-based ESL model in which direct instruction in learning strategies plays an important role. This model was designed for students with limited English proficiency who are in their last year of either an ESL or a bilingual program, and who need a "bridge to the mainstream." For these students, selected content area instruction is provided, using language development instructional approaches and learning strategies. The model has been described more thoroughly elsewhere (Chamot and O'Malley 1986, 1987, in press) and is the foundation for instructional materials in social studies (Chamot 1987a,) and mathematics (Chamot and O'Malley 1988a,). It has also been used in teacher training in a number of locations throughout the country and is being implemented in whole or in part in a number of school districts.

The final chapter summarizes what we have learned from our research and theoretical developments and charts the future direction for work on learning strategies in second language acquisition research, theory, and practice.

2 A cognitive theory of learning

This chapter describes the rationale for advancing a cognitively based theory in second language acquisition and presents the foundation for the theory as it relates to constructs that will be discussed in later chapters. We suggest that second language acquisition cannot be understood without addressing the interaction between language and cognition, and indicate that at present this interaction is only poorly understood. Second language theorists have not capitalized on the available body of research and theory that has already been worked out in cognitive psychology. The chapter first identifies second language processes as having parallels with the way in which complex cognitive skills are described in cognitive theory. Aspects of cognitive theory are discussed that relate to memory representation and to the process of acquiring complex cognitive skills. The theory on which we rely most extensively is augmented in order to describe more adequately processes that occur in second language acquisition. We go on to discuss the way in which cognitive theory addresses specific language comprehension and language production processes, and conclude by indicating that cognitive theory can extend to describe learning strategies as complex cognitive skills. Finally, we introduce the major types of strategies on which we rely in later chapters.

Background

The fields of linguistics and cognitive psychology each contain separate paradigms for describing second language acquisition. Linguistic theories assume that language is learned separately from cognitive skills, operating according to different principles from most learned behaviors (e.g., Spolsky 1985). This assumption is represented in analyses of unique language properties, such as developmental language order, grammar, knowledge of language structures, social and contextual influences on language use, and the distinction between language learning and acquisition. Language and linguistic processes are viewed as interacting with cognition but nevertheless maintaining a separate identity that justifies investigation independent from cognitive processes (e.g., Wong

Fillmore and Swain 1984). Varied social processes may also be brought into theory formulations that are related to motivation for learning (see Cummins 1986; Gardner 1979; Schumann 1984; Wong Fillmore and Swain 1984). Cognitive processes, when represented at all in these theories, are typically concerned with various aspects of cognitive style and other predispositions for learning (see Wong Fillmore and Swain 1984).

These theoretical developments in second language acquisition serve as a general reference point but are not useful in explaining the role of cognitive processes in second language acquisition, because they fail to treat cognition and learning in the context of the larger and more extensive body of theory and research that has evolved in cognitive psychology. One of the principal cognitive processes that has not been addressed in these theories is learning strategies, or the "behaviors and thoughts that a learner engages in during learning that are intended to influence the learner's encoding process" (Weinstein and Mayer 1986, p. 315). Theory development in second language acquisition that addresses cognitive processes remains limited despite recent interest in the relationship between language and cognition (McLaughlin et al. 1983; Nagle and Sanders 1986; Spolsky 1985), and more specific theoretical interest in the role of learning strategies in second language acquisition (e.g., Bialystok 1978; Bialystok and Kellerman 1986).

The second paradigm for theory development in second language acquisition emerges from cognitive psychology and is based in part on information processing and in part on studies and theory that have evolved over the past fifteen years or so on the role of cognitive processes in learning. The role of learning strategies in the acquisition of information generally can be understood by reference to the information processing framework for learning. The purpose of this framework is to explain how information is stored in the memory and particularly how new information is acquired. In its simplest form, the framework suggests that information is stored in two distinct ways, either in *short-term memory*, the active working memory that holds modest amounts of information only for a brief period, or *long-term memory*, the sustained storage of information, which may be represented as isolated elements or more likely as interconnected networks (Lachman, Lachman, and Butterfield 1979; Shuell 1986; Weinstein and Mayer 1986). In some representations, *working memory* is used to describe short-term memory as a way of denoting the active use of cognitive procedures with the information being stored (Anderson 1985).

In this cognitive psychology paradigm, new information is acquired through a four-stage encoding process involving selection, acquisition, construction, and integration (Weinstein and Mayer 1986). Through *selection*, learners focus on specific information of interest in the environment, and transfer that information into working memory. In *ac-

quisition, learners actively transfer information from working memory into long-term memory for permanent storage. In the third stage, *construction*, learners actively build internal connections between ideas contained in working memory. The information from long-term memory can be used to enrich the learner's understanding or retention of the new ideas by providing related information or schemata into which the new ideas can be organized. In the final process, *integration*, the learner actively searches for prior knowledge in long-term memory and transfers this knowledge to working memory. Selection and acquisition determine *how much* is learned, whereas construction and integration determine *what* is learned and how it is organized.

The role of learning strategies in this formulation is to make explicit what otherwise may occur without the learner's awareness or may occur inefficiently during early stages of learning. Individuals may learn new information without consciously applying strategies or by applying inappropriate strategies that result in ineffective learning or incomplete long-term retention. Strategies that more actively engage the person's mental processes should be more effective in supporting learning. These strategies may become automatic after repeated use or after a skill has been fully acquired, although mental processes that are deployed without conscious awareness may no longer be considered strategic (Rabinowitz and Chi 1987).

The two-stage framework of short-term and long-term memory and the four mental processes described previously were not intended to meet the need for a theory to explain the role of cognition in second language acquisition. The framework has been applied most regularly to problem solving, vocabulary learning, reading comprehension, and the acquisition of factual knowledge, but not to the full range of phenomena that form the totality of language. A theory is needed that addresses multiple aspects of language for integrative language use in all four language skill areas – listening, speaking, reading, and writing – and that addresses language acquisition from the earliest stages of second language learning to proficient use of the target language. Further, the theory must be able to address language comprehension and production as central issues, as is required to represent topics of concern in second language acquisition research. The two-stage, four-process explanatory framework of learning presented earlier was not designed to address these concerns.

A specific advance beyond this framework emerged with the formulation in cognitive theory of mechanisms for representing complex cognitive skills. There are a number of ways to represent the competence that underlies performance of a complex cognitive skill such as language, including rational task analysis (Gagné and Paradise 1961), interrelated procedural networks (Brown and Burton 1978), and production systems (see Anderson 1980, 1983, 1985). Our discussion will focus on Anderson's production systems for five reasons:

1. Anderson's work integrates numerous concepts from prevailing notions of cognitive processing that give the theory generality and currency with regard to existing views in the field (see, for example, Shuell 1986).
2. Theoretical developments in production systems cover a broader range of behavior than other theories, including comprehension and production of oral and written texts as well as comprehension, problem solving, and verbal learning.
3. The theory distinguishes between factual knowledge and procedural skills in both memory representation and learning.
4. The theory can be expanded to incorporate strategic processing as part of the description of how information is learned.
5. The theory has been continually updated, expanded, and revised in a number of recent publications (e.g., Anderson 1983, 1985).

We then review Anderson's (1983, 1985) information processing theory of cognition and memory, as well as those of other cognitive theorists, and show how these theories can be used for discussing second language acquisition.

Language as a cognitive skill

The approach taken in our work is that second language acquisition is best understood as a complex cognitive skill. The theoretical framework in which we discuss second language acquisition therefore is based on a comprehensive model of cognitive skill learning. This approach has several advantages. First, considerable research in cognitive skill acquisition has occurred in recent years in such disciplines as cognitive psychology and in the information processing aspects of computer sciences (Anderson 1981; Gagné 1985). By applying relevant theories and models developed in these other disciplines to the study of second language acquisition, we are able to provide a comprehensive and well-specified theoretical framework that is consistent with related work. A second advantage to viewing second language acquisition as a cognitive skill is that the level of specificity and the "dynamic" or "process" orientation of models of skill acquisition allow us to provide a more detailed process view of second language acquisition than is provided by most current models of second language learning (see Chamot and Stewner-Manzanares 1985a; McLaughlin 1987a). A third advantage is that viewing language acquisition as a cognitive skill provides a mechanism for describing how language learning ability can be improved.

A fourth and related advantage is a pedagogical one, and pertains to the development and use of learning strategies in second language instruction. Anderson (1983, 1985) has described cognitive skill acquisition as a "three-stage" process, using a "production system" notation to specify the dynamics of the system during the skill acquisition process. This framework is particularly useful in the current context because it helps to identify and test the existence and applicability of specific learning strategies that are appropriate at various stages in the skill acquisition process. Nevertheless, as will be seen, the straightforward, three-stage process suggested by Anderson has some limitations, which become particularly evident when language is the complex cognitive skill under investigation.

Representation in memory

Anderson (1983, 1985) distinguishes between what we know *about*, or "static" information in memory, and what we know *how to do*, or "dynamic" information in memory. All of the things we know about constitute *declarative knowledge*, and the things we know how to do are *procedural knowledge*.

DECLARATIVE KNOWLEDGE

Examples of things we know about include the definitions of words, facts (such as "George Washington was the first president of the United States"), and rules (such as "*i* before *e* except after *c*"). Declarative knowledge need not be verbal. Although it often takes the form of abstract propositions, declarative knowledge can also take the form of temporal strings (cf. Tulving 1983), such as our memory for the order of events – that is, which things came earlier and later in our lives – or the form of images (cf. Gagné and White 1978), such as our memory for what a zebra looks like or the arrangement of our living room. Although the following rule of thumb is not always true, declarative knowledge can usually be expressed verbally, or "declared." Thus, we typically are able to describe the contents of declarative knowledge.

Declarative knowledge is maintained in long-term memory in terms of meaning instead of precisely replicated external events. While images and temporal strings play a role in memory, as suggested before, the most significant mode of storing information in memory for the analysis of language is through *propositional representations* (patterned after Kintsch 1974). Propositional representations maintain the meaning of information while ignoring unimportant details. Each proposition is denoted by a *relation* followed by an ordered list of *arguments*. In an example used by Anderson (1985),

Nixon gave a beautiful Cadillac to Brezhnev, who is leader of the USSR.

the relations correspond to the verbs (*give, is*), adjectives (*beautiful*), or other relational terms (*leader of*), while the arguments correspond to the nouns (*Nixon, Cadillac, Brezhnev*). The full ordered list of relations and arguments necessary to describe the proposition expressed in this sentence is usually expressed in parentheses and would include the agent of giving, the object given, the recipient of the giving, and the time of the giving, as in (*Give, Nixon, Cadillac, Brezhnev, Past*). In a propositional analysis, each complex sentence such as this one is differentiated into a number of simpler propositions on which the truth of the main proposition rests, such as

Nixon gave a Cadillac to Brezhnev. The Cadillac was beautiful. Brezhnev is the leader of the USSR.

These simpler propositions and their respective relations and arguments can be used to generate another original sentence, whose essential meaning would not change, such as

The leader of the USSR, Brezhnev, was given a Cadillac by Nixon and it was beautiful.

Anderson indicates that relations and arguments in a propositional analysis can be represented schematically by a *propositional network*, as illustrated in Figure 2.1. Each proposition in Figure 2.1 is shown as a circle, which is connected by labeled arrows to its relations and arguments. The basic unit or element of the propositional network is a *node*, as shown in the figure by the circles. The arrows connecting each node to its relations and arguments are referred to as *links*. The nodes are similar to the more commonly used term *ideas.* and the links are similar to what have more often been referred to as *associations*. The advantage of schematic representations of propositional networks lies in their depicting graphically the connections (associations) among the elements (ideas).

Representation of information in memory in terms of propositional networks has a number of important features. First, propositions can be organized hierarchically. The argument *Cadillac* is a specific instance of the broader set of arguments that exists for *cars*, and cars are characterized by certain properties such as being; a means of transportation, a four-wheeled vehicle, driver-controlled, and so forth. *Cadillac* is also an instance of arguments for *expensive* objects. Similarly, the USSR is an instance of countries possessing a communistic economy with which the United States, the country of which Nixon was president, has had considerable disagreements.

A second important feature of the propositional network is *spreading activation*, or the activation of additional concepts by evoking a single concept. When the label *Cadillac* appears, other associations with which

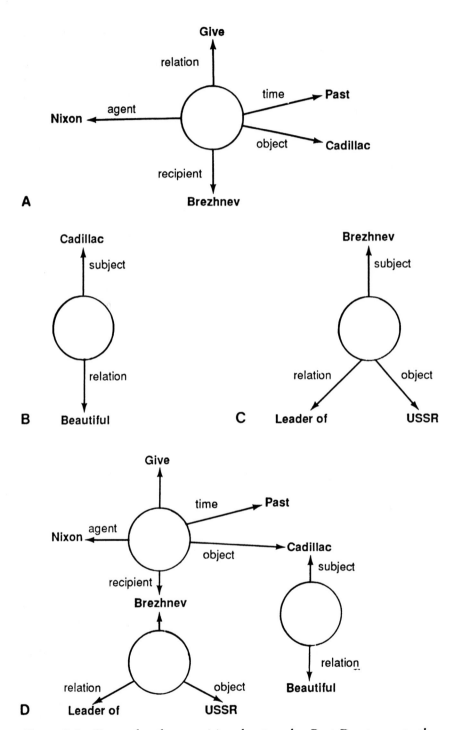

Figure 2.1   Example of propositional networks. Part D represents the combined networks A–C. (Adapted from Anderson 1985, p. 117.)

it is linked are activated in addition to those identified in the sentence. The same process occurs with the mention of Brezhnev. These hierarchies add information to the meaning of the sentence and may be used in understanding how the individual responds to the proposition. Giving an expensive vehicle to the leader of a country that was in disagreement with the United States may be seen as questionable. Thus, the sentence may produce a raised eyebrow of curiosity that might not have appeared had Nixon given the Cadillac to the leader of a country known to be on friendlier terms with the United States at the time. The important point is that these associations reside in the listener rather than in the sentence being communicated, are linked hierarchically to the initial concept, and are activated depending on their relationship in the prop-ositional network to the initial concept. Anderson suggests that working memory is defined as the range of nodes reached by spreading activation.

Larger units of meaning than can be represented by propositional networks require a *schema,* or a configuration of interrelated features that define a concept. The features or attributes used to define the concept *wheel* (as in tires for a car) may consist of the following interconnected list:

superset: object that rolls
material: rubber tire, mounted on metal inner wheel
contents: air
function: movement
shape: round, doughnutlike
size: 6"w x 27"d to 8"w x 36"d (approx.)
location: on axle of car

The schema for a wheel therefore consists of the specific values that a wheel has for these and perhaps other attributes. Schemata may be composed of propositional networks, but differ from them in two ways. First, any of the attributes in a schema may take on different values. For example, the concept *wheel* would be linked hierarchically within the superset *object that rolls* to the concepts *ball* and *cylinder,* each of which has its own values for the features indicated. Second, networks in schemata are interconnected with other networks. Each of the values specified for *wheel* has its own attributes that link it hierarchically to other concepts, as the concept *air* is linked to oxygen, hydrogen, and nitrogen.

The principal value of schemata is that they facilitate making infer-ences about concepts. If we hear the concept *wheel,* and the reference clearly is to the tires on a car, we understand that the wheel is round, is made of rubber, and has other features specified in the hierarchical organization. This inferential process is based on probabilities in that the wheel size may be substantially different if the car is a go-cart or a grand prix racer. Stated differently, the value of schemata is that they enable us to organize and understand new information. Upon hearing the word *wheel*, we can juxtapose the concept relative to other important and related concepts and thereby develop a broader understanding than is evident from the information supplied by any particular sentence.

New events tend to be encoded with respect to schemata, which can be used to infer information that is missing in recall. The probabilistic nature of schemata indicates that recall will be accurate if the inferences match the situation, but will be inaccurate if the inference and the situation fail to match. Thus, schemata may either assist or detract from accurate recall.

PROCEDURAL KNOWLEDGE

The term *cognitive skill* is used by Anderson (1980) to refer to the ability to perform various mental procedures. Our ability to understand and generate language or apply our knowledge of rules to solve a problem would be examples of *procedural knowledge*. Anderson argues that as we use the same knowledge over and over again in a procedure, we can lose our access to the rules that originally produced or enabled the procedure, and thus lose our ability to verbally report or "declare" these rules. Whereas declarative knowledge or factual information may be acquired quickly, procedural knowledge such as language acquisition is acquired gradually and only with extensive opportunities for practice. The representation of procedural knowledge in memory is a key issue in cognitive theory and is contained in what Anderson (1983, 1985) refers to as *production systems*.

PRODUCTION SYSTEMS

One of the problems in developing an effective and useful theory of cognitive skill acquisition has been understanding and explaining how complex cognitive skills are represented in human memory. Anderson (1983) argued for a unitary theory of the mind or a common cognitive system for all higher-level mental processes. This position is in direct contrast to the opinion of many theorists, including Chomsky (1980), who argue that the mind has specific faculties associated with language and perhaps with other special symbolic systems, such as numbers.

Recently, studies on artificial intelligence have made an important contribution to cognitive psychology by developing sets of procedural formalisms that serve as models of how complex cognitive skills can be represented in memory using uniform principles of representation. One such representational system, a production system, is briefly described here. Anderson argues that all complex cognitive skills can be represented as production systems. Computer simulations using production systems have been developed for a number of cognitive skills, including such seemingly diverse skills as reading (Thibadeau, Just, and Carpenter

1982), playing chess (Newell and Simon 1972), and solving algebra story problems (Bobrow 1968). In its most basic form, a production has a "condition" and an "action." The condition contains a clause or set of clauses preceded by IF, and the action has a clause or set of clauses preceded by THEN. Consider, for example, the following production for pluralization (Anderson 1980):

If the goal is to generate a plural of a noun, and the noun ends in a hard consonant, THEN generate the noun + /s/.

Note that one of the conditions for this production refers to an internal goal, an important point because as internal goals or states are satisfied or change for the learner, the IF clause will match different sets of stored conditions and the learner will execute different sets of actions. Condition-action pairs (or productions) such as this one can initially be represented in declarative form, and gradually, through practice, can be compiled into production sets and fine tuned to the point of automatic execution. Such a representational system can be used to represent specific procedures in any domain (math, physics, chess, language, and so on) as well as general strategies, or domain-independent problem-solving procedures. Moreover, the relationships among elements of a skill can be clearly specified, and the conditions that must exist for a particular skill to operate can be made explicit (see Gagné 1985 for a discussion of production system notation in the representation of basic skills).

Stages of skill acquisition

The important question that follows from the description of procedural knowledge in Anderson's theory is: "How does one proceed from the rule-bound declarative knowledge used in performance of a complex skill to the more automatic proceduralized stage?" Anderson (1983, 1985) described three stages of skill acquisition: the cognitive, associative, and autonomous stages.

COGNITIVE STAGE

For most learners, skill learning begins with the cognitive stage. During this stage, the learners are instructed how to do the task, observe an expert performing the task, or attempt to figure it out and study it themselves. This stage involves conscious activity on the part of the learner, and the acquired knowledge at this stage is typically declarative and can be described verbally by the learner. For instance, one can memorize vocabulary and the rules for grammar when learning to speak a second language, or learn from observation when to use an unanalyzed chunk of language appropriately, just as one can memorize any other set of facts. This knowledge enables the learner to describe how to communicate in the second language, but the knowledge by itself is inadequate for skilled performance, since the performance at this stage is very deliberate and tends to be laden with errors.

ASSOCIATIVE STAGE

During this second stage, two main changes occur with respect to the development of proficiency in the skill. First, errors in the original declarative representation of the stored information are gradually detected and eliminated. Second, the connections among the various elements or components of the skill are strengthened. Basically, during this stage the declarative knowledge is turned into its procedural form. However, the declarative representation initially formed is not always lost. Thus, even as we become more fluent at speaking a foreign language, we still remember its rules of grammar. Performance at this stage begins to resemble expert performance, but may still be slower and errors may still occur.

AUTONOMOUS STAGE

During the third, or autonomous, stage, the performance becomes increasingly fine-tuned. The execution or performance of the skill becomes virtually automatic, and errors that inhibit successful performance of the skill disappear. The skill can often be executed effortlessly, and there is much less demand on working memory or consciousness at this stage. Thus, as we become skilled drivers, we shift gears smoothly and automatically, without consciously applying rules. In fact, skilled drivers are typically able to drive and carry on a conversation at the same time, indicating that very little conscious processing is being devoted to driving (or perhaps to talking). The skill has become automatic and the driver is able to monitor its effective execution with very little effort. Similarly, as we become more proficient in a second language, we are able to comprehend and produce utterances with little difficulty. It is important to note that skilled performance improves gradually. While a fact can often be learned in one trial, a complex skill such as second language acquisition can only be mastered after a relatively long period of practice.

This specific, three-stage theory of skill acquisition assumes that individuals will learn the rules underlying performance of a complex skill as a precursor to competent and automatic skill execution. This process of skill acquisition is referred to as *knowledge compilation* and contains two basic components: *proceduralization* and *composition* (Gagné 1985). In proceduralization, the learner generates a propositional representation of a sequence of actions and converts this propositional representation into production systems. Composition consists of combining several productions that have already become automatic into a single production and serves to overcome the limitations of short-term memory, since the shorter action sequences that have already become automatic no longer impose demands on memory space. The limitations of short-term memory and the complexity of representing skill sequences in it are fundamental to why complex skills take a long time to learn.

Two other important aspects of this three-stage theory are *controlled* and *automatic processing* (LaBerge and Samuels 1974; Posner and Snyder 1975; Schneider and Shiffrin 1977; Shiffrin and Schneider 1977). Cognitive tasks may be conceived of as involving controlled processes, which require the attention of the learner, and automatic processes, which do not require the attention of the learner. In controlled processing, the skill performance entails activation of nodes in a sequence that is directed through attentional processes requiring the use of short-term memory. Accordingly, performance of the skill involves conscious effort, as in the cognitive stage of learning. Important portions of short-term memory are consumed by execution of the skill, and there is little capability remaining to perform additional skills. In automatic processing, nodes in long-term memory containing action sequences are activated, and the sequences can be performed without demands being placed on short-term memory. The activation is a learned response that has been built up over a considerable period of time, as is true in the autonomous stage described earlier. A complex skill can be performed without conscious or deliberate effort if it is processed automatically. Controlled and automatic processing are reflected in Anderson's cognitive and autonomous stages of learning.

Complements to the stage-related theory of learning

In this section we examine what appear to be three basic difficulties with Anderson's description of the stagewise acquisition of complex cognitive skills: the rule-bound nature of learning the theory expresses, the insistence on a single process to explain all forms of learning complex cognitive skills, and the possibility that the theory leads to an inefficient system of instruction.

LEARNING BY FORMAL RULES

The theory's reliance on a rule-bound system of learning is evident in Anderson's suggestion that declarative knowledge can become proceduralized through practice, and the implication that declarative knowledge for second language acquisition principally consists of the formal rules of language. Anderson (1980) uses the following example to draw the distinction between declarative and procedural knowledge in the context of second language acquisition:

When we learn a foreign language in a classroom situation, we are aware of the rules of the language, especially just after a lesson that spells them out. One might argue that our knowledge of the language at that time is declarative. We speak the learned language by using general rule-following procedures applied to the rules we have learned, rather than speaking directly, as we do in our native language. Not surprisingly, applying this knowledge is a much slower and more painful process than applying the procedurally encoded knowledge of our own language. Eventually, if we are lucky, we can come to know a foreign language as well as we know our native language. At that point, we often forget the rules of the foreign language. It is as if the class-taught declarative knowledge had been transformed into a procedural form. (p. 224)

Although Anderson does not indicate that this is the only way in which second language acquisition occurs, he gives no other examples to suggest that other processes are involved. The principal difficulties with this description are that not all the rules of languages construction are known, certainly not by most learners of a second language, and not all of the rules individuals use in second language acquisition are the ones taught in classrooms. Furthermore, not all second language acquisition occurs initially in classrooms, and not all second language classrooms focus on grammatical rules. Thus, the rules followed by a beginning learner may not be the easily identifiable rules of "grammar" but may emerge out of the individual's experiences, and thus represent an ad hoc usage rule.

The cognitive theory of acquiring complex cognitive skills that Anderson proposes is sufficiently flexible in our view to accommodate informal rules, or rules generated uniquely by individuals to explain their experiences with a language as well as to explain the more formal use of rules in proceduralization. This is demonstrated in Chapter 3, which illustrates how production systems can be used to explain communicative competence and its manifestations in sociolinguistic knowledge, discourse knowledge, strategic knowledge, and grammatical knowledge. Individuals generate their own rules for language formations, whether learning takes place within or outside formal classroom environments, and they use these rules in language comprehension or production whenever they are needed. The learner's selection of a rule should be independent of whether the rule is formal or informal, but selection should depend upon the rule's utility in assisting the individual to address the communication task at hand. As individuals can shift from one rule to the next and may do so with minimal demands on attention when the skill has become proceduralized (see Chapter 3), they may shift from a grammatical to a sociolinguistic rule depending on the task demands.

UNITARY PROCESS FOR LEARNING COMPLEX SKILLS

While there are some theorists who question whether separate processes are necessary to explain the acquisition of declarative and procedural skills (e.g., Rabinowitz, personal communication), indicating that a single process will suffice, our own view is that the representation of second language acquisition would be extremely difficult without production systems, as will be seen in Chapter 3. Nevertheless, there are others who indicate that even additional processes are required to explain the full complexity of learned phenomena. For example, Rumelhart and Norman (1978) suggest that learning a complex cognitive skill may entail at least three processes. The first process is *restructuring*, or the development of novel structures for interpreting new information and for reorganizing existing knowledge. This contrasts with learning that entails *accretion*, or the gradual accumulation of new information by matching new data to existing schemata; and *tuning*, or the refinement of existing knowledge based on modifications of available knowledge structures. Tuning is referred to as the "evolution" of existing memory structures and results in the ability to perform a task "more easily and effectively."

Accretion seems characteristic of Anderson's cognitive stage of learning and applies more to declarative than to procedural knowledge. Tuning, a continuous process, may entail gradual refinement and increased automaticity of a skill through practice, as in Anderson's shift from the associative stage to the autonomous stage (see Anderson 1985). Tuning consists of sharpening the performance of cognitive skills (such as chess, problem solving, or language) or of physical skills (such as typing, driving a car, and playing sports). However, Rumelhart and Norman do not distinguish between declarative and procedural knowledge in describing learning processes. For example, they freely mix declarative and procedural knowledge when discussing tuning, which they claim can be represented by becoming a better typist, a procedural skill, according to Anderson's classification, or by a young child learning that not all animals are "doggies," an example of declarative knowledge. Tuning appears to be the only one of the three types of learning processes that includes procedural skills, and it may itself involve three distinct processes: improving the accuracy with which concepts are matched to a schema, generalizing the schema to new instances, or differentiating among particular instances when a schema is inappropriate. Examples in second language acquisition of each of these types of tuning can be easily identified. With a general schema for asking permission in class, a learner might match a concept, such as getting a teacher's attention, to the schema, generalize the schema so as to determine how to get the attention of a teacher in another classroom, and differentiate the schema from the one necessary to get a friend's attention.

In contrast to accretion and tuning, restructuring assumes prior accretion of knowledge categories and interconnected schemata linking the concepts involved. It entails the creation of new structures or schemata that reorganize these linkages or add new ones. Restructuring is the principal mechanism by which new structures or schemata are created, and it occurs only after long exposure to the material on which it is based. Rumelhart and Norman note that restructuring is required when existing memory structures cannot account for existing knowledge. The process involves "erecting new schemata specifically designed for the troublesome information or ... modifying (tuning) old ones" (p. 45). Restructuring can be represented in Anderson's theory as one of the processes involved in acquiring or transferring declarative knowledge.

The question we wish to underscore is whether accretion, tuning, and restructuring represent unique forms of learning or can be represented through existing mechanisms in Anderson's theory. We have noted earlier that accretion entails adding new information to existing schemata, and tuning is parallel to what Anderson calls proceduralization, except that Rumelhart and Norman do not distinguish between declarative and procedural knowledge. The distinction between accretion and restructuring mechanisms is not alien to Anderson's theory but simply consists of two ways in which the long-term memory store of declarative knowledge is modified. There remains essentially one way in which complex cognitive skills are acquired in Anderson's theory – proceduralization – and one way in Rumelhart and Norman's – tuning. However, Anderson's description has the advantage of not confusing declarative with procedural knowledge, and differentiates the acquisition of procedural knowledge (i.e., complex cognitive skills) into three stages.

IMPLICATIONS FOR INSTRUCTION

Another possible limitation of Anderson's stagewise theory of learning complex cognitive skills is that it may lead to ineffective instructional approaches. As Gagné (1985) notes, requiring students to learn rules as declarative knowledge before they can perform the steps in a complex skill is a tedious way to learn. Students prefer to perform the skill as early as possible, irrespective of the familiarity of the rules. The desire to perform the complete skill independently of the thoroughness with which the rules have been learned may result from the awkwardness of having to revert back to the rules when the next step in complete execution of the skill has been forgotten. The time demands required for continually checking the rules for execution of the next step can be frustrating and give the individual the feeling that the learning of the skill has been fragmented and incomplete. The frustration will be exacerbated when there is a practical necessity to perform the skill in an applied setting, as is often true of language. Another difficulty with this process for learning is that not all of the rules for performing a complex cognitive skill such as language have been identified or are easily formulated into words. The complexity of language rules and the difficulty of committing them to memory is another reason why second languages take an extended period of time to master. This complexity may also be a good reason why second language learners generate interlanguage rules and produce intermediate forms of the target language (e.g., Selinker 1972).

Gagné suggests that a far more efficient procedure for learning a complex cognitive skill is through cued performance, with repeated opportunities for practice of the complete skill. Effective instruction of complex cognitive skills could include modeling the desired performance and providing cues for the student at critical points where the complete skill has been forgotten, thus avoiding the necessity of continually referring to the rules. Students learning a complex skill requiring composition would be required to practice the skill components regularly so as to be able to perform them automatically. Fluent performance of the skill components is essential for composition to occur. In support of this, Gagné cites work indicating that slowness in recalling basic number facts is associated with poor computational performance on complex arithmetic problems (Tait, Hartley, and Anderson 1973), and slow word decoding is related to poor reading comprehension (Perfetti and Lesgold 1979).

In second language acquisition, this description by Gagné of cued performance and modeling could as easily describe the audiolingual method as it could communicatively based instructional approaches. In the audiolingual method, the process of learning a language is seen as the acquisition of a set of habits that permits a speaker to respond correctly to a given stimulus (Chamot and Stewner-Manzanares 1985a). The learner practices imitating grammatically accurate language models and patterns until they can be produced automatically. Students repeat isolated units of language that are modeled by the teacher to illustrate grammatical constructions. Discrete component parts of the four language skills (listening, speaking, reading, and writing) are mastered first, and the student progresses gradually toward integrative aspects of language. The teacher's role is to model the correct forms and to provide cued feedback to students to fine-tune their acquisition of accurate structures and pronunciation, much as in Gagné's description.

While the audiolingual approach focuses on grammatically correct constructions, communicative approaches have as their general objective the development of the ability to use a second language to communicate meaning (Chamot and Stewner-Manzanares 1985a). Aspects of communicative approaches considered important are the development of interpersonal communication skills and command over sociolinguistic, discourse, and strategic competence. In addition, communicative approaches have begun to emphasize the incorporation of reading and writing activities into the classroom, but with the view that learners interact with these textual forms as they would with another person.

In contrast to the role of the teacher in an audiolingual classroom, where the focus is on accuracy, the teacher in a communicatively oriented classroom provides cued feedback to elicit meaningful communication. The teacher may model language functions and use in specific socio-linguistic settings, emphasizing the interpersonal goals that language can be used to accomplish and the ways in which meaning can be conveyed. Feedback provided to students is in terms of the meaning conveyed ("I didn't understand, try to say it a different way") rather than in terms of accuracy of structure or pronunciation ("Say it this way"). While the role of the teacher in a communicative classroom is different from that in an audiolingual classroom, the instructional procedures may be quite similar in terms of modeling and the use of cued feedback for language production. The common teacher role of modeling in the two types of classrooms suggests that students are encoding entire phrases appropriate to the teacher's emphases, in one case focusing on the accuracy of pronunciation or structure, and in the other case focusing on the meaning conveyed. Because the focus in a communicatively oriented classroom is on meaning, and accuracy of phonology or structure is of less immediate concern, the role of modeling and cued feedback need not be assumed by an ideal model – the teacher alone – but can be assumed by other students. Thus, cooperative learning is a natural extension of a communicative approach but is difficult to justify in an audiolingual classroom.

The question that needs to be answered is whether or not additional learning processes must be formulated beyond those specified in Anderson's theory in order to account for learning through modeling. To our knowledge, Anderson does not talk about modeling as a mechanism for learning. It should not be surprising that observational learning is absent from a theory that is largely based on information processing models and computer simulation. But cognitive theory does allow for learners to encode chunks of language that convey important meanings in specific interpersonal contexts or that are accurate with regard to structure or phonology. Furthermore, the mental processes that occur during modeling can entail matching known rules to the language input or formulation of idiosyncratic rules to understand and retain language for which no rules seem to apply. Essentially, the problem is one of understanding the mental processes that occur during listening comprehension, an issue addressed in the following section, which the theory is adequate to explain. Thus, no new mechanisms seem to be necessary to explain the type of learning Gagné suggests is more efficient than a stagewise proceduralization of rules, only a clearer specification of the mental processes associated with learning a language from a model's input.

Faerch and Kasper (1985) note that learning through imitation is one of two basic processes involved in the acquisition and automatization of a second language, particularly throughout the phases of acquisition during which familiarization with interlanguage rules is established. Imitation requires that the learner be able to store unanalyzed blocks of language in short-term memory and shift them to long-term memory for later use. The obvious limitations of short-term memory constrain the extent to which modeling can be used to produce spontaneous language without combination and proceduralization of the component blocks. The second basic process in second language acquisition is hypothesis testing. Hypothesis formation and hypothesis testing are based on the learner's prior linguistic knowledge, that is, knowledge of language rules in the first or the second language or of some other language. The effective use of prior linguistic knowledge from the first or some other language results in interlingual transfer, while the application of knowledge from within the language results in intralingual transfer. Inferencing skills are involved to the extent that the individual anticipates the extension of prior knowledge to new situations. Learners are said to test hypotheses in at least one of four ways:

1. Receptively, by comparing hypotheses to second language input;
2. Productively, by using the hypothesis to generate language and assessing the feedback;
3. Metalingually, by consulting a native speaker or text; or
4. Interactionally, by making an intentional error to elicit a repair from a native speaker.

The learner is in a position to assess and revise a hypothesis based on the information received from one or more of these hypothesis testing ventures. Ellis (1986) suggests that learners formulate two competing hypotheses and decide between the two of them based on the accumulated evidence from experience over time. The purposes of formal instruction may be to guide the process of hypothesis formation and testing, to limit the range of feasible hypotheses, and to select the second language input and identifying cues that will lead to effective hypothesis formation. This analysis of instruction, which stresses the active role of the learner, complements Gagné's suggestion that complex cognitive skills may be acquired effectively through modeling, practice, and cued feedback. In the next section, we examine comprehension processes that may be occurring in the learner in response to language input from teachers and other sources.

Language comprehension

Language comprehension is generally viewed in cognitive theory as consisting of active and complex processes in which individuals construct meaning from aural or written information (Anderson 1985; Byrnes

1984; Call 1985; Howard 1985; Pearson 1985; Richards, 1983). Anderson (1983, 1985) proposes that the mental processes necessary for comprehending aural and written texts are sufficiently similar that comprehension of both can generally be discussed as a common phenomenon. He then differentiates comprehension into three interrelated processes: perceptual processing, parsing, and utilization. The processes are recursive in that uninterrupted shifts may occur from one process to the next and then back to the previous process, and they overlap with and are consistent with listening comprehension processes identified in the second language literature (e.g., Call 1985; Clark and Clark 1977; Howard 1985) and with comprehension processes identified in the literature on reading (e.g., Anderson and Pearson 1984; Pearson 1985).

In *perceptual processing*, attention focuses on the oral or written text, with portions of the text being retained in short-term memory. The capacity limitations of short-term memory prevent specific word sequences from being retained longer than a few seconds, as new information to which the person attends replaces the old information in short-term memory. While the text is still in short-term memory, some initial analyses of the language code may begin, and encoding processes may convert some of the text to meaningful representations. During this process, attention may be directed selectively to aspects of the task or the context that will be useful in comprehension. In listening, these aspects might be pauses and acoustic emphases that provide clues to segmentation, while in reading they might be punctuation or paragraph separations. In either listening or reading, the individual may focus on contextual factors such as the immediate task characteristics (e.g., scanning for information versus reading for meaning) and the type of text being used (expository or narrative text).

In *parsing*, the second listening comprehension process, words and phrases are used to construct meaningful mental representations of text. Individuals first *decode* individual words by matching the aural or visual pattern of the word with its representation in the declarative knowledge stored in long-term memory (Gagné 1985). The result of decoding is *lexical access*, or a matching between words in short-term memory and a type of dictionary in long-term memory that enables us to identify the meanings of individual words. Considerable variation exists in the amount of information retained in long-term memory, the way in which information in long-term memory is organized, and the access individuals have to that information (Rabinowitz and Chi 1987).

The basic unit of comprehension is a *proposition*, a meaning-based representation, retained in long-term memory, of the original sequence of words. Although the representation is an abstraction of the original sequence of words, it can be used to re-create the original sequence or at least the intended meaning of the sequence, as was noted earlier. At least part of our ability to parse based on meaning originates in our understanding of the structure and rules of language, which enables us to formulate propositional representations. For example, fundamental distinctions between the active and passive voice, tenses used in communicating past and current actions, and conditional as contrasted with unconditional phrases enable us to analyze and represent the connection between language input, intent, and meaning in terms of propositions. When individuals have established a propositional representation of a phrase, this meaning is then integrated with the meaning of other propositions to form a more comprehensive understanding of the text (Gagné 1985). Anderson (1985) refers to this combination of phrases that have already been parsed as *concatenation*.

Segmentation, or differentiation of language input into words or phrases, is essential for detecting meaning in either aural or written language. The size of the unit or segment (or "chunk") of information processed depends upon the learner's knowledge of the language, general knowledge of the topic, and how the information is presented (Richards 1983). The principal clue for segmentation in comprehension processes is meaning, which may be represented by one or some combination of syntactic, semantic, or – in listening – phonological features of the message (Anderson 1983, 1985). There is an interplay between various kinds of knowledge in segmentation, although semantic information seems to be more effective than syntactic information in reducing sentence response time in listening (Byrnes 1984).

The third process, *utilization*, consists of relating a mental representation of the text meaning to declarative knowledge in long-term memory. This process is referred to as *elaboration* in other descriptions of the reading process (Gagné 1985). Declarative knowledge is stored in long-term memory in terms of either propositions or schemata. The process by which this knowledge is accessed, *spreading activation,* activates nodes in long-term memory that have a meaningful connection with the new information that has been parsed. Utilization is the key to comprehension and the basic determinant that facilitates it. In any message, there may be an interplay between information we already know and information that is entirely new. Anderson (1985) refers to this as a distinction between *suppositions*, or ideas that the speaker or writer supposes we already know, and *assertions*, or information the speaker or writer considers either new or warranting emphasis. There are linguistic devices for conveying that information is supposed or asserted. Supposed information tends to be conveyed in the subjects of sentences, and asserted information tends to occur in predicates. Stress, however conveyed, is an indicator of asserted information. For example, the definite article *the* before a noun phrase suggests supposed information, while the article *a* indicates that new information will follow.

Individuals make use of two types of declarative knowledge to identify the meaning of propositions: real world knowledge and linguistic knowledge (Richards 1983). Real world knowledge, or facts, experiences, and impressions concerning a topic, is used to elaborate on new information and give it greater meaning. The more additional processing one does that results in "related, or redundant propositions, the better will be memory for the material processed" (Reder 1980, p. 7). Two special types of declarative knowledge are *scripts*, or special schemata consisting of situation-specific knowledge about the goals, participants, and procedures in real-life situations; and *story grammars,* or schemata representing the discourse organization of fables, stories, and narratives. These schemata enable the person attempting to comprehend a passage to anticipate what will occur next, to predict conclusions, and to infer meaning where portions of the text are imperfectly understood. Individuals who make use of real world schematic knowledge to develop expectations of text meaning are using *top-down* processing (Howard 1985). They are drawing upon information in memory or upon an analysis of meaning-based contextual features of the text to project additional meanings.

Linguistic knowledge may also be stored as schemata or propositions, but the information stored consists of a lexicon of word meanings and a body of grammatical or syntactic rules. Individuals who analyze each individual word for its meanings or grammatical characteristics and then accumulate meanings to form propositions are using *bottom-up* processing (Howard 1985). This type of processing leads to three types of inefficiencies. First, the meaning of any word often depends on the context in which it is used. An individual attempting to comprehend either written or aural text would need to process any word more than once if it was found later not to bear the meaning originally determined, which seems more likely to occur if each word is analyzed in isolation of its context. A second type of inefficiency is that lexical access will be faster if the context can be used to narrow the range of possible meanings that must be explored in long-term memory. That is, the route through memory pathways to the specific word meaning will be quicker if the context is provided (Gagné 1985). And third, bottom-up processing, or processing words without using context to project additional meaning, can be expected to have inefficiencies since individuals who do make predictions about text meaning tend to have greater comprehension (Palincsar and Brown 1984).

Bialystok and Ryan (1985) have suggested that two orthogonal dimensions of cognitive skill are the basis for linguistic knowledge: analyzed knowledge and cognitive control. Both dimensions are continua and extend from low to high values. The knowledge dimension may contain varying levels of knowledge about features such as units of speech, the relationships between forms and meanings, and awareness of syntax (Bialystok 1986). The control dimension involves the selection and coordination of information to solve a linguistic task. The information selected will vary depending on the difficulty of the task and the time available to complete it. Difficult tasks require more highly analyzed linguistic knowledge, according to Bialystok and Ryan. In second language acquisition, we would add that the difficulty of the task depends upon the proficiency of the learner. It seems likely that less proficient learners will be more inclined to use bottom-up processing than top-down processing, because their linkages to long-term memory in the second language have yet to be established. During the early stages of learning the second language, learners are building connections between the new language and knowledge about concepts that were acquired in their first language. The Bialystok and Ryan dimensions, to the extent that they rely upon linguistic knowledge rather than meaning-based concepts, are an analysis of bottom-up processing rather than top-down processing.

In sum, language comprehension is viewed in cognitive theory as an active, constructive process that applies equally to listening or to reading. The comprehension process progresses through stages of perceptual analysis, parsing, and utilization of the meanings uncovered in oral or written text. At each of the stages, complex processing and strategic analysis takes place that assists the individual in detecting or inferring meanings and in relating the information to existing knowledge. The various ways in which existing knowledge is stored, whether as real world knowledge or linguistic knowledge, will be used to aid in interpreting the text's meaning. To the extent that individuals rely upon meaning-based representations of knowledge to analyze and predict the content of text, they are using top-down processing, while if they use rely upon individual word meanings or grammatical characteristics, they are using bottom-up processing. Cognitive theory suggests that effective processing of text requires the use of both top-down and bottom-up processing (Howard 1985).

Language production

In cognitive theory, language production is seen as an active process of meaning construction and expression. Anderson (1985) indicates that language production can be divided into three stages, as can language comprehension. He points out that although the stages of comprehension and production are analogous (though in reverse order), in fact important differences exist in terms of the underlying mental processes. In addition, as Vollmer and Sang (1983) have indicated, greater knowledge of syntax is required in production than in comprehension, which again suggests that language reception and production are not mirror images of each other.

The three stages of language production Anderson identifies are:

1. *Construction*, in which the speaker/writer selects communication goals and identifies appropriate meanings. In writing, this phase is termed *planning*, and comprises the prewriting stage (Hayes and Flower 1980; Scardamalia and Bereiter 1986).
2. *Transformation*, in which language rules are applied to transform intended meanings into the form of the message. In writing, both composition and revision take place during this stage.
3. *Execution*, in which the message is expressed in its audible or observable form. In writing, this stage corresponds to the actual physical process of producing the text, whether handwritten, typed, or word-processed.

These three stages can be recursive after the initial communication goal is established. That is, once a speaker or writer has decided what to communicate, he or she may go back and forth between the processes of construction, transformation, and execution as the message is developed.

Anderson (1985) describes the features of the construction and transformation stages, which involve higher-level processes, but merely identifies the execution stage as involving "the mouth and the hands" (p. 375). For the second language learner and teacher, the execution stage takes on a far greater significance, especially with speech, as considerable time and effort is spent in improving the accuracy of students' pronunciation so that they will be comprehensible to other speakers of the target language. The execution stage can also be extremely important in developing the handwriting skills of second language learners who are either not literate in their native language or whose native language is written with a different graphic system. We will return to second language issues after a discussion of the first two stages of language generation – construction and transformation.

In *construction*, an individual decides what to say. This decision is based on the goals the speaker or writer has for language production. Once a person has decided on the goals to be served through language generation, the second step is to select the facts to be expressed. This entails a search through declarative knowledge and identification of information appropriate to the functional goal established. The third step in the construction stage is to decide how to structure the information selected.

In structuring the information to be expressed, the speaker or writer uses various types of knowledge, including discourse knowledge, understanding of the audience, and sociolinguistic rules. Discourse knowledge involves the ability to call up various types of schemata, such as story grammars if the language to be generated is a narrative, or event scripts (Schank and Abelson 1977) if the language will be used to participate in a sequence of habitual actions, such as a service encounter in which a purchase is made. Schank and Abelson's (1977) model of the formation of knowledge structures that allow an individual to organize common and recurring life experiences (such as service encounters) includes plans, goals, and scripts. While originally intended to describe language comprehension, the model has implications for language production as well. Event scripts begin as plans, which consist of knowledge of how goals are achieved. For example, a child may have as a goal the successful negotiation of the purchase of a chocolate ice-cream cone. The child plans the type of language needed to achieve this goal based on similar experiences or observations of others, then carries out the plan. After engaging in this type of negotiation a number of times, the child has developed an event script for buying chocolate ice-cream cones, which can then be modified for other flavors of ice cream and eventually for other types of service encounters. In a second language context, the event script may have developed somewhat differently, as plans originally developed in the first language may have to be modified linguistically and conceptually, even though the goals may remain the same.

Anderson (1985) indicates that linear discourse organization is typically used when structuring speech. When a speaker decides to describe events, the information is presented in a linear order according to the sequence in which the events happen, but even when the description is of a place, speakers impose a linear order on the description by noting each feature of the place as if making a tour of it (Anderson 1985).

In writing, organization at both the sentence and the text level is an important contributor to the successful communication of meaning and hence to the quality of the written product (Gagné 1985; Scardamalia and Bereiter 1986). At the sentence level, cohesive devices signal relationships within the sentence and refer back to previously mentioned ideas. Gagné (1985) points out that different amounts of declarative knowledge are used for different types of cohesive devices. For example, cohesive links using syntactical markers such as pronoun referents or conjunctions require procedural rather than declarative knowledge. On the other hand, cohesive links using lexical markers such as synonyms and those using event scripts require that the appropriate schemata be available in declarative knowledge. At the text level, degree of coherence, or the way in which the entire text is structured logically, differentiates between novice and expert writers. Difficulties in coherence may be due to lack of sufficient procedural knowledge (how to organize text) or lack of declarative knowledge (the store of relevant information to organize) (Gagné 1985). Thus, knowledge of various levels of discourse is essential in the construction or planning stage of writing.

In drawing upon knowledge of the audience, the speaker or writer must assess what the audience's prior knowledge of the topic is likely to be, and then structure the information to be produced accordingly. The accuracy of this assessment appears crucial to conducting a successful conversation. If the speaker provides too much information that the listener already knows, the listener is likely to be bored; if too little information is provided, the listener is likely to be confused. The sociolinguistic rules underlying a conversation have been identified by Grice (1975) as a series of maxims to be satisfied. These include providing the right amount of information (neither too little nor too much), being truthful unless obvious sarcasm is intended, being relevant to the topic, and being clear rather than obscure. A similar situation prevails in writing, where an accurate understanding of the audience is necessary for successful communication at all levels of writing, from a business letter to a novel.

In *transformation*, the second stage of language production, the speaker or writer who has decided what to say must convert the information into meaningful sentences. This process is similar to the parsing process during comprehension, when the incoming language is segmented into meaningful units. Anderson (1985) cites a number of studies of oral production in which pauses occur at phrase boundaries, indicating, in his view, that language is generated in phrases as well as being comprehended through parsing of such constituents. Production systems for language generation correspond to production systems for language comprehension, as discussed earlier in this chapter under procedural knowledge. These language-generation production systems are, like other types of procedural knowledge, goal-oriented IF-THEN statements that constitute a program for a given action to take place when certain conditions exist (Gagné 1985). In a conversational exchange, production systems can be used to describe both language comprehension and language production (see Chapter 3, Table 3.1).

In writing, the transformation stage has been termed *translation* (Flower and Hayes 1980; Gagné 1985). Translation refers here to converting intentions or plans into a mental representation rather than to rendering equivalent meanings between one language and another, as translation is generally thought of in second language acquisition. During translation, the writer forms a representation of the goals, ideas, and organization plan developed in the construction or organization stage. This mental representation consists of sentences and sentence fragments that will be written down during the third stage, *execution*. While executing the written product, the writer may pause and return to the previous stages to alter or make new plans as the writing progresses. Expert writers focus on the emerging meaningfulness of their text, while young and novice writers focus on mechanical aspects such as handwriting, spelling, or grammar (Scardamalia and Bereiter 1986). Gagné

(1985) points out that during the translation stage it is useful for a writer to have automatic mechanical skills of this sort so that attention can be freed for developing the cohesion, coherence, and knowledge of audience that improve the quality of writing.

The reviewing or revising process in writing is included by Anderson (1985) as part of transformation, his second stage of language production. In the reviewing process, the writer undertakes two activities – evaluation and revising (Flower and Hayes 1980; Gagné 1985). The writer first evaluates what has been produced in terms of the original goals set, thus returning to the first stage of the writing process (construction). Then the writer returns to the second stage (transformation) and revises the written product in light of the evaluation.

A model of language production quite similar to Anderson's (1985) has been proposed by Clark and Clark (1977) and applied to second language production by Littlewood (1979) and Ellis (1986). This is also a three-stage model, in which the first stage consists of planning, the second of articulating the language components to the plan, and the third the physical production of the utterance. The first two stages are recursive, as the individual moves back and forth between planning what to say and articulating how to say it. The planning stage consists of establishing a goal for communication and developing plans at the discourse, sentence, and constituent levels. This stage alternates with the articulatory stage, in which the speaker selects the meaning for each constituent, specifies its basic syntactic structure, selects first the content and then the function words and affixes, and finally identifies the phonetic realization of the constituent to be communicated. At this point the "motor program," or physical production of the utterance, takes place.

Turning to the second language speaker and writer, we find a number of parallels with first language processes. The novice second language learner cannot develop all aspects of the planning and articulatory stages simultaneously, and therefore selectively uses only those aspects that have already been proceduralized. This results in two basic planning strategies, semantic simplification and linguistic simplification (Ellis 1986). In semantic simplification, the second language learner selects those constituents that can be expected to convey the basic meaning, perhaps with the aid of paralinguistic cues such as gestures. An example of the semantic simplification that might be used by a second language learner requesting a specific food item is:

"You give me _____."
(*Speaker points to potato salad at a picnic.*)

In linguistic simplification, the speaker's omissions are syntactic rather than semantic and include elements such as verb and noun endings and function words. Ellis (1986) points out that linguistic simplification implies that the syntactic form is known by the speaker (one cannot simplify what is not yet acquired), but may not always be used. This variability in second language (L2) use is a characteristic of interlanguage, and it can be explained through Anderson's (1985) second stage of learning procedural knowledge, the associative stage, in which learners begin to fine-tune their performance as they gradually detect and eliminate their errors. This error detection and correction takes place, in Ellis's view, during the articulatory stage of language production, in which the learner monitors output either during any of the phases of the articulatory stage or after the articulation program has been completed. Thus, Ellis divides strategies for language production into planning strategies, which involve either semantic or linguistic simplification, and correcting strategies, which involve monitoring.

In sum, language generation is viewed in cognitive theory as an active and meaning-based process that applies to both speaking and writing. The generation process consists of three stages analogous to the stages of language comprehension, but with important differences. In cognitive theory the first two stages, construction and transformation, have been described in terms of setting goals and searching memory for information, then using production systems to generate language in phrases or constituents, much like parsing in language comprehension. Second language theorists have used first-language production theory as a basis for explaining production at both the early and later stages of second language acquisition (Ellis 1986; Littlewood 1979). Both cognitive and second language theorists indicate that language generators move back and forth between the planning or construction stage and the articulation or transformation stage as they actively develop the meaning they wish to express through speech or writing.

Learning strategies as cognitive skills

In this section we define and classify learning strategies and indicate how the strategies can be described within the framework of Anderson's cognitive theory (especially Anderson 1983). Anderson does not distinguish learning strategies from other cognitive processes, perhaps because his theory focuses on describing how information is stored and retrieved, not on how learning can be enhanced. However, if one's purpose is to facilitate learning and teaching, there are advantages to isolating component mental processes that can be imparted to learners as ways to make learning more effective. If learning strategies themselves are a learned skill, the processes by which strategies are stored and retrieved for future use must be identified. In Anderson's theory, strategies can be represented the same way as any other complex skill, and described as a set of productions that are compiled and fine-tuned until they become procedural knowledge.

Definition and classification

Learning strategies, according to Weinstein and Mayer (1986), have learning facilitation as a goal and are intentional on the part of the learner. The goal of strategy use is to "affect the learner's motivational or affective state, or the way in which the learner selects, acquires, organizes, or integrates new knowledge" (Weinstein and Mayer 1986, p. 315). This broad description of learning strategies may include any of the following: focusing on selected aspects of new information, analyzing and monitoring information during acquisition, organizing or elaborating on new information during the encoding process, evaluating the learning when it is completed, or assuring oneself that the learning will be successful as a way to allay anxiety. Thus, strategies may have an affective or conceptual basis, and may influence the learning of simple tasks, such as learning vocabulary or items in a list, or complex tasks, such as language comprehension or language production.

The distinctions among learning, communication, and production strategies are particularly important in second language acquisition (Faerch and Kasper 1984; Tarone 1981). The focus of interest with learning strategy research has been on language acquisition, while research on production and communication strategies has more often referred to language use. As Tarone (1981) notes, learning strategies are attempts to develop linguistic and sociolinguistic competence in the target language. The motivation for use of the strategy is the desire to learn the target language rather than the desire to communicate. Production strategies are used to accomplish communication goals; they reflect an interest in using the language system efficiently and clearly without excessive effort. Examples of them are prefabricated patterns and discourse planning. Communication strategies are an adaptation to the failure to realize a language production goal. They therefore serve an important role in negotiating meaning between individuals (Tarone 1981). Communication strategies are particularly important in negotiating meaning where either linguistic structures or sociolinguistic rules are not shared between a second language learner and a speaker of the target language. For example, communication strategies might entail approximations, mime, circumlocution, or message abandonment. While generally agreeing that communication strategies emerge from the failure to realize a language production goal, Faerch and Kasper (1984) assert that communication strategies may entail a "psycholinguistic" solution to the communication problem instead of one which relies upon the negotiation of meaning. Examples of psycholinguistic solutions are the reduction of language complexity in order to avoid errors, and expression of the communicative goal in a different way but at the same level of complexity. Tarone cites another type of strategy, perception strategies, which are attempts to interpret incoming utterances efficiently, for example by focusing attention on word endings, stressed syllables, or redundancies in speech. These distinctions are useful, but – as Tarone notes – occasional overlap between definitions may occur under special circumstances, as when an individual's motivation for using a strategy is unclear.

The subset of learning strategies that is concerned with conceptual processes that can be described in Anderson's cognitive theory is of principal interest in our analysis. Affective strategies are of less interest in an analysis such as ours which attempts to portray strategies in a cognitive theory. For purposes of discussion, however, we present a classification scheme that includes the full range of strategies identified in the literature. The examples we select concentrate on strategies that are applicable in comprehension.

Learning strategies have been differentiated into three categories depending on the level or type of processing involved (O'Malley et al. 1985a). *Metacognitive strategies* are higher order executive skills that may entail planning for, monitoring, or evaluating the success of a learning activity (Brown et al. 1983). Metacognitive strategies are applicable to a variety of learning tasks (Nisbet and Shucksmith 1986). Among the processes that would be included as metacognitive strategies for receptive or productive language tasks are:

1. Selective attention for special aspects of a learning task, as in planning to listen for key words or phrases;
2. Planning the organization of either written or spoken discourse;
3. Monitoring or reviewing attention to a task, monitoring comprehension for information that should be remembered, or monitoring production while it is occurring; and
4. Evaluating or checking comprehension after completion of a receptive language activity, or evaluating language production after it has taken place.

Cognitive strategies operate directly on incoming information, manipulating it in ways that enhance learning. Weinstein and Mayer (1986) suggest that these strategies can be subsumed under three broad groupings: rehearsal, organization, and elaboration processes (which may include other strategies that rely at least in part upon knowledge in long-term memory such as inferencing, summarizing, deduction, imagery, and transfer). Cognitive strategies may be limited in application to the specific type of task in the learning activity. Typical strategies that have been discussed in the cognitive category for listening and reading comprehension are:

1. Rehearsal, or repeating the names of items or objects that have been heard;
2. Organization, or grouping and classifying words, terminology, or concepts according to their semantic or syntactic attributes;
3. Inferencing, or using information in oral text to guess meanings of new linguistic items, predict outcomes, or complete missing parts;
4. Summarizing, or intermittently synthesizing what one has heard to ensure the information has been retained;
5. Deduction, or applying rules to understand language;
6. Imagery, or using visual images (either generated or actual) to understand and remember new verbal information;
7. Transfer, or using known linguistic information to facilitate a new learning task; and
8. Elaboration – linking ideas contained in new information or integrating new ideas with known information (elaboration may be a general category for other strategies, such as imagery, summarization, transfer, and deduction).

Social/affective strategies represent a broad grouping that involves either interaction with another person or ideational control over affect. Generally, they are considered applicable to a wide variety of tasks. The strategies that would be useful in listening comprehension are:

1. Cooperation, or working with peers to solve a problem, pool information, check notes, or get feedback on a learning activity;
2. Questioning for clarification, or eliciting from a teacher or peer additional explanation, rephrasing, or examples; and
3. Self-talk, or using mental control to assure oneself that a learning activity will be successful or to reduce anxiety about a task.

These three types of strategies – metacognitive, cognitive, and social/affective – are summarized in Table 2.1. As compared to the strategies in Table 1.1 identified by Rubin (1981) and by Naiman et al. (1978), which emerged largely from interviews with good language learners, the strategies shown in Table 2.1 emerged from research in cognitive psychology based on interviews with experts and novices on psychological tasks and from theoretical analyses of reading comprehension and problem solving. There is some overlap between the two sets of strategies in categories such as monitoring, asking for clarification, inferencing, and practice or rehearsal. As would be expected, there are also some differences. Some of the strategies identified in second language acquisition (Table 1.1) are general techniques for functioning effectively in the language, such as "production tricks," and others are general tactics for learning, such as "creating opportunities for practice" and "responding positively to learning opportunities or exploiting learning environments." In contrast, the strategies mentioned in the cognitive literature

TABLE 2.1. PRELIMINARY CLASSIFICATION OF LEARNING STRATEGIES

Generic strategy classification	Representative strategies	Definitions
Metacognitive strategies	Selective attention	Focusing on special aspects of learning tasks, as in planning to listen for key words or phrases.
	Planning	Planning for the organization of either written or spoken discourse.
	Monitoring	Reviewing attention to a task, comprehension of information that should be remembered, or production while it is occurring.
	Evaluation	Checking comprehension after completion of a receptive language activity, or evaluating language production after it has taken place.
Cognitive strategies	Rehearsal	Repeating the names of items or objects to be remembered.
	Organization	Grouping and classifying words, terminology, or concepts according to their semantic or syntactic attributes.
	Inferencing	Using information in text to guess meanings of new linguistic items, predict outcomes, or complete missing parts.
	Summarizing	Intermittently synthesizing what one has heard to ensure the information has been retained.
	Deducing	Applying rules to the understanding of language.
	Imagery	Using visual images (either generated or actual) to understand and remember new verbal information.
	Transfer	Using known linguistic information to facilitate a new learning task.
	Elaboration	Linking ideas contained in new information, or integrating new ideas with known information.
Social/affective strategies	Cooperation	Working with peers to solve a problem, pool information, check notes, or get feedback on a learning activity.
	Questioning for clarification	Eliciting from a teacher or peer additional explanation, rephrasing, or examples.
	Self-talk	Using mental redirection of thinking to assure oneself that a learning activity will be successful or to reduce anxiety about a task.

tend to look more like underlying mental processes and, as will be seen in the next section, can be discussed in terms of theoretical processes involved in learning.

Strategies as cognitive processes

At least two sets of questions about learning strategies are raised by Anderson's cognitive theory. The first concerns the way in which strategies can be described within the context of the theory. That is, where do the strategies appear in the theory, what terms are used to refer to them, how do they function, and what role do they serve? The second set of questions concerns how the strategies may be learned by a person who does not presently use them on a task where they might facilitate learning. Are strategies like other learned information, what type of information do they most resemble, how are they stored, and how can they be learned and retained for use with a variety of tasks?

METACOGNITIVE STRATEGIES

Procedural knowledge is the basic mechanism through which control over cognition is exercised in Anderson's theory. Lachman et al. (1979) differentiated between declarative knowledge and procedural knowledge by using a computer analogy – the former resembles stored data, while the latter represents the software program. Procedural knowledge as represented in production systems is used to examine, test, and modify the procedural system as well as to extend the system's range of control. Production systems by definition have a goal statement as the condition (IF) preceding an action (THEN), and therefore provide direction in planning future thoughts or behavior. Planning is a key metacognitive strategy for second language acquisition, involved in directing the course of language reception and production.

Planning, to Anderson, is a procedure for conflict resolution among competing action statements that applies to the conditional (IF) clause in the production system. Planning may be influenced by goals or by input features that seem most useful for performing a task. The significance of goals is suggested in the distinction between top-down processing, which capitalizes on known information, and bottom-up processing, which starts with features of the input. Learners are often viewed as top-down processors who successively refine higher-level goals into achievable actions. Anderson suggests that individuals may also plan opportunistically and alternate between top-down and bottom-up processing, depending on the task demands. This view is consistent with our characterization of listening comprehension, where an individual may alternate processes depending on the difficulty of the specific language items contained in the text, or at which stage of learning the individual happens to be functioning with any item of input. We also indicated that top-down processing can involve attending to the overall meaning of phrases and sentences rather than their linguistic features, as would be involved in bottom-up processing.

Two other metacognitive processes that are described in Anderson's (1983) theory are selective attention and monitoring. *Attentional processes* are an important part of the perceptual processing that occurs during listening comprehension in Anderson's theory. They are limited in both scope and capacity, as evidenced in the difficulty individuals have in processing more than one complex task at a time and in holding in short-term memory more than a modest amount of information. However, highly practiced skills may require little attention and involve automatic processing, while skills that are less practiced require the full attention of the listener and involve controlled processing. Listeners to a second language may be unable to distinguish between word and phrase boundaries in the early stages of L2 acquisition. The listener seeks but is unable to locate identifiable segments of the oral text on which to focus attention. The inevitable result of this difficulty in attention is poor comprehension. Given that attentional processes are limited, training in learning strategies that includes selective attention for key words, phrases, or word/phrase boundaries could be an important facilitator of the learner's efforts.

Monitoring, in Anderson's view, is a response to ambiguity in comprehending language where an individual selects a best guess of the message's meaning based on available information. This was reviewed when we discussed parsing, where we indicated that a listener may have to monitor subsequent input relative to the initial guess and perhaps retrieve and modify earlier comprehension errors. Inferencing skills are clearly involved in the way that Anderson uses the term *monitoring*. It is also involved in control processes and in opportunistic planning, because a learner will analyze task demands to determine the task difficulty and the appropriateness of using top-down or bottom-up processing.

We made the point earlier that monitoring was described incompletely by Anderson and suggested that this construct has considerable potential for adding to the description of the learning process. The issue that needs to be addressed more explicitly in a theory concerned with comprehension processes is the cues to which individuals attend that assist learning. For example, Markman (1981) has identified internal monitoring signals, such as perceived absence of structure and perception of inconsistencies, that learners can use in detecting failure to comprehend verbal materials. Nisbet and Shucksmith (1986) suggest that monitoring is the key process that distinguishes good learners from poor learners. In their view, monitoring is the ability to analyze the demands of the task and to respond appropriately, that is, to recognize and manage the learning situation.

Monitoring can be described as being aware of what one is doing or bringing one's "mental processes under conscious scrutiny and thus more effectively under control" (Nisbet and Shucksmith 1986, p. 7). Weinstein and Mayer (1986) add that monitoring involves setting goals for learning and deploying alternative procedures when the goal is not met. They also present evidence emphasizing the central role monitoring plays in effective learning and supporting the responsiveness of monitoring to strategy training.

COGNITIVE STRATEGIES

Anderson's (1983) theoretical analysis of cognition includes descriptions of a number of strategylike cognitive processes, including imagery, organization, inferencing, elaboration, deduction, and transfer. Elaboration plays a key role in describing both deduction and transfer.

To Anderson, images are one of three ways in which information is stored in memory; the others consist of temporal strings and propositions. Spatial images are subject to the same short-term memory limitations as propositions and consequently are retained in terms of an abstraction of the original object or scene. Anderson's theoretical description of images is concerned primarily with topics such as the ability of individuals to match patterns similar to an original figure, perhaps rotated or segmented, and to identify patterns with and without supporting organization or context. The importance of images in comprehension processes is that they may assist in recalling verbal materials.

Anderson (1980) suggests that verbal-imagery linkages may be useful in learning vocabulary, as in the *keyword method*, but dismisses the usefulness of connections between visual images and meaningful verbal information as is found in authentic texts. The keyword method is common in second language vocabulary learning and is used by developing an English-language homophone for the second language vocabulary word (e.g., "cart" for the Spanish word "carta," or letter) and imagining some meaningful interaction between the two that is linked to the meaning of the second language word (e.g., a letter being pushed in a shopping cart). Weinstein and Mayer (1986) implicitly support this distinction by classifying imagery as a strategy that is useful for "basic learning tasks" such as vocabulary or word lists. The keyword method has been found to be successful for these kinds of materials in foreign language learning (Atkinson and Raugh 1975; Pressley et al. 1981).

Anderson (1985) also reports evidence indicating that the *method of loci*, a visual mnemonic device used to remember an ordered sequence of items, is effective in assisting recall of unconnected verbal materials. The method of loci is used by imagining a fixed path through a familiar area (e.g., home to school) and imagining that the items to be remembered (e.g., vocabulary words) are interacting with well-known fixed objects along the path. A vocabulary word such as "biscuit" might be associated with a neighbor's house and the neighbor would be imagined eating the biscuit. Other items in the list would be associated with some other specific location and action. Anderson concludes that strategies that capitalize on the inherent meaningfulness of information are more useful than attempting to represent the information visually, given the capacity limitations of short-term memory.

This issue should not be considered closed for two reasons. First, other investigators have shown that by directing subjects to form mental images, the subject's ability to supply missing words for paraphrased items from a reading passage was improved (Kulhavy and Swenson 1975). It is quite possible that the additional elaborations formed while pausing to create an image were the key factors in making imagery instruction more effective than simple directions to study the passage. As Gagné (1985) notes, imagery instructions should not be ignored by teachers, since these instructions are so easy to give. A second reason why the use of mnemonic devices with meaningful prose materials should not be dismissed is that elaborations may not always be possible. Levin (1982) points out that learners may not be able to formulate meaningful elaborations from expository texts when the materials are unfamiliar, highly complex, or otherwise difficult to remember. Anderson's suggestion to capitalize on the inherent meaningfulness of the materials would appear to be difficult under these circumstances. Mnemonic devices might be preferable for storage and retrieval with this type of information. Additionally, one could rely upon grouping as a strategy to begin the process of building schemata that will assist later in forming meaningful elaborations. A repertoire of both comprehension-directed approaches and memory-directed techniques might be advantageous for the well-prepared learner (Levin 1982).

Anderson's (1985) discussion of organization or grouping as a strategy for comprehension is embedded in his description of parsing productions. Individuals attending to extended oral or written texts segment or chunk information into words or phrases depending on the level at which the information is most meaningful. As we noted previously in our discussion of selective attention, learners may focus on either meaning-related aspects of words or linguistic characteristics. Organizational strategies are also useful for building connections between related ideas, as is discussed later under elaboration.

Strategic uses of inferencing are addressed only in part by Anderson's theory. While he indicates the role inferencing plays in recall, the focus is either on the contributions to comprehension made by prior knowledge (schemata) or on the characteristics of text that make it ambiguous instead of on inferencing strategies learners can use to deal with ambiguity. Inferencing has rich possibilities in comprehension tasks, as suggested by Sternberg's work on training individuals to use cues that assist comprehension (Sternberg 1985; Sternberg, Powell, and Kaye 1982). Sternberg notes that the high correlation found between tests of vocabulary and intelligence may result from the fact that vocabulary tests are indirect measures of the ability to acquire new knowledge or the ability to infer meanings of unfamiliar words from context. Sternberg suggests that, in addition to the usual linguistic cues, there are a variety of cues in a text that individuals can use to infer meaning of a word in context, such as classifications, attributes, causal relations, or temporal or spatial relations. The learner should weigh the importance of the word for overall text comprehension before applying the cues, selectively combine information from the cues to derive the definition, and compare the definition in its context with existing knowledge for related words or concepts. Sternberg has developed a training program in which these strategies are embedded (Sternberg et al. 1982).

Possibly Anderson's strongest contribution to cognitive strategy applications is his discussion of elaboration with meaningful texts. Elaborated memory structures are powerful aids to recall that exert their influence through spreading activation. The influence may occur by: (1) redirecting activation away from interfering paths and toward paths which lead to the target concept; (2) spreading activation toward concepts that were part of the study context; and (3) enabling a reconstruction of the original text through inferences based on information available at the time of recall. That is, individuals can enhance memory for concepts if they increase the number of related ideas that are present at the time of study or increase the number of related ideas that are present at the time of recall. Either approach will work, and each will contribute even further to recall if the related ideas are part of a schema constructed out of prior knowledge through which a broader range of elaborations is available. Anderson indicates clearly in his discussion of elaboration that individuals can be encouraged successfully to elaborate on meanings to enhance memory with meaningful information.

Elaborated structures are the foundation for describing deductive strategies and transfer. Schemata that are based on rules (linguistic or paralinguistic) for language use enable deductions to be made about meanings of words or phrases. The learner may apply grammatical rules, discourse rules, sociocultural rules, or rules developed idiosyncratically to gain an understanding of extended oral text. These schema-based rules are part of declarative knowledge, but they may become procedural knowledge with increased language proficiency. A second type of schema is based on world knowledge; it enables the person to transfer information to the present learning environment that will assist in comprehension, efficient storage into an existing schema, or retrieval at the time of recall. As discussed earlier, world knowledge can originate in either the first or second language.

STRATEGY REPRESENTATION AND ACQUISITION IN COGNITIVE THEORY

Learning strategies are complex procedures that individuals apply to tasks; consequently, they may be represented as procedural knowledge which may be acquired through cognitive, associative, and autonomous stages of learning. As with other procedural skills at the different stages of learning, the strategies may be conscious in early stages of learning and later be performed without the person's awareness. Rabinowitz and Chi (1987) suggest that strategies must be conscious in order to be "strategic"; consequently, they should no longer be considered as strategic behavior once they are performed automatically. Because strategies are complex skills, a person attempting to apply an unfamiliar strategy to a demanding task will have difficulties in controlled processing that can be anticipated from performing two complex tasks simultaneously. It is for this reason that teaching students to use new strategies with cognitive tasks is extremely difficult.

Strategy applications resemble production systems with a condition (IF) and one or more action (THEN) clauses, as in the following examples:

IF the goal is to comprehend an oral or written text,
and I am unable to identify a word's meaning,
THEN I will try to infer the meaning from context.

IF the goal is to comprehend a concept in a written text,
and I know the concept is not at the beginning,
THEN I will scan through the text to locate the concept.

IF the goal is to comprehend and remember an oral passage,
and I have heard a complete passage or thought expressed,
THEN I will summarize the passage to ensure I understand it.

IF I have heard a complete oral passage expressed,
and I am unable to summarize the passage,
THEN I will ask the speaker to repeat the passage.

Because controlled processing places an extra burden on attentional processes, the learner might easily be inclined to reduce the cognitive load by not performing the strategy or by using a more familiar but less efficient strategy. In the example just cited, the person might guess at the meaning without using contextual clues, which would probably lead to an incorrect inference. The learner who sees the task as too familiar or too difficult may not be inclined to use a new strategy, but may rely upon automatic problem solution strategies (productions) that have already been learned. Guessing without using contextual clues is a good example of this. Thus, one of the dilemmas of strategy training is that learners will avoid new strategies with tasks that are too difficult or too easy.

In Anderson's theory, the transfer of strategies to similar tasks – generalization of the production system – is based on a pattern-matching condition in which the learner recognizes similarities between new tasks and tasks involved in former strategy applications. If the learner recognizes these task similarities, the conflict over which alternative productions (i.e., other strategies) to select is resolved, and the learner is more likely to apply the production representing the familiar strategy. However, if the learner does not recognize the similarities, the use of a new strategy is possible.

One of the principles in Anderson's theory that helps resolve the conflict between competing productions is goal dominance, or the salience of a goal for one production over another. Productions that refer to a current goal take precedence over productions that might apply because of strength of association. Thus, a learner with an explicit goal to use a strategy included in training will be able to apply it to the task even though other productions (strategies) may be competing. What is required, however, is intentional control over the learning situation. Perkins (1989) describes this pattern matching and explicit control leading to strategy transfer as the "high road," and contrasts it with the "low road" to strategy transfer, which consists of repeated cued practice opportunities using a specific strategy with a particular task.

A number of writers have commented on the difficulty of strategy training and the problem of furthering strategy transfer (Derry and Murphy 1986; Nisbet and Shucksmith 1986). Derry and Murphy distinguish between detached training, which trains students to use strategies independent of the context provided by any specific curriculum, and embedded training, which trains students to use strategies with specific subject matter courses. Whereas detached training may be generalizable across a variety of subject areas, it may fail in promoting strategy use beyond the immediate training environment. Conversely, whereas embedded training may encourage strategy use in specific subject areas, it may fail in promoting strategy use in other subject areas. Nisbet and Shucksmith refer to this as the "skills dilemma," and suggest that it can be overcome by making the transferable elements in different subject areas explicit for the learner. Derry and Murphy (1986) suggest the use of an "incidental learning model" that consists of "well-planned, short programs of detached strategies training, including tactics and tactics-utilization training, followed by unobtrusive prompting in the actual instructional environment" (p. 32).

Our earlier discussion of the advantages of learning a complex cognitive skill from modeled performance of the complete task suggests the advantage of embedded training accompanied by explicit strategy training. One example of a training program in which strategies are embedded in the task but strategy training is both modeled and explicit is the "reciprocal teaching" for reading comprehension as described by Palincsar and Brown (1984). In this approach, the teacher models for a small group of students the following activities with a reading text:

1. Reading a single paragraph as a group silently;
2. Briefly summarizing the paragraph;
3. Identifying and discussing one or more questions about the paragraph;
4. Leading a discussion to clarify any uncertainties about specific sections of the paragraph; and
5. Predicting the contents of the paragraph to follow.

After a number of repeated sequences of modeling the performance, the teacher then gives each student in turn an opportunity to be the teacher. Strategies appearing and being modeled in this activity include summarizing, questioning, clarifying, and predicting. Palincsar and Brown reported improvements in comprehending expository academic texts on a number of indexes for seventh graders who had been identified as needing special help in reading comprehension relative to comparable students who had not received this type of training. Furthermore, strategy transfer was found on similar tasks for summarizing and detecting ambiguities in the text but not for identifying important themes or predicting questions. While Calfee and Drum (1986) caution that the findings are limited to small instructional groups and to expository texts that are shorter than those found in the usual subject area book, the study illustrates the advantage of embedding strategies in the context of an instructional activity while at the same time providing explicit directions to use the strategies. More will be said of this approach in later chapters.

Conclusions

This chapter began with the assertion that second language acquisition could not be understood completely without a description of the interaction between language and cognition. The chapter built a theoretical foundation for discussing second language acquisition as a complex cognitive skill. We relied for the most part on Anderson's cognitive theory, but found it necessary to augment portions of the theory with concepts expressed by other cognitive theorists. Anderson's theory and the other theories we identified were used to describe memory representation in terms of declarative and procedural knowledge and to describe the process of acquiring a complex cognitive skill such as language. It was particularly in the storage of information in memory that language and cognition were seen to be inextricably interrelated, whether in the representation of declarative or procedural knowledge. The distinction between declarative and procedural knowledge has been acknowledged in the second language acquisition literature (see Faerch and Kasper 1987), but has not been expanded into a useful component of theory development. Cognitive theory views declarative knowledge as being acquired most effectively by building upon prior knowledge, whereas procedural knowledge may be learned more effectively through cued practice with the complete skill or with portions of it that can be compiled.

The cognitive theories gave a descriptive view of language comprehension which indicated that comprehension of both oral and written texts is an active, constructive process that progresses from attentional and encoding processes through utilization of the meaning interpreted. Language production was seen as involving selection and organizational processes required to express meaning. Learning strategies were also viewed in cognitive theory as complex cognitive skills. We presented an initial learning strategy classification scheme and analyzed specific strategies based in cognitive information processing theory. Using comprehension strategies as examples, we discussed different types of strategies within the theoretical model developed by Anderson. This discussion served to illustrate which strategies correspond to mental processes and also helped clarify the distinction between metacognitive strategies and cognitive strategies. The next chapter builds upon the theory formulations indicated here and describes some of the specific constructs that have been of topical concern in the second language acquisition literature.

The theoretical statements we have relied on most heavily in this chapter are not the only views in cognitive psychology and certainly do not represent the end point of theoretical development. We indicated some of the competing views in this chapter when describing procedures involved in learning complex cognitive skills, but concentrated on one particular approach for reasons already indicated. Newer concepts of memory processes are emerging, however, and one or more of these may show greater promise for studying second language acquisition in the future (e.g., McClelland and Rumelhart 1986; Rumelhart and McClelland 1986; Schank 1982).

3 How cognitive theory applies to second language acquisition

In the previous chapter we argued that second language acquisition cannot be understood adequately without reference to the interaction between language and cognition. We indicated that language and cognition interact through the way that concepts are stored in memory, both in declarative and in procedural knowledge, and discussed the influence of stored knowledge on the comprehension of language where new concepts or ideas are presented. Perhaps most significantly, cognitive theory was shown to provide explanatory concepts for language acquisition as well as for language comprehension and production. One other important part of the foundation for describing second language acquisition is that strategies for learning can also be described within the framework provided by cognitive theory. As will be seen, this is an essential step in being able to describe further the process of second language acquisition.

In this chapter we apply cognitive theory to a set of prevalent constructs that have emerged in the second language acquisition literature. We confront the notion that second language acquisition must be explained by reference to a special set of principles or constructs that depend on the notion that language is a unique phenomenon operating outside the usual range of explanations offered for other types of behavior. These constructs include common underlying proficiency, transfer, metalinguistic awareness, interlanguage, automatic processing, communicative competence, and the distinction between acquisition and learning. For each construct, we define the term, explain why it is important in second language acquisition, and then provide a theoretical examination of the construct based on cognitive theory. While the list of constructs is far from exhaustive, the intention here is not to survey and reexamine the entire field of second language acquisition but to apply cognitive theory to a reasonable representation of items and concepts not previously analyzed from a common framework. One of the advantages in using a common theory to explain these separate constructs is that it shows the constructs are interrelated in ways that would not otherwise be evident. Another advantage is that suggestions for research emerge from the theory that have not been part of the prevailing thought in second language acquisition.

Background

The second language acquisition literature is replete with significant constructs that have emerged through researcher or practitioner analysis. Many of these constructs have appeared in the literature as interesting but isolated ideas that do not seem to have any relationship with each other or with any reasonable theoretical foundation. In other cases, a theory or some semblance of theory has been erected on the foundation of a single construct reported in the literature, but no relationship has been drawn to other constructs or theories. In very few cases has there been any analysis of the relationship between theory development in second language acquisition and theoretical explanations of the same phenomena offered in other disciplines. A description is needed in which these constructs are examined within a single theory that can explain how and why they occur without inventing new or special theories just for the explanation of a single phenomenon. For our purposes, we believe that the cognitive theory described in the previous chapter will serve as an excellent vehicle for this analysis. We do not suggest that the theory is adequate to explain all phenomena in both first and second language acquisition at this stage of its development, only that it serves as a useful approach for understanding the constructs we have attempted to analyze thus far.

McLaughlin (1987a) draws the distinction between inductive and deductive theories in describing different approaches that have been taken in theories of second language acquisition. Inductive theories are bottom-up in the sense that they start with the data and then construct principles or laws to explain phenomena. With new empirical data, additional principles are presented to explain the findings of observations or research. Thus inductive theories may accumulate numerous principles, depending on the variation and breadth of studies that have been performed in the specific area. The principles or laws are interrelated and become part of a network of relationships that serve the purposes of explanation and prediction.

Deductive theories, in contrast, are top-down in that laws emerge as deductions from a small set of basic principles. Deductive theories often start with a broader range of behavior they wish to explain and are concerned with complete behavioral processes. These theories are not empirically driven in the same sense as inductive theories and may begin with a rational explanation for the phenomenon the theorist wishes to examine. The explanation is formulated in terms of laws, which are then used to develop additional laws which explain an increasing range of observed phenomena. Thus, a deductive theory is not restricted to empirically derived laws but may independently develop new definitions, causal statements, or predictions of the behavior in question, which are only later confirmed or modified by research.

McLaughlin suggests that theories of second language acquisition can be placed along a continuum from inductive to deductive and that most can be positioned at the inductive end, with the exception of Krashen's Monitor Model (e.g., Krashen 1977, 1980, 1981, 1982; Krashen and Terrell 1983), which was developed more as a deductive theory. However, with the exception of some of McLaughlin's own work (viz., McLaughlin 1987a, b; McLaughlin et al. 1983; McLeod and McLaughlin 1986), theories of second language acquisition have not relied upon the significant body of research in cognitive psychology. Insofar as cognitive theory emerged both from research and from information processing theory, it can be considered both inductive and deductive.

Some of the second language acquisition work has given tacit recognition to concepts in cognitive theory, but has not fully exploited them to describe as many constructs as might be possible. An example of this is the recognition given by Faerch and Kasper (1985, 1987) to the distinction between declarative and procedural knowledge. They indicate that declarative knowledge in second language acquisition consists of "interlanguage" rule knowledge, such as rules for phonology/graphology, morphology, and syntax; rules for pragmatics and discourse knowledge; and rules for social interaction. *Interlanguage* is the intermediary form of a second language that often contains elements of both the native and the target language (Selinker 1972; Selinker and Lamendella 1976). The purpose of procedural knowledge is to activate declarative knowledge and to increase it through learning. Thus, consistent with prevailing notions in cognitive theory, declarative knowledge tends to be static while procedural knowledge takes an active role in transforming facts and data stored as declarative information. According to Faerch and Kasper, procedural knowledge can be differentiated into five separate components:

1. Reception procedures, such as the use of inferencing to extrapolate meaning;
2. Production procedures, such as planning and monitoring speech production;
3. Conversational procedures, such as following linguistic principles that produce coherent text, performing discourse regulatory functions, and using repairs to remove communication blocks;
4. Communication strategies, which are intended to solve problems in speech comprehension, and may involve pauses in communication or direct appeals for clarification; and

5. Learning procedures, such as the development of interlanguage knowledge through hypothesis formation and testing, and learning through modeling or imitation.

The first four of these component procedures involve assessment of the speaker's language and organization of planned responses, while the last involves the learning and automatization of the language system. As Faerch and Kasper suggest, most declarative knowledge is activated in a conscious manner, while procedural knowledge tends to be automatic and is activated without awareness, except when the language user experiences interruptions in communication due to failures in comprehension or production. Some of the primary purposes of second language research to Faerch and Kasper are to elucidate the components of declarative knowledge that influence second language acquisition, to identify relatively automatic procedures that under ordinary circumstances would occur without awareness, and to determine the extent to which procedural knowledge is unique or common to the native language and the second language. The question of research methodology then becomes one of analyzing the approaches to investigation that will accomplish these purposes.

The principal limitations of the Faerch and Kasper analysis are in not expanding their examination of cognitive theory beyond this preliminary familiarization with the distinction between declarative and procedural knowledge, and in including only linguistic information in their analysis of declarative knowledge. As we pointed out in Chapter 2, to include only linguistic information in the analysis of declarative knowledge leaves the theorist focusing on bottom-up processing because of the attention given to formal aspects of language rather than to meaning. Furthermore, Faerch and Kasper did not discuss the process by which learning strategies become proceduralized, a major issue in cognitive theory. The value of Faerch and Kasper's formulations lies in the broad range of linguistic behaviors to which they were able to apply the distinction between declarative and procedural knowledge, and in recognizing that learning strategies are represented in memory as procedural knowledge.

An example of less explicit acknowledgment of cognitive theory occurs in Bialystok and Ryan's (1985) proposal that two orthogonal dimensions of cognitive skill underlie linguistic knowledge: analyzed knowledge and cognitive control. The two dimensions can be portrayed pictorially as four quadrants representing different levels on the knowledge or control dimensions (Figure 3.1). We had discussed aspects of this proposal in the prior chapter as it relates to language comprehension, although Bialystok and Ryan have applied this framework to a number of other issues, such as the development of metalinguistic skills. A high level of both knowledge and control procedures is necessary in the solution of

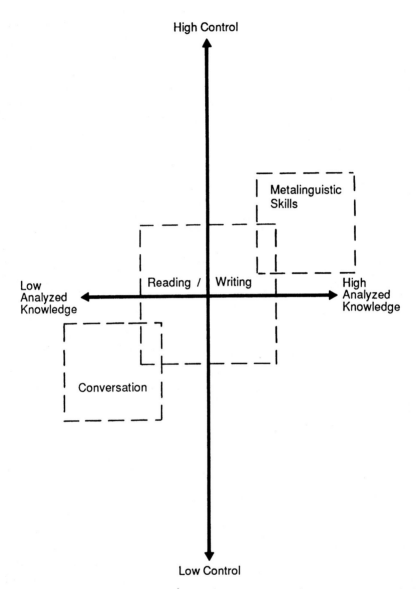

High Control

Low
Analyzed
Knowledge

Metalinguistic
Skills

Reading / Writing

High
Analyzed
Knowledge

Conversation

Low Control

Figure 3.1 A cognitive framework underlying the development of language abilities. (Adapted from Bialystok and Ryan 1985, p. 232.)

metalinguistic problems, that is, metalinguistic problems entail high levels of analyzed knowledge and high levels of control. In contrast, ordinary conversational interactions may require very little analyzed knowledge and few control mechanisms. Falling between these two extremes are ordinary reading and writing tasks, which require moderate amounts of analyzed knowledge and control procedures. Applying a control procedure transforms the information accessed on the knowledge dimension so that it can be applied to the immediate linguistic task. What is analyzed by the control dimension is not the knowledge itself but the representation of that knowledge as shown in propositional representations, consistent with cognitive theory. As Bialystok and Ryan note in applying their theory to metalinguistic tasks:

> More formal cues are involved in solving a metalinguistic task than in participating in a conversation. It is the ability to accomplish this selection, to know what information is required, to retrieve it, and to coordinate it into a solution within given time constraints that is the responsibility of cognitive control. (1985, p. 235)

The knowledge dimension has parallels with declarative knowledge and the control dimension has parallels with procedural knowledge, as Bialystok and Ryan note. However, these authors claim to differ from Anderson's (1978, 1982) use of these terms in at least three ways. First, Bialystok and Ryan do not allow that procedural knowledge is represented internally any differently from declarative knowledge, even though procedural knowledge is often executed automatically. As an example, reading at the beginning levels is said to be the same fundamental task as at the highest levels of knowledge and control, involving the same elements of the skill but with more proficiency along the control dimension. Another way of stating this is to indicate that Bialystok and Ryan would not use production systems to represent procedural knowledge but presumably would find constructs associated with declarative knowledge, such as schemata and propositional knowledge, to be adequate. Thus, the only difference between beginning and more proficient readers would be the degree of automaticity achieved in execution of the task. A second source of difference is that Bialystok and Ryan claim to have a unique identification with a developmental orientation, which they indicate does not characterize Anderson's work. This developmental orientation is manifested in changes in the knowledge dimension resulting from analysis of the information stored and changes in the control dimension resulting from "the expansion of procedures and the fluency of experience" (1985, p. 246). For example, one of the key factors resulting in modifications in the knowledge dimension is literacy, which not only produces new knowledge about processes entailed in reading and writing but also promotes the ability to apply linguistic knowledge. The third difference between Bialystok and Ryan's views and those of Anderson is that Bialystok and Ryan claim that conscious awareness of processing is not an essential part of their system, whereas Anderson indicates that awareness is evident at the cognitive stage of learning, but less likely as procedural skills become automatic. Bialystok and Ryan suggest that conscious awareness may occur with simple tasks but may also exist at the highest levels of analyzed knowledge.

Bialystok and Ryan are not alone in suggesting that procedural knowledge need not be represented internally by different processes than have been illustrated for declarative knowledge, and that there is no reason to posit a distinct form of memory representation for skills that have become procedural (e.g., Rabinowitz 1987). Their argument that skilled reading differs from beginning reading only in terms of the degree of automaticity entailed in execution of the task is at odds with the cognitive theory of reading comprehension (e.g., Pearson 1985; Pearson et al. 1984), which indicates that skilled reading is characterized by complex processing strategies that do not appear among less skilled readers. It is our view that the use of production systems to represent procedural knowledge is necessary to fully characterize the way in which these processing strategies operate, as we indicated in Chapter 2. Further, as we will show later, the use of production systems has some advantages in allowing the description of communicative competence and other aspects of second language acquisition, which we believe would otherwise be quite difficult.

The claim that Bialystok and Ryan make in having a unique identification with developmental theory should be updated, considering some of Anderson's more recent writings (e.g., Anderson 1983, 1985) showing the proceduralization of knowledge through tuning and the modification of declarative knowledge through its interaction with procedural knowledge. It is the interaction between declarative and procedural knowledge that produces the kind of transformation Bialystok and Ryan attribute to developmental theory. The point they make concerning conscious awareness results, we believe, from some terminological differences in talking about procedural skills. Because procedural skills are often performed without awareness, requiring few demands on short-term memory, does not mean that the skill performance will go unnoticed if there are reasons to analyze the skill or the component knowledge used in performing the skill, as Faerch and Kasper (1987) suggest, and as we will show in our research in later chapters. One reason to analyze the skill might be that the person encounters a comprehension problem, or is distracted or interrupted and must refocus attention to the task.

The final difficulty with the approach Bialystok and Ryan have taken in analyzing metalinguistic skills is that without reference to an independently grounded theory, their argument for the relationship between metalinguistic skill and the two dimensions they have proposed sounds threateningly like a tautology. That is, they have argued that one can define metalinguistic skills by reference to the two dimensions, but they also argue that one can define the two dimensions by the types of skills analyzed at each level on the two continua.

The most explicit acknowledgment of cognitive theory in the second language acquisition literature is in McLaughlin's work relating skilled language production to information processing theory (e.g., McLaughlin 1987a, b; McLaughlin et al. 1983). McLaughlin views second language learning as the acquisition of a complex cognitive skill, consistent with the view expressed in the previous chapter. One of the principal concepts in this view is that individuals acquire mastery over complex new skills through performing aspects of the skill that require little processing capacity, freeing attentional processes for other aspects that demand conscious effort. Aspects of the skill that are performed without conscious effort are referred to as automatic processes and result from the activation of memory associations that have already been thoroughly learned. Those components of the skill requiring more deliberate effort are controlled processes and entail new learning of associations. Controlled processes place demands upon short-term memory, while automatic processes free portions of working memory for new learning. Second languages are learned, as with other complex cognitive skills, through the "gradual integration of subskills as controlled processes initially predominate and then become automatic" (McLaughlin 1987a, p. 139).

McLaughlin (1987a) examines a number of applications of cognitive theory to second language acquisition, including *lexical retrieval*, syntactic processing, reading, speaking, and discontinuities in the process of second language acquisition. In lexical retrieval, individuals retrieve precise meanings of words appropriate to specific contexts from among a range of possible alternative meanings. The questions raised in the second language acquisition literature about lexical retrieval concern the manner in which the meanings are retrieved and whether the retrieval entails automatic or controlled processing. For example, do individuals who are more proficient in a second language process lexical items differently compared to individuals who are less proficient, or do they simply perform the retrieval more quickly? One research approach used in addressing these questions is the lexical decision task, which entails collecting precise measurements on the speed with which individuals signal that they recognize the meaning of a target word, preceded by prompt words which have varying levels of relationship to the target, flashed on a screen. By reducing the amount of time between the prompt and the target word, the experimenter can control whether controlled or automatic processes are used by the individual. Furthermore, under conditions involving automatic processing, the experimenter can manipulate the prompt word to determine if semantically related as contrasted with less related prompts produce semantic facilitation, or shorter response times. The following findings summarize some of the conclusions reached in McLaughlin's review:

1. Only balanced, as compared with dominant, bilinguals (those dominant in their native language) showed the same degree of semantic facilitation in both languages under the automatic processing condition. Dominant bilinguals were also noted to read more slowly in their second language than in their first language.
2. Even after years of exposure to a second language, the processing speed of individuals fails to match the processing speed achieved in their native language. This is true even though the individuals are overtly balanced bilinguals.
3. More proficient bilinguals seem to use different lexical processing strategies than less proficient bilinguals. The more proficient bilinguals (and native speakers) make vocabulary recognition errors that suggest the use of semantic encoding, while less proficient bilinguals make vocabulary recognition errors that suggest the use of acoustic (phonemic) encoding. This indicates that the less proficient bilinguals have yet to make automatic processing based on word meaning a formal part of their second language repertoire.

These findings reveal the way in which cognitive theory can be applied to second language acquisition processes. What these studies suggest is that retrieval mechanisms in long-term memory are based on connections established for word meanings, and that access to these pathways may be available at the beginning levels of proficiency but becomes automatic only after repeated practice and may never reach the level of automaticity achieved for processing the first language. The findings also indicate that retrieval processes among individuals who are more proficient in a language are based on meaning, whereas individuals at the beginning level of proficiency process language based on sound similarities among words. These studies and the conclusions reached here have importance for some of the research discussed in later chapters that addresses the way in which second language learners process information while involved in tasks of the kind that they typically receive in school.

McLaughlin also reviewed differences in syntactic processing between proficient and less proficient speakers of a second language. One of the questions addressed in these studies concerned the way in which individuals process continuous text while reading or listening in terms of attention to meaning as contrasted with structure and form in the text. One of the studies McLaughlin reviewed used a letter-deletion task in which individuals crossed out certain letters in the text. While individuals who were less proficient in the second language crossed out the letter in both content (meaning) and function (e.g., connectors or articles) words with approximately equal frequency, individuals who were native speakers of the language crossed out the letter in content words while tending to ignore the letter's occurrence in function words. Thus, native speakers focused their attention on meaning-based aspects of the text, while least proficient non-native speakers expended mental processing effort on aspects of the text that may not have been necessary to extract meaning. This suggests that the native speakers had achieved a degree of automaticity in reading and that they simplified the processing task to devote greater attention to meaningful portions of the text.

Another study focused on recognition of changes in text that had been made to semantic as contrasted with syntactic portions of the original reading passage. Presumably, native speakers of the language would process syntactic information automatically and as a result may have less perfect recall of those portions of a passage than would non-native speakers. The findings indicated that while native speakers showed better recognition of semantic rather than syntactic changes to the original text, non-native speakers were better able to determine whether the form of a sentence had been changed rather than the meaning. The findings suggested that native speakers of a language focus on meaning and process the structural aspects of text automatically. Individuals with less proficiency in the language devote both attention and processing energy to encoding both meaning and structure.

McLaughlin (1987b) has also applied cognitive theory to reading comprehension in second language acquisition, consistent with a long line of cognitive research with native speakers of English performed by others (e.g., Anderson and Pearson 1984; Pearson 1985; Samuels and Kamil 1984). The cognitive basis for reading comprehension has been an essential factor in understanding how native English speakers learn to read and how readers process text. Whereas reading comprehension was once thought of as a process of representing with reasonable accuracy the information contained in a text, more recent views of reading focus on the constructive elements of the process and acknowledge that what is retained is the result of a dynamic interaction between the reader, the task, and the context. The reader's prior knowledge and strategies for reading (scanning, summarizing, etc.) may vary depending on the perceived reading task (e.g., to remember information versus to follow directions), and the approach the reader takes may vary depending on the context or situation (e.g., preparing for a test versus reading for pleasure). Consequently, comprehension and retention of textual materials will be influenced by prior knowledge, the purpose for reading, the strategies used, and the expected application of the information. More proficient readers vary their strategies depending on the nature of the task and the context, while less proficient readers either deploy fewer strategic processes with the task or follow strategies that are not appropriate for either the task or the context.

McLaughlin (1987b, c) adds to this view by identifying reading processes that differentiate native from non-native speakers of a language and by stressing the importance of restructuring (Rumelhart and Norman 1978). Restructuring is a process by which second language learners replace previous strategies with new approaches instead of simply performing the same reading processes more quickly as they become more proficient. If increases in automaticity or proceduralized knowledge would explain why readers become more proficient, one should find a degree of continuity in comprehension across different types of reading tasks accompanying increased skills in a second language. In particular, as learners become more proficient in a second language and become more skilled in reading, their errors should be meaning-based because they have automated the components of reading concerned with form. However, McLeod and McLaughlin (1986) found that although advanced students of English as a second language (ESL) made fewer errors on a cloze test than beginning ESL students, their errors nevertheless did not appear to be based on meaning, in contrast to the more meaning-based errors made by native English speakers. This suggested that the advanced ESL students were not approaching the task strategically by using top-down processing, that is, by using contextual clues to extract meaning from text. Instead, they appeared to be using specific lexical access without the advantage of context to aid in their comprehension. On the assumption that they were able to use context to extrapolate meaning in their native language, McLeod and McLaughlin suggest that there was evidence of the need for these students to restructure their approach to reading in the second language by using strategies that had been found effective in the first language.

The notion of restructuring contrasts with the position expressed by Bialystok and Ryan (1985), who had indicated that proceduralization entails accelerating learning processes performed more slowly by novices at the task. The question McLeod and McLaughlin have raised in their work is when and how second language learners begin to use strategies that will assist their comprehension and retention of information. As will be seen, our own studies address this and other questions related to learning strategies in second language acquisition for both receptive and productive language tasks. The position we take is that an explanation of the difficulty in transferring strategies from first to second language tasks is best understood as a problem of transferring procedural skills as opposed to one of adopting a new schema, as is suggested in McLaughlin's analysis of restructuring. Nevertheless, there remains a possibility that some amount of restructuring is also involved in the recognition that a procedural skill can be applied to a new context.

McLaughlin (1987a) further builds the application of cognitive theory to second language acquisition in his description of speaking skills. McLaughlin relies on Levelt's (1978) suggestion that speaking is an example of a complex cognitive skill that can be differentiated into various hierarchical subskills, some of which might require controlled processing while others could be processed automatically. For example, speaking entails hierarchic goals to express specific intentions, to decide on a topic, to formulate a series of phrases, to retrieve the needed lexicon, to utilize appropriate syntactic rules, and to meet pragmatic conventions. We expand on this view later in this chapter in discussing how communicative competence can be represented through production systems. McLaughlin also notes that learning a second language is more than a simple process of refinement of a complex skill; it may entail restructuring or imposing a new organization on information already stored in long-term memory. This restructuring often results in greater efficiencies in producing the skill or in applying the skill in novel situations through the realizations that emerge from establishing new links between the skill and other associations. Examples of restructuring in second language acquisition, as described by McLaughlin, are interlanguage, where individuals restructure transitional grammars that are seen to violate more recently acquired principles, or the use of new learning strategies, where individuals apply strategies to second language acquisition which they had previously found effective with native language tasks.

In our analysis of learning strategies as procedural knowledge, such transfer could be explained by adapting IF-THEN production systems underlying use of the learning strategy in the first language (L1) to new conditions in the second language (L2), applying the production system with sufficient regularity so that it becomes proceduralized. This is difficult to accomplish because of the load added to short-term memory processing requirements, which already are burdened by trying to decode the new language. Restructuring may be involved if one's metacognitive schema for understanding how reading comprehension tasks are performed includes the recognition that strategic modes of processing are important, and one extends this schema with the realization that strategic modes of processing are as important in L2 as they are in L1. However, the actual use of strategic processing in L2 remains a procedural skill, and the primary difficulty in extending the strategies from L1 to L2 is probably one of transferring procedural knowledge, not of restructuring declarative knowledge. This explanation avoids what we see as a difficulty in extending restructuring to procedural knowledge when it seems better designed to explain phenomena associated with declarative knowledge.

Our primary contention in this chapter is that there is much more that remains to be described, apart from the preliminary concepts introduced earlier, that will illustrate not only the varied uses of cognitive theory for explanation of second language constructs but also help in analyzing both learning and instruction. We begin with a description of applications of declarative and procedural knowledge to second language acquisition and then discuss extensions of the stagewise theory of learning a complex cognitive skill.

Relationship of cognitive theory to specific constructs

Although the developments in cognitive theory indicated earlier were not intended to describe second language acquisition, a number of direct applications can be identified. These applications extend considerably the suggestions made by Faerch and Kasper and build upon McLaughlin's analysis of second language processes in cognitive theory. The original concepts presented here are based on a manuscript that was part of a four-year investigation of learning strategies (O'Malley et al. 1985a; O'Malley et al. 1985b; O'Malley, Chamot, and Walker 1987). This discussion was originally developed to examine the number and variety of second language constructs that could be explained using cognitive theory and is expanded here to include recent refinements in our thinking.

Declarative knowledge

At least three sets of questions concerning second language acquisition are raised by Anderson's (1983, 1985) discussion of declarative knowledge in memory. These questions concern: (1) how meaning in two languages is represented in memory, and how the transfer of knowledge in a first language (L1) to second language (L2) expression takes place; (2) whether some types of knowledge are more easily transferred to the L2 than others; and (3) how metalinguistic information is stored and influences performance for bilinguals.

REPRESENTATION OF MEANING

In second language acquisition, theorists have argued whether bilingual individuals have two separate stores of information in long-term memory, one for each language, or a single information store accompanied by selection mechanisms for using the L1 or L2 (McLaughlin 1984). If individuals have a separate store of information maintained in each language, they would select information for use appropriate to the language context or the language being used at the time. Transfer of information acquired in the L1 to L2 applications would be difficult because of the independence of the two memory systems. An individual at the early stages of proficiency in the L2 would either have to translate information from the L1 to the L2, or relearn the

L1 information in the L2, capitalizing on existing L1 knowledge where possible. In Anderson's theory, information stored in memory has a meaning-based representation independent of a specific language and would be stored as declarative knowledge through either propositional networks or schemata.

The argument for separate propositional networks and schemata associated with each language is consistent with the notion of domain-specific language skills. Speakers of an L1 often acquire vocabulary and structures for specific domains appropriate to interactions in their profession, family, social group, or shopping place. The domain-based meanings represent schemata in that unique concepts, linkages, propositions, and networks are involved in each domain. Learners may acquire one or more of these domain-specific capabilities in the L2 by direct exposure or by training, but be ineffective in communicating in other domains because of the highly specific nature of the language involved. Thus, domain-specific language proficiency may be constructed out of experience and not established by direct transfer from L1 proficiency. Hakuta (1986) adds to this picture of memory storage related to the L1 and L2 by suggesting that memory systems will be discrete to the extent that they are directly language-related, as in poetry, but will entail transfer of information from the L1 to the L2 if they are not so highly language-related, as in content area knowledge.

The notion of common propositional networks and schemata for both languages is consistent with Cummins's (1984) proposed common underlying proficiency in cognitive and academic knowledge for bilinguals. He argues that what is originally learned through the L1 does not have to be relearned in the L2, but can be transferred and expressed through the medium of the L2. Cummins's view of common underlying language proficiency is consistent with Anderson's suggestion that nodes are based on meaning instead of a direct replication .of language. Nodes that access meaning in long-term memory may be non–language-specific but have built-in features that signal one language or the other, as McLaughlin (1987a) has suggested. In other words, the selection of the L1 or L2 for comprehension or production is performed in short-term memory, whereas concepts are stored in and retrieved from long-term memory as non–language-specific generalized meaning. Second language learners may be able to transfer what they already know from the L1 into the L2 by: (1) selecting the L2 as the language for expression, (2) retrieving information originally stored through the L1 but presently existing as non–language-specific declarative knowledge, and (3) connecting the information to the L2 forms needed to express it. The first and third steps would be functions that occur in short-term memory. In fact, learning strategy research (O'Malley et al. 1985a, b) indicates that students of English as a second language consciously and actively transfer information from their first language for use in the L2.

TRANSFER OF DECLARATIVE KNOWLEDGE

A second question raised by Anderson's theory is whether there is variation in the effectiveness or ease of transfer of declarative knowledge from the L1 to the L2. Is all declarative knowledge originally acquired in an L1 context equally easy to transfer and access through the L2, or do particular characteristics of the declarative knowledge make a difference? Anderson's descriptions of the ways in which declarative knowledge can be represented in memory provide clues to the answer to this question.

Anderson indicates that declarative knowledge may be represented in memory as schemata, or organizational frameworks. He describes two major types of schema – organization by natural categories and organization by events. Natural category schemata are based on real world phenomena, such as classifications of plants, animals, minerals, quantities, and other aspects of the natural world. A natural category schema would appear to be easily transferable to expression through a second language because the information describes observable reality. (This assumes that the person has learned about natural phenomena from a scientific rather than a naive point of view, since the latter may not always be accurate.)

Schemata organized by events include both personal recollections of event sequences and the sequence of events that characterize the discourse organization of a story. Story scripts (or story grammars) have been shown to be strongly influenced by culture. For example, in Western culture stories traditionally deal with a hero who sets out to accomplish a definite goal. By accomplishing the goal, he or she attains a reward, which is often material. In traditional Japanese stories, on the other hand, the protagonist is not goal-oriented, and adventures and rewards that come about do so as a result of the protagonist's intrinsic merit (Matsuyama 1983). Second language learners who have internalized one type of story schema may find it difficult to understand a differing schema, not because of language factors but because of cultural expectations.

Another type of event organization described by Anderson (1980) is referred to as social cognition. Persons organize their knowledge about individuals or groups according to certain perceived characteristics. This type of schematic organization of knowledge may lead to stereotyping, because one person's individual knowledge about a group may rely on data limited to personal experience or biased information. The formation of stereotypes may also be culturally linked, so that the schemata developed to characterize a certain group through the L1 may not be relevant to characterize the same group through the L2. A stereotype transferred to a second language context may interfere with accurate communication in the L2.

Thus, the way in which declarative knowledge is organized in memory may have a substantial impact on the L2 learner's ability to transfer it effectively and accurately into the new language. The educational implications for second language learners are that concepts related to natural categories such as science, mathematics, and technical subjects may be easier to transfer to the L2 than concepts related to culturally affected areas such as literature or social studies, or concepts related to domain-specific knowledge.

REPRESENTATION OF METALINGUISTIC KNOWLEDGE

A third question raised by Anderson's views on declarative knowledge is how metalinguistic information among bilingual persons is stored and how this information influences performance. One of the primary features defining metalinguistic awareness is an understanding of the arbitrary uses of language. Bilinguals may be expected to have an advantage in understanding arbitrariness in language use and, accordingly, in metalinguistic awareness (De Avila and Duncan 1979). Metalinguistic awareness will be manifested particularly in fluent bilinguals, and these individuals will share advantages not only in verbal skills but in problem-solving tasks (Tunmer, Pratt, and Herriman 1984). Bilingualism has been viewed as a "three-dimensional insight" into language that a monolingual rarely experiences (Lambert 1981). Advantages found among bilinguals have included enhanced concept formation and mental flexibility, as in the ability to switch object names and to use the new names in sentences (Cazden 1972; Feldman and Shen 1971; Ianco-Worrall 1972).

Bialystok and Ryan (1985) argue that metalinguistic tasks have been so poorly defined in the second language literature that they cannot be understood without reference to their knowledge and control dimensions used in processing the tasks. We earlier suggested that this line of reasoning is circular, since the dimensions are then defined in terms of the tasks being processed. Nevertheless, one important contribution of this view is in acknowledging the procedural aspects of metalinguistic processing, which our earlier work on this topic (O'Malley et al. 1987) had not discussed.

One way to describe metalinguistic awareness in cognitive theory is as a new schema constructed to link independent schemata in the L1 and L2 that reference the same domain. That is, an individual with domain-specific knowledge in two languages may begin to see the different ways in which the same concept can be expressed in the L1 and

L2. The person then establishes a new schema that differentiates applications of each language to identical concepts. This type of learning may also be represented by what Rumelhart and Norman (1978) refer to as restructuring of knowledge developed in the L1 and L2. Two types of restructuring are described by Rumelhart and Norman: *patterned generation* of schemata, or patterning new schemata on old ones by making a copy with modifications; and *schema induction*, or inducing a new schema from regularities in the temporal or spatial configurations of old schemata. Most learning probably occurs through patterned generation, as takes place in classrooms when teachers introduce analogies, metaphors, or models. Schema induction is a form of learning by contiguity in which certain configurations of schemata tend to co-occur in a recognizable pattern, which leads to the development of a new schema. This form of learning is said to be rare because of the difficulty in discovering or recognizing similarities in existing schemata and the requirement that the schemata occur contiguously. We suggest that metalinguistic knowledge is an example of schema induction, where the individual sees similarities in the pattern by which two languages are comprehended or produced when the languages co-occur or are contiguous. Second language acquisition is more likely than most other forms of learning to result in the co-occurrence of schemata from the two languages because both schemata may be evoked whenever the meaning-based representation is stimulated. However, metalinguistic knowledge may also result from patterned generation if a teacher provides the model for the comparison between the languages.

This explanation of metalinguistic awareness is based on the notion that separate memory systems are developed in each language. Let us assume for the moment that knowledge is stored with unitary, meaning-based propositions, consistent with Cummins's notion of common underlying proficiency. A bilingual person with common underlying proficiency would use an executive function to select the language in which the meaning is expressed, depending on contextual factors or task demands (see McLaughlin 1984). In essence, meaning is not inextricably tied to specific lexical, structural, or any other characteristic of a specific language. Underlying meanings may have more than one language schema linked to them. For example, a person could easily have a single propositional representation for informal greetings, but have independent language schemata in Spanish and in English to represent the meaning. Metalinguistic schemata would serve the purpose of linking these independent language schemata based on analyses of the different ways in which an exchange of greetings transpires, perhaps contrasting the degree of informality, the number of expressions necessary to establish the salutation, differences in the use of second-person pronouns, and so on. Thus, whether one prefers a unitary view of underlying meaning or maintains that there are separate memory stores for each language, meta-linguistic knowledge can be explained with reference to cognitive theory.

The development of metalinguistic awareness may be related to the conditions necessary for acquiring the second language effectively. Cummins (1979) notes that the cognitive benefits of bilingualism may depend on children reaching a minimum level of bilingualism (his "threshold" hypothesis), and that the level of competence achieved in the L2 may depend on the proficiency of the child in the L1 at the time when intensive exposure to the L2 begins (his "interdependence" hypothesis). In cognitive theory, schemata linking knowledge based on independent language systems would not have sufficient connections to establish metalinguistic awareness unless Cummins's threshold and interdependence conditions are met. Failure to meet Cummins's two conditions could also detract from the ability to transfer information from the L1 to the L2 in that schemata established in the L1 may not have sufficient internal linkages to provide an adequate foundation of information. Without a threshold having been met and adequate exposure to the second language having been provided, the learner may have difficulty developing the metalinguistic connections that could be involved in learning the second language.

Procedural knowledge

The distinction between declarative knowledge and procedural knowledge has both theoretical and practical importance in second language acquisition. Knowing about language as a grammatical system, which involves knowing the rules underlying syntax, semantics, and phonology, is not a sufficient condition for knowing how to use the language functionally, as many teachers and students of foreign languages have discovered. In order to use a language for communicative purposes, procedural knowledge is required. Instructional approaches need to provide for communicative activities that focus on language as a skill instead of on language as an object of study. Two implications of the distinction between declarative and procedural knowledge that will be discussed here are: (1) the extension of procedural knowledge as represented in production systems to communicative competence in the L2; and (2) the transfer of both declarative and procedural knowledge from the L1 to the L2, as is required in the view of common underlying proficiency described by Cummins (1981).

COMMUNICATIVE COMPETENCE

Canale and Swain (1980) define the four components of communicative competence as the ability to use grammatical, sociolinguistic, discourse, and strategic skills. This definition indicates that it is important to con-

TABLE 3.1. A PRODUCTION SYSTEM FOR COMMUNICATING IN A
SECOND LANGUAGE

P1*   IF the goal is to engage in conversation with Sally,
      and Sally is monolingual in English,
      THEN the subgoal is to use my second language.

P2   If the goal is to use my second language,
      THEN the subgoal is to initiate a conversation.
      (sociolinguistic competence)

P3   IF the goal is to initiate a conversation,
      THEN the subgoal is to say a memorized greeting formula.
      (discourse competence)

P4   IF the goal is to say a memorized greeting formula,
      and the context is an informal one,
      THEN choose the appropriate language style.

P5   IF the goal is to choose an appropriate language style,
      THEN the subgoal is to say, "Hi, how's it going, Sally?"
      (sociolinguistic competence)

P6   IF the goal is to say, "Hi, how's it going, Sally?"
      THEN the subgoal is to pay attention to pronouncing the sentence as
      much like a native speaker as possible.
      (grammatical competence for pronunciation)

P7   IF the goal is to pronounce the sentence as much like a native speaker
      as possible,
      THEN the subgoal is to check whether my pronunciation is accurate
      enough to communicate the meaning.
      (sociolinguistic competence)

P8   IF the goal is to check whether my pronunciation is accurate enough to
      communicate the meaning of my greeting,
      THEN the subgoal is to pay careful attention to Sally's response.
      (sociolinguistic competence)

P9   IF the goal is to pay careful attention to Sally's response,
      and her response indicates that she has understood my meaning,
      THEN the subgoal is to wait for Sally to finish her conversational turn.
      (discourse competence)

P10   IF the goal is to wait for Sally to finish her conversational turn, and
      she completes her turn with a question,
      THEN the subgoal is to understand her question.
      (grammatical competence)

P11   IF the goal is to understand Sally's question,
      THEN the subgoal is to compare what she says to what I already
      know in English and to my general knowledge of how conversations
      work.
      (grammatical competence and sociolinguistic competence)

TABLE 3.1. *(continued)*

P12 IF the goal is to compare Sally's question to what I already know,
and the match is good enough to understand her meaning,
THEN the subgoal is to answer with the information requested.

P13 IF the goal is to answer with the information requested,
and I want to form a grammatically correct sentence,
THEN the subgoal is to pay attention to word order and noun and
verb endings as I respond.
(grammatical competence for syntax and strategic competence)

P14 IF the goal is to pay attention to word order and noun and verb
endings,
and I notice (or Sally's reaction suggests) that I have made a mistake
that impedes comprehension,
THEN the subgoal is to correct my mistake.
(sociolinguistic and grammatical competence)

P15 IF the goal is to correct my mistake,
THEN "pop the goal" (e.g., go back to P13).

P16 IF the goal is to continue the conversation with Sally,
and she responds with a question that I don't understand,
THEN the subgoal is to ask her to repeat or paraphrase.

P17 IF the goal is to ask Sally to repeat or paraphrase her question,
and this time I understand the question,
THEN "pop the goal" (e.g., go back to P12).

P18 IF the goal is to continue the conversation with Sally,
and she begins telling a long story about her activities,
THEN the subgoal is to pay attention to her pauses and linguistic
markers and interject comments appropriately.
(discourse and strategic competence)

---

*P1 stands for the first production system, P2 for the second, and so on.

sider the idea of a *rule* in its broadest sense. Rules apply to all aspects
of a language and are not limited to systematic rules of grammar. Furthermore, rules may be learned either through informal means, or in
formal classroom settings through direct instruction; they may be self-
generated; or ad hoc rules may be needed to understand or produce
language for specific purposes.

Table 3.1 is an example of a set of of production systems that illustrate
some of the different types of rules that need to be applied by the second
language learner in order to be communicatively competent, as communicative competence is defined by Canale and Swain (1980). Specific
examples are presented of rules covering sociolinguistic competence,
discourse competence, and strategic competence. Thus, rules of grammar

are only a part of the declarative knowledge required by a competent user of the second language. By using production system notation, additional aspects of language use can be specified and described. Table 3.1 shows how a production system might be used to generate and maintain a particular conversation in a second language between an intermediate-level speaker of English and a native English speaker. The purpose of this example is to illustrate how even a brief conversational exchange is subject to complex rules on a number of aspects of language, of which grammer is only one.

The example in Table 3.1 illustrates the goal-directed characteristics of communication interactions and the adaptability of goals as the conversation progresses. Although only one set of goals is illustrated, the speaker may change goals and move the conversation in different directions at any time. In this example, the speaker restates portions of the communication that were misunderstood by the listener. The intent to communicate begins at the production system designated P1, where the speaker establishes a goal to communicate with another person in the speaker's second language. P2 identifies a subgoal to use the second language, leading to P3, which concerns selection of an appropriate greeting. Thus, goals may be embedded in other goals and provide connecting links in the production system. In P6 the speaker initiates the conversation by expressing the greeting, and in P10 the listener responds by presenting a question. The exchange continues in P13, with the speaker's miscommunication in the second language. In P14 the speaker recognizes that a mistake has been made and in P15 tries to formulate the P13 utterance again. (The phrase "pop the goal" is used by Anderson [1983] to indicate that the sequence shifts from the current goal to one preceding it in the hierarchy.) The communication continues at P18, with the listener initiating an extended story requiring attention by the initial speaker.

A general model of a conversation would contain multiple branching and exit opportunities in addition to a hierarchical structure with subroutines reflecting subgoals that depend on the choice made at a given branching opportunity. The choice selected at one turn determines the next production set, which then creates a new set of choices. For example, among the choices evident is the possibility of ending the conversation at any point. The native speaker of English has a number of gambits that can be used to end a conversation in a socially appropriate way, such as "Well, I've got to go now," or "Hey, it was great seeing you." Such discourse markers and their underlying meaning may be unknown or misunderstood by individuals with limited English proficiency, resulting in their inability to end a conversation appropriately or to recognize that the other person is ending the conversation. As a result, the limited English speaker may explore a number of possible meanings for such utterances before reaching an accurate conclusion. This exploration may require new production sets just to interpret the communication, each of which may have new goals and choices.

Individuals applying rules to a communication as described in Table 3.1 may do so efficiently despite the level of detail required to delineate individual steps in the interaction. The rules governing individual productions in some cases may be based on procedural rather than declarative knowledge and may have been forgotten by the person. Furthermore, as we will point out later, rules that are represented by procedural knowledge may be performed automatically, without conscious deliberation, although some rules may still require conscious application in the production. Whether any single production is represented by declarative or procedural knowledge will most likely depend on the learner's prior exposure to rule systems, the transfer of comparable rules from the L1, and the person's prior opportunities for communicative practice in contexts where sociolinguistic and strategic competence are needed.

Stages of skill acquisition

Anderson's (1980) three stages of skill acquisition (cognitive, associative, and autonomous) have important implications both for understanding the process of second language acquisition and for developing instructional approaches. At least four issues in second language acquisition can be examined through the theory of cognitive skills acquisition: (1) the parallel between stages and second language constructs; (2) the learner's awareness of learning processes; (3) the rate of language acquisition for selected learning tasks; and (4) the retention or loss of language over time.

PARALLEL BETWEEN STAGES AND SECOND LANGUAGE CONSTRUCTS

The parallel between stages and second language constructs can be shown by delineating second language processes occurring at each stage. What is important to remember in the following description is that Anderson (1983, 1985) views the stagewise acquisition of a complex cognitive skill as a shift from declarative to procedural knowledge, or as the "proceduralization" of knowledge. During the cognitive stage, the second language learner engages in conscious mental activity in order to find meaning in the new language. This conscious mental activity may focus on different aspects of the L2, depending on the context of learning. The learner's attention may focus on the functional use of language in learning that takes place informally outside the classroom. Learners in these contexts have been observed to respond to and use appropriately

entire phrases or sentences whose component parts are not yet understood (Ventriglia 1982). For example, a learner might be aware of the
functional consequences of "Heygimmedeball" and even note that it has
similarities with "Heygimmedepencil," but be unaware of the grammatical components involved in the continuous string of sounds. In a
sense, learners are opportunistic and grasp onto meaningful chunks of
language that they can understand and that appear to have important
consequences. In a classroom setting, on the other hand, the learner's
attention may be directed by the teacher to the formal aspects of the
language, to its sound system, to vocabulary, to functional use of language chunks in communicative activities, or to a combination of these
aspects of language. Whatever the characteristics of the input are, however, the learning process at the cognitive stage would be the same –
intensive attention to the new language and deliberate efforts to make
sense of it.

This intensive attention to the new language that characterizes the
cognitive stage may explain why many learners go through a silent period
or delay language production at the beginning of their exposure to the
L2 (Krashen 1980). Beginning-level learners may find it easier to focus
on understanding and remembering different parts of the new language
by silently attending to it instead of by being distracted by the demands
of immediate language production.

In the second, or associative, stage of skill learning, learners begin to
develop sufficient familiarity with the knowledge acquired in the first
stage so that it can be used procedurally. This stage appears to correspond with what second language theorists term *interlanguage*, the not-
yet-accurate use of the target language by the L2 learner (see Selinker
1972; 1984). Interlanguage is characterized by errors that are gradually
corrected as learners become more proficient at detecting discrepancies
between their language production and the models that they encounter.
It is a temporary system, restructured as the learner tests hypotheses
about the new language, and adds, drops, or modifies rules as a result
of these trials. At this intermediate stage, the L2 learner is able to use
the language for communication, although imperfectly, but may find
difficulties in using the new language as a tool for learning complex
information, because active attention is still being given to strengthening
the language skill itself, which reduces the amount of attention that is
free to deal with incorporating new information into declarative
knowledge.

When second language learners reach Anderson's third stage of language learning, they are able to process language autonomously, or
without reference to the underlying rules. In other words, their performance in the language is very like that of a native speaker. In second
language acquisition, this third stage has been called automatic pro-

cessing (McLaughlin et al. 1983). At this point, the learner focuses on using the language for functional purposes, whether these are social, academic, or technical. Because language can be processed automatically, the learner is able to process new information at the same time that language is in use. In other words, parallel processing becomes possible.

As we have noted in the previous chapter, we believe that this basic stagewise explanation of how learning occurs needs to be augmented in the case of language acquisition and perhaps with other complex cognitive skills as well. There are difficulties in limiting a theory of second language acquisition to a learning system that is bound to formal rule systems, because many of the rules for second language acquisition appear to be self-generated in an idiosyncratic manner (e.g., Selinker 1972, 1984) and because instructional systems to teach complex skills relying on formal rules as a precursor to expert performance may be highly inefficient and even counterproductive (Gagné 1985). We are not convinced that reorganization is different from some of the processes that can be described under Anderson's theory. We see nothing inconsistent between reorganization as described by Rumelhart and Norman (1978) or McLaughlin (1987b) and Anderson's (1983, 1985) description of procedural knowledge, since the transfer of production systems seems to be a useful way of explaining how reorganization of procedural knowledge occurs. Because we have discussed these concepts earlier, we will not elaborate on them at this point.

CONSCIOUS AWARENESS

The second issue that can be analyzed using a cognitive theory of skill acquisition concerns conscious awareness of learning. The internal processing that takes place during these stages may explain the role of conscious learning effort in different language contexts. Krashen (1982) uses the term "acquisition" to refer to language proficiency gained through unconscious processes in unstructured language interactions outside the classroom, and "learning" to refer to language skills gained through conscious processes in the structured environment provided by classrooms. In the cognitive theory of complex skill acquisition, learners in unstructured language contexts might be more inclined to parse language into chunks based on meaning or language functions instead of on language structures. The learner tends to be consciously aware of rule applications during initial stages of acquisition and unaware of rules once proficiency has been achieved. Nevertheless, the learner may be unaware of specific rule applications, merely repeating phrases that have immediate functional utility for a specific context. This does not mean that initial learning occurs without conscious awareness, only that the formal linguistic or other rule on which the language usage is based may be unknown to the learner. The person will be very aware of many aspects of the learning process and may even apply specific strategies to aid in learning, such as relating new information to prior knowledge, comparing a new linguistic item to an item in the L1, and so on.

Whether one believes in a stagewise theory of second language acquisition or in learning that involves accretion, tuning, and restructuring, there are similarities between these views in the shift that occurs from controlled processes to automatic processing (see, for example, Anderson 1985; Faerch and Kasper 1987; McLaughlin 1987a). The critical determinants of whether controlled or automatic processes are used seem to be the degree to which the procedural skill has been learned and the task familiarity or novelty of the information being processed. A highly learned skill with a familiar stimulus is likely to be associated with automatic processing, but may be associated with controlled processing when there is a change in the nature of the task or unfamiliar information is introduced. Poorly learned skills are likely to be associated with controlled processing, except in the circumstance where subskill components have been practiced sufficiently with repeated information (Shiffrin and Schneider 1984). In second language acquisition, an individual who is presented with unfamiliar language elements may shift from automatic to controlled processing. While Shiffrin and Schneider (1984) avoid use of the term *consciousness* in their discussion of controlled and automatic processing, Faerch and Kasper (1987) join Anderson (1985) in suggesting that automatic mental processes are performed without awareness with familiar information, but that the processes become conscious when the learner encounters novel or unfamiliar material. In contrast, Bialystok and Ryan (1985) indicate that the notion of consciousness is irrelevant to the processes' knowledge and control dimensions, since individuals may consciously analyze a relatively simple task but also consciously analyze a metacognitive task at the highest levels of the two dimensions. The question concerning awareness of mental processing bears upon research methodology in second language acquisition, since without awareness of otherwise automatic processes, learners would never be able to describe how they learn. What cognitive theory indicates is that awareness and conscious control depend on the familiarity of the skill being applied and the nature of the information that is processed, not whether the information is learned in a classroom or in a supposedly natural language environment, as Krashen suggests.

Thus, where Krashen's linguistic theory predicts unconscious learning, cognitive theory predicts awareness. Evidence supports the view that beginning and intermediate L2 learners are aware of strategies used outside the classroom as well as those used in school settings (O'Malley et al. 1985a). Further, where Krashen differentiates between acquisition and learning, cognitive theory sees the distinction as unnecessary and unparsimonious. Because different language skills may be acquired at different rates, as pointed out later, a learner might be unaware of conceptual processing for more advanced individual skills even though overall proficiency is at the beginning or intermediate level. Language processing without awareness therefore could occur in either classroom or nonclassroom settings, depending on the level of the skill. Analysis of the cognitive processing that goes on even in unstructured learning environments provides opportunities to understand language acquisition in generalizable terms parallel to other complex skills. A cognitive model of second language acquisition sees active conscious processes involved in all language settings, at least in the initial stages of learning. These processes can be described and used to assist learning instead of being relegated to the uncertainty of unconscious mechanisms.

RATE AND TYPE OF LANGUAGE SKILL

The third issue that can be examined with a theory of skills acquisition is the rate and type of language skill acquired. Given that language is a highly complex system, involving not only grammar, semantics, and pronunciation but also rules of usage and discourse, learners may acquire different aspects of the new language sequentially. For instance, a learner might move through the three stages of skill acquisition initially with those aspects of the new language that are most accessible. For some learners, this might be the sound system or grammar rules. For others, it might be sociolinguistically appropriate chunks of the new language, and for others it might be communication tricks that keep a conversation going. As these "easy" features move from the cognitive stage through the associative stage and then become autonomous, the learner begins to have more and more attention freed to focus actively on some of the "harder" features of the new language, as well as content information, through the medium of the new language.

The relative difficulty of different language features could serve as a basis for "chunking" with L2 learners. Individuals might treat a difficult chunk with rule-based procedures that are applied at the cognitive stage, while processing what is perceived as easier using procedures at the associative or autonomous stage. Thus, a learner might alternate processing associated with different stages of learning depending on the perceived difficulty of language chunks. What is perceived as easy or difficult could vary between learners, and might depend on factors such as age, context of learning, learning style, affective considerations, prior declarative and procedural knowledge, and ability to deploy effective learning strategies.

RETENTION AND ATTRITION

A fourth issue that a cognitive theory of skill acquisition can address is language retention or attrition after exposure or formal instruction in the language ceases. This usually applies to the loss of a second language in a first language environment, as in foreign language instruction, or to the loss of a first language in a second language environment, as in language loss among immigrant populations. However, other possibilities are evident, such as the loss of a first or second language due to aging (Weltens 1987). Research on second language attrition has attempted to identify which aspects of a language are forgotten after a period of disuse, the rate at which these aspects are lost, if the sequence of forgetting parallels the initial learning sequence, and if the conditions under which the language was initially learned affect retention. Research on language attrition indicates that both the initial competence gained in a second language and the amount of subsequent practice opportunities affect how much of the language is lost or retained over time (Lambert and Moore 1984; Oxford 1982).

A cognitive theory of skills acquisition would predict that aspects of the language that are at the first or cognitive stage of skills acquisition and are therefore represented by declarative knowledge would be forgotten first, whereas those aspects of the language that have become automatic or proceduralized would be retained. The theory also predicts that retrieval of words from long-term-memory depends on *depth of processing* (Craik and Tulving 1975), or the extent to which words have been applied in a number of semantic or syntactic contexts.

The issue that needs to be addressed is: Which language skills are declarative and which skills are procedural? Vocabulary is identified with concepts and thus can be represented as declarative knowledge. Sociolinguistic competence involves knowing about cultural norms, styles, and registers; it may also be represented as declarative knowledge. In contrast, grammatical competence – whether phonological, morphological, or syntactical – is characterized in Anderson's (1980) theory as procedural knowledge. As we noted earlier, Faerch and Kasper (1985) suggested that procedural knowledge includes receptive skills, production skills, conversational procedures, communication strategies, and learning strategies. The general implication is that the way in which knowledge was learned and is represented will influence retention. The distinction may be useful in planning the types of skills relearning in a second language should focus on and the types of learning activities that should be emphasized during initial instruction.

Unfortunately, none of the studies on language retention appears to have drawn the distinction that would be required between different types of declarative and procedural knowledge (Weltens 1987). Further, the studies did not report whether different linguistic levels (e.g., phonology, morphology, syntax, and lexicon) measured in the same subskill area (reading, writing, listening, speaking) are affected by attrition in the same way. Nor did these studies appear to have determined whether different language functions (explaining, describing, getting another's attention) or areas of communicative competence (sociolinguistic and discourse competence as well as linguistic competence) are affected differentially by attrition.

Despite the lack of data from second language acquisition research on retention of declarative versus procedural knowledge, a study of the ability of college students to retain various kinds of materials presented in a zoology course sheds at least some indirect light on this issue (Tyler 1934). Students were presented single one-hour lectures over a semester and then measured for learning before and after the course and at a 15-month delayed interval following the conclusion of the course. They showed the most dramatic losses when it came to identifying technical terms and naming parts of animals, both declarative knowledge. In contrast, in applying principles and interpreting experiments, both procedural skills, the students showed almost no loss, even over the 15-month period. We know of no more recent or more relevant study of the long-term retention of procedural relative to declarative knowledge. While this is meager substance for applications to second language acquisition, clearly some new directions for research on attrition are required to build on this isolated piece of information.

Conclusions

Viewing second language acquisition as a cognitive skill offers a number of advantages. First, it can provide a comprehensive and well-specified theoretical framework for second language learning. The theory has evolved over an extended period in cognitive psychology, is well supported by an extensive body of research, and provides insights into second language acquisition that would not be otherwise evident. Second, the theory can explain a number of useful constructs that have been discussed in the second language literature as relatively isolated phenomena and place them within the context of a broader theoretical statement. These constructs include common underlying proficiency, transfer, metalinguistic awareness, interlanguage, the rules of communicative competence, automatic processing, the acquisition versus learning distinction, and language retention. Third, the theory can be adapted to provide a detailed process view of second language acquisition. Whereas previous theories have been silent or at best taciturn on the cognitive processes involved in second language acquisition, this theory provides far more information about the linguistic phenomena that occur during the stages of acquiring a complex cognitive skill.

A final advantage of the theory is that greater focus is given to a number of new directions for research. The first direction concerns knowledge representation, or the ways in which information is stored in memory. With regard to declarative knowledge, the theory has raised but not resolved the question of whether knowledge is stored separately in two languages or as a single system. There are obvious implications here for how the theory will explain common underlying proficiency, transfer, and metalinguistic awareness, among other constructs. The theory still needs further specification concerning the ways in which propositions are organized and differentiated from schemata, and the role of schemata in retention. With regard to procedural knowledge, the theory raises questions about the basis for production systems in the L1 and L2, the relationship between production systems and language-based rule systems (in the broadest sense), and the commonality of production systems in the L1 and L2.

The second direction for research suggested by the theory is to analyze in far greater detail the mental processes occurring during second language acquisition, the correspondence between mental processes and stages in acquiring a complex cognitive skill, and the ways in which production systems parallel sociolinguistic, discourse, and strategic rules as well as grammatical rules. The interest in production systems applies not just to learning but also to retention and language loss. That is, the information retained or lost may be analyzed in terms of whether it is declarative or procedural knowledge.

A third direction for research concerns second language instruction and the procedures that will lead to more effective learning. One of the major implications of cognitive theory is that the way in which individuals process information must be considered along with the way in which teachers teach if we are to understand the instructional process. A greater focus in second language acquisition research on learner processes under different instructional approaches seems warranted.

4 Learning strategies: methods and research

In previous chapters we established the foundation for describing second language acquisition and learning strategies as complex cognitive skills within a cognitive-theoretical framework. This theoretical foundation is necessary for the research on learning strategies in second language acquisition we present in this and later chapters to have substance and meaning in a broader framework than would be provided by simply demonstrating that students report using learning strategies or that the strategies can be taught. We use the theory in this chapter to build a rationale for analyzing findings from the descriptive research, and in later chapters we use it to specify the conditions under which strategy training is likely to be effective.

Research on learning strategies is based on the assertion that strategies begin as declarative knowledge that can become proceduralized with practice and, like complex cognitive skills, proceed through the cognitive, associative, and autonomous stages of learning. At the cognitive stage, the strategy application is still based on declarative knowledge, requires processing in short-term memory, and is not performed automatically. The student may have a firm recollection of using the strategy with a specific task. In this case, research on how the strategy is used should be relatively easy and presumably could be performed through virtually any form of data collection, such as interviews or questionnaires. However, if the strategy application has become proceduralized and the strategy use is performed automatically, the student may not be aware of using the strategy, and data collection might require specialized techniques that interrupt ongoing mental processes. Although it may be legitimate to question whether or not automatic use of learning techniques qualifies as being strategic (Rabinowitz and Chi 1987), similar mental processes are presumably being used when the strategy is still declarative knowledge, albeit automatic strategy application occurs more quickly and autonomously, and without the intervening use of short-term memory. Thus, some of the primary purposes of research in second language acquisition, as Faerch and Kasper (1987) have noted, are to determine the ways in which declarative knowledge influences second language acquisition, to isolate relatively automatic procedures in second language acquisition that ordinarily would occur without awareness, and to determine the processes that are unique to the native language or shared in common with the second language. While Faerch and Kasper have suggested that these purposes apply to all types of declarative and procedural knowledge in second language learning, the discussion that follows limits these principles to research on learning strategies alone.

A framework for data collection on learning strategies

The need for a framework to describe data collection methodologies in learning strategies research is evident, considering the varied degrees of success of different methodologies in eliciting strategies and the varied types of strategies that might emerge depending on the data collection procedure employed. The following framework, a minor variant on the criteria for classifying introspective methods in second language research suggested by Faerch and Kasper (1987), contains six elements:

1. The strategy or strategies which are the objective of data collection,
2. The language skill or task of interest,
3. The temporal relationship between the strategy use and the data collection,
4. The level of training required for the informant to respond,
5. The elicitation procedure, and
6. Whether or not the data collection is performed individually or in a group.

We point out how these elements apply to different data collection procedures, such as observations, questionnaires, interviews, and other forms of eliciting information from students, and conclude by analyzing some of the concerns that have been expressed about introspective or self-report methods of data collection.

Objective of data collection

The major objective of data collection in studying learning strategies is to elicit information about the ways in which the strategies are used with specific second language tasks by various learners operating under different types of conditions. However, beyond this primary objective, there may be at least three secondary objectives: (1) to focus on strategies that are represented as declarative or as procedural knowledge; (2) to identify overt or covert strategies; or (3) to distinguish among executive strategies (which we call metacognitive strategies), strategies that operate directly on the learning materials (cognitive strategies), and strategies that require the presence of another person (social strategies) or involve affective control during learning (affective strategies).

DECLARATIVE VERSUS PROCEDURAL KNOWLEDGE

Strategies that are only recently learned or discovered are likely to operate under a deliberate rule-based system and function as declarative knowledge, while strategies that have been used repeatedly are most likely operating as procedural knowledge. As we have seen, complex cognitive skills such as learning strategies are often acquired gradually over repeated opportunities for cued practice, but may be performed autonomously or without reference to the original rule when they are thoroughly learned (Gagné 1985). However, we suspect that highly effective language learners transfer at least some strategies they have learned earlier on similar tasks, or combine strategies to maximize learning, and may perform these functions automatically from the onset. Because strategies that have become proceduralized may be operating automatically through connections in long-term memory, the process does not enter short-term memory (Ericsson and Simon 1987) and may be inaccessible for introspective report.

The process of data collection using introspective reports is complicated considerably in analyzing proceduralized strategies, but may be facilitated under three conditions. First, in second language acquisition, learners often experience tasks that vary in difficulty for them, as when portions of a communication are easily understood while other portions are far more demanding. Under these conditions, the person may tend to use learning strategies consciously for the more demanding portion of the task, while processing the less demanding portions automatically. The conscious processing becomes available for introspective analysis. A second condition that may facilitate data collection with a proceduralized learning strategy is that certain types of tasks such as responding to dictation and producing original writing require deliberate processing. Under these circumstances, the learning strategies will be accessible to introspection, and the learner should be able to provide an account of the strategy even though the strategy may occur automatically with another task. And finally, an individual may be interrupted mid-task so that processes that otherwise would occur automatically might be available for introspection. This approach is not easy to implement with certain kinds of language tasks, however, since informants who are in the midst of oral production in a second language may find it exceedingly difficult to explain what they are thinking while at the same time generating the required language. The demands on short-term memory could easily be so complicated as to prevent either the learning strategy description or the language task from being performed effectively.

OVERT VERSUS COVERT BEHAVIOR

Some strategies occur overtly and are relatively easy to observe, whereas other strategies occur only covertly and require introspective forms of data collection in which the informant provides a description of the strategy used. Examples of overt strategies include note taking and referencing skills, such as using a dictionary. As we discuss later, strategies that occur overtly cannot qualify as mental processes. Nevertheless, the mental processes underlying these overt strategies could easily entail such strategic modes of processing as self-monitoring, summarizing, and inferencing (among other strategies). It is for this reason that we group these overt activities as learning strategies.

STRATEGY TYPE

The intent of data collection may be to obtain information on all types of strategies, to focus on one specific category of strategy (metacognitive, cognitive, or social/affective), or to focus on a specific strategy (e.g., self-monitoring). The usual procedure has been to generate information on all strategies, although other approaches are possible, as when the investigator is trying to determine the way in which a specific strategy is used with a specific language task. Wenden (1983), for example, asked informants questions about the types of metacognitive strategies they used in second language acquisition. The broadest range of coverage for strategy use can be obtained with questionnaires and guided interviews because of the structure given to the questions, whereas the narrowest range of strategy coverage seems likely to occur with think-aloud procedures, because the data collector is constrained from using prompts for additional strategies by the nature of the approach.

Language task

The investigation of learning strategies in second language research may concentrate on the student's first or second language, on any of the four language modalities (listening, speaking, reading, or writing, or some combination of these), or on other aspects of the language task. For example, the investigation might concentrate on specific tasks that typically occur in second language classrooms irrespective of the modality, such as following directions (which may entail both listening and writing) or learning grammar (which could involve all four language skills). Each of these possibilities is discussed in the following sections.

FIRST OR SECOND LANGUAGE

Investigations may attempt to obtain information on strategies that are used in the first language or the second language, or may attempt to compare strategies used in the first or second language. The typical focus of investigation in second language acquisition research has been to analyze learning strategies used in acquiring a second language. However, by comparing the strategies used in a first and second language with identical tasks, such as reading, the investigator can obtain critical information about the extent to which the learner has internalized procedures that have been found to facilitate learning in the first language and transferred them to the second language. We reported in Chapter 3 on McLaughlin's (1987b) descriptions of students' failure to transfer reading comprehension strategies used in the first language to the second language even though the individuals appeared to be balanced bilinguals and transfer of strategies would have been expected.

LANGUAGE MODALITIES

The focus of research on learning strategies might be on all four language skills or only on one or more language modalities. The typical approach in studies of second language acquisition has been to collect information on all four language skills – listening, speaking, reading, and writing. The early work on learning strategies by Naiman et al. (1978) elicited information from respondents concerning each of the four language skills using multiple data collection procedures, which included observations, interviews, and questionnaires. The respondent can be asked to describe uses of strategies in general with second language acquisition or can be asked to describe the strategies used with specific language tasks.

In our own work, we have varied the data collection approach depending on the purpose of the study and the depth with which we wished to elicit information about strategies used with individual language skills. When greater depth was required, we tended to focus on a single language skill, such as listening comprehension. However, when a broad survey of language skills was of interest, we asked informants about strategies they used with all language skills. The broadest survey of language skills we performed, as will be discussed later, was to analyze through observations the language tasks that typically occurred in the second language classroom and then ask questions of students in these classrooms about strategies used with all of these tasks. Many of these language learning activities crossed modalities, as in preparing a brief speech (where the student may have written the speech out prior to delivering it) and listening to a teacher's lecture (where many students report taking notes as well as listening). This approach proved useful, because students could relate to the type of task they were asked to discuss through analysis of their experiences in the classroom.

SPECIFICITY OF THE TASK

Respondents can be asked to describe their strategies in general in second language acquisition or can be asked to describe their strategies with specific language learning tasks. In reporting strategies in a diary, for example, the individual probably describes strategies that are practiced on isolated tasks that seem difficult or important or on functional tasks experienced in context. In contrast, while reporting strategies in questionnaires or during a think-aloud, the strategies reported are specific to the task indicated by the investigator. In the work on classroom strategies mentioned previously, we asked questions about discrete-point and integrative language tasks that occur in classrooms and about functional language tasks that typically occur outside the classroom (e.g., answering the telephone, applying for a job).

One unique form of think-aloud that has been introduced recently is a think-aloud on a variant of the cloze test, referred to as a C-test (Feldman and Stemmer 1987; Grotjahn 1987). Whereas a cloze test may have every ninth word deleted from passages of varying length, the C-test has the second part of every second word deleted from what are usually short texts on different topics. This type of test is more likely to elicit the respondent's knowledge of structural rules in the second language. Grotjahn combined the C-test methodology with a think-aloud approach because of both an interest in the underlying mental processes occurring while students responded to the test and uncertainty about what the test was actually measuring.

Temporal relationship

The contiguity of data collection with the task on which the student is asked to report uses of learning strategies is a critical determinant of the type of information that can be expected. Faerch and Kasper (1987) distinguish three distinct types of data collection along this dimension: (1) *simultaneous introspection,* or concurrent performance of the task and reporting on the strategies used; (2) *immediate retrospection,* or introspection about a task that was just completed; and (3) *delayed retrospection,* or analysis of strategies used with previously completed tasks. Simultaneous introspection occurs with think-aloud tasks, where the informant is asked to report on the strategies being used while the task is being performed. The advantage of this data collection approach is that strategies that occur only fleetingly in short-term memory can be identified and reported. This approach would be suitable for receptive tasks or for writing, but would be difficult to use in reporting on strategies used while speaking. Immediate retrospection, however, could be used with speaking as well as with any of the other modalities and occurs when the person is interrupted just as the language task is completed. Delayed retrospection occurs when the person is asked to reconstruct the types of strategies used with language tasks long after the task has been performed, as with diary studies, questionnaires, and some interviews.

A fourth possible distinction along the temporal dimension is *predic-*

tive introspection, or stating what one might do in an anticipated learning event (Brown et al. 1983). The work we described earlier, in which we asked students to report on strategies used with a broad range of language tasks occurring in classrooms, used a delayed retrospection approach.

The possibility exists that simultaneous introspection will change the nature of the thought processes so that the informant is reporting a modified version of what actually occurs while thinking. Ericsson and Simon (1987) distinguish between a "talk-aloud" data collection procedure and "think-aloud." In the talk-aloud procedure, the verbal reporting of the informant is expected to parallel the thought processes, as in performing simple arithmetic or solving a problem in logic. The respondent is reporting on information that is needed to solve the problem as it enters into short-term memory. In this case, silent thought would be no different from overt thought processes and may in fact occur within roughly the same time frame as silent thought processes. In the think-aloud procedure, however, the informant encodes the mental processes immediately after they occur and then takes time to describe them to the investigator. Thus, the description is not contemporaneous with the problem solution process, and overtly describing the problem solution takes longer than solving comparable problems silently. This description of think-aloud procedures characterizes data collection with second language acquisition in which informants describe each strategic step in learning or comprehending information immediately after it occurs. Respondents are typically interrupted at various points as they are listening and asked to describe what they were just thinking rather than asked to perform a task simultaneously while reporting on their thought processes. The critical point with think-aloud procedures is that the mental processing the informant reports on is still accessible in short-term memory.

Informant training

Most data collection techniques for investigating learning strategies do not require prior training of informants. Prior training has not been used with questionnaires, guided interviews, and other techniques that give structure to the informant's task. However, part of the problem of obtaining adequate samples of strategies with diaries or interviews may be incomplete training of the informant so that the person is uncertain what to report, how often to report it, and how much to report. Furthermore, if the informant reports information independently of cues or prompts, the person may have difficulty remembering details. Informant training is strongly recommended for the think-aloud procedure (Ericsson and Simon 1987) because of the potential confusion over what to report in the interview. In our own work, we have followed the recommendation by Ericsson and Simon (1987) to use a warm-up procedure prior to the actual think-aloud data collection session. The initial part of the warm-up consists of a problem that the respondents solve aloud, while later the respondents are given verbal tasks about which they are asked to think aloud. We reserve one full session for training, and then provide a review of training at the start of each data collection session. The advantages in training are to familiarize informants with the data collection procedures and to any equipment that may be used in recording the informant's report, and to ensure that all informants are using the same verbal report procedure.

In performing work on second language acquisition strategies, the investigator must decide on the language in which to provide the warm-up period. In our own work we have allowed respondents at the intermediate level of proficiency in the second language to warm up on tasks in their first language and then switch to the same language in which the task is performed (the second language) when reporting on their learning strategies. In addition to the warm-up portion of the data collection, Ericsson and Simon (1987) refer to the use of interviewer reminders throughout the data collection when the informant becomes silent or strays from talking about strategies. For example, even trained respondents sometimes begin to describe the content of the passage to which they have attended when thinking aloud instead of describing their thoughts while attending to the passage. Interviewer comments such as "Keep talking" and "What are you thinking about?" are useful probes to encourage respondents to continue describing their strategies.

Elicitation procedures

There are at least three aspects of the elicitation procedure that have an important influence on data collection – the language in which the data are collected, the degree of structure given to the task, and whether the elicitation is oral or in writing.

LANGUAGE OF DATA COLLECTION

The customary approach in studies of second language acquisition has been to permit respondents to use their native language in describing their language learning strategies. In our own work, where we performed retrospective interviews with students of English as a second language, we encouraged students with beginning level skills in English to use their native language in describing their strategies, and gave the option to students at the intermediate level to decide on the language in which they preferred to be interviewed. Generally, students at the intermediate level preferred to use English. In contrast, when we interviewed students learning foreign languages in the United States, even the intermediate level students were interviewed in their native language (English). In think-aloud interviews, as we noted previously, we permitted informants with intermediate level skills in the second language to warm up in their native language. This has the advantage of familiarizing the respondent with the introspection process and facilitates transfer of the process to the second language. A reasonable degree of proficiency in the second language should be evident if think-aloud data are to be collected in the second language, since the short-term memory demands for processing information about learning strategies could easily limit the type of information generated about the strategies or the person's approach to the task.

DEGREE OF STRUCTURE

A high degree of structure in the data collection means that the instrument will have a strong influence on the content of the informant's report, whereas a low degree of structure indicates that the instrument has little influence on the specific content. Procedures with the highest degree of structure are questionnaires and rating scales, which may determine not only the type of strategy but also the type of task and the setting where the strategy is used. For example, a questionnaire can determine that the strategy is used with a vocabulary or a listening task, and that the task appears in a classroom or while the informant is involved in a functional activity such as listening on the telephone. A number of investigators have reported on learning strategies based on the use of questionnaires in both the second language literature (e.g., Oxford 1986; Politzer and McGroarty 1985) and the psychological literature (e.g., Weinstein, Schulte, and Cascallar 1983; Zimmerman and Pons 1986). In contrast to the structure derived from the use of questionnaires, a diary may leave open the specific language task involved or the setting in which the task is performed. Think-aloud data collection and other interview procedures delimit the task and the context but leave open the nature of the strategies that are reported. Wenden (1983) has expressed concern that self-reported strategies fail to lend themselves to rigorous analysis or classification due to the subjectivity of self-reports.

With data collection procedures that have little structure, one of the major sources of difficulty is in classifying strategies accurately from open-ended responses. In data collection with either interviews or think-aloud procedures, we tape-recorded informant responses and wrote complete transcripts to ensure that the classification of strategies is performed with acceptable levels of interrater reliability. With retrospective interviews, we made transcripts of a sample of the tapes for use in training individuals to code directly from the audio recording of the interview. With think-aloud interviews, however, we transcribed the entire interview, in part because of the difficulty of establishing interrater reliability directly from the taped interview but also because of the richness of the informant responses. Transcribed interviews give the data analyst copious amounts of data to review and code. Grotjahn (1987) reported having 2,000 pages of transcripts on verbal protocols obtained from introspective reports. While questionnaires fail to provide the depth of information yielded in interviews, the data produced are far more manageable and easier to analyze.

ORAL OR WRITTEN RESPONSES

Responses that are requested in writing may consist of diaries or more structured approaches such as questionnaires. Various investigators (e.g., Rubin 1981) have attempted to use diaries, for they may contain reasonably complete records of informant impressions about daily second language interchanges. However, diaries have the disadvantage of containing far more information than is needed for a straightforward analysis of learning strategies, and they often contain information that is of little value for learning strategy analyses. Rubin attempted to counteract this problem by giving her informants directions for completing the diaries. The advantage of questionnaires is in delimiting the responses to information that is relevant and in simplifying data manipulation, since computers can be used for data coding and analysis. In contrast, responses requested orally may be extremely difficult to record accurately, requiring tape or video recording equipment and complete transcripts of interview protocols for subsequent analysis. The potential for inaccuracy if the interviewer attempts to code strategy occurrences immediately after the informant mentions them or at the close of the interview is far too great to permit. We have used audio recordings in our own work to avoid this difficulty. As we already noted, however, the researcher must then decide whether to transcribe the full set of interviews or only a sample for the purpose of establishing interrater reliability.

The primary advantage with interview data collection is the richness of the description obtained of the respondent's use of learning strategies. The researcher obtains in-depth information about the use of strategies with individual tasks that would be difficult to obtain using other techniques, including diaries. We have found that students are all the more motivated to respond in an interview because they are pleased to have someone take a personal interest in their learning processes. We have usually prefaced the data collection in interviews by saying that what we learn from the research will be used to help other students like themselves. Students rarely have an opportunity to discuss the way that they think about learning or to provide this type of assistance to future students attempting to learn a second language.

Individual versus group data collection

The final characteristic of data collection used to identify learning strategies in second language acquisition research is whether the data are collected individually or in a group. This issue usually arises only with interviews, since most diaries are reported individually and most questionnaires and observations are performed with groups. Retrospective interviews are relatively easy to conduct with small groups of three to five students, whereas think-aloud interviews are typically conducted individually. We have found that retrospective interviews with students of high school age can be performed in small groups, and that students build on the response provided by other students by adding strategies of their own. We used this procedure with a guided interview about the special methods students used to learn specific academic tasks, which we had observed in their classrooms. Although other investigators have discussed data collection on the learning strategies of younger children (e.g., Brown, Bransford, Ferrara, and Campione 1983), we have not interviewed younger children ourselves and would be hesitant to do so in groups.

The principal disadvantage in conducting group interviews is that the strategies reported are difficult to relate to individual learning outcomes, as has been performed with questionnaires (e.g., Politzer and McGroarty 1985; Zimmerman and Pons 1986). The identity of individual students is often lost in tape recordings of the interview, and the students' reported strategies are influenced by what other students have said. Thus, there can be little confidence in associating specific strategy applications with individual students. In contrast, with either individual interviews or questionnaire responses, the researcher can obtain independent information on the student's performance on a language learning task or over a course of instruction and relate this to the strategies reported.

Multiple data collection procedures

Because different types of data collection procedures may lead to different conclusions about the character and use of learning strategies, some investigators have used multiple approaches to data collection (e.g., Naiman et al. 1978). We have used multiple data collection techniques in our own work consistent with the purpose of the study. In our earlier studies we were attempting to obtain a broad survey of the types of strategies students used, and we collected data with both small group interviews and questionnaires. One of the conclusions we reached from these studies is that the strategies reported depend on the data collection methodology. This seems disconcerting only if one ignores the extreme differences in the way that questions are asked of respondents using these different methodologies. When these differences are acknowledged, finding varying results from different data collection procedures can be expected. More recently, when we have focused in depth on the ways in which strategies are used with individual tasks, we have used think-aloud procedures combined with individual interviews and group-administered questionnaires.

Issues in the use of self-report data

Concerns about the use of data based on verbal report have been expressed in the psychological literature since the early part of this century (Ericsson and Simon 1987). Early studies were easy prey for behaviorists because they assumed a high degree of isomorphism between verbal reports and underlying mental processes. When differences appeared in the verbal reports of the same mental phenomenon as described by different investigators, little agreement could be reached on the nature of the underlying mental processes, and the procedures were criticized for being unscientific. With the recent emergence and increased credibility in these data collection procedures, especially since the 1970s, concerns have been expressed anew on at least two accounts: the veridicality of verbal reports with underlying mental processes, and potential changes in mental processes resulting from the questions asked during data collection.

Seliger (1983) raised concerns about the veridicality of verbal reports with the processes they purportedly represent in commenting upon an earlier study reported by Cohen and Hosenfeld (1981). The study used questionnaires to obtain retrospective data concerning strategy use in second language acquisition. Seliger specifically questioned whether the learner will have success in reporting on unconscious levels of processing, or is simply reporting on the *products* (e.g., utterances, translations) of underlying processes that are inaccessible. The learner observes the product and surmises how it might have been produced, but probably does not describe what transpired at the time of production. Furthermore, according to Seliger, the informant's description of an underlying process is likely to be misinterpreted by the examiner, who will probably view the description as referring to processes other than those the learner intended. Verbal reports are considered in this view to be useful information about how learners *use* what they know rather than as a means of uncovering underlying learning processes.

Cohen's (1984) rejoinder to these concerns is based on three arguments. One is that Seliger's (1983) own work in analyzing mental processing relied on only loosely formulated retrospective questions instead of concurrent interviews in attempting to reconstruct the use of linguistic rules. Because subjects were unsuccessful at remembering the rule while succeeding at a linguistic task, Seliger had concluded that there is a poor correspondence between recall of mental processes (such as interlanguage rules) and language production. Cohen points out that the data collection technique (retrospection) may have been poorly matched to the problem. Not only should a concurrent introspection approach have been used, but Seliger should have inquired more specifically about the linguistic elements he intended to elicit. Second, informants can be more successful at detecting underlying mental processes than Seliger allowed because the extent of conscious processing is greater than Seliger claimed. Because we ignore much of mental processing does not mean that it is inaccessible. Third, the linguistic processes involved in learning or problem solving should be as accessible as the problem-solving approach itself. Cohen cites Ericsson and Simon's (1980) analyses of various studies in which verbal reports coincided with mental processing on a variety of cognitive tasks, including classification, problem solving, and the ability to state a rule governing problem solution.

There remains a second problem in self-report data, which is that the process of inquiring about the strategies may change the nature of the mental processing, particularly during think-aloud interviews. Ericsson and Simon (1987) note that the major change in thinking that occurs during think-aloud interviews is that the "rate of thinking has to be slowed down to allow for the additional time required for verbalization of the thought" (p. 51). They reach this conclusion based on two types of analysis. One is by analyzing concurrent and retrospective verbal reports against a priori plausible thought sequences that emerged in a task analysis. While concurrent introspection yielded mental processes that were reasonably parallel with the task analysis, retrospective data collection appeared to delete important elements, suggesting that processing was more complex than individuals were able to recall. A second type of analysis is through inspection of findings from redundant observations, as are found in analyses of eye movements and verbal reports. This type of analysis, in fact, suggested that there was acceptable convergent validity from the independent methods of analysis. Brown et al. (1983) have noted that thinking aloud may not alter the underlying reasoning process, but may nevertheless have either a salutary or detrimental influence on learning. Good problem solvers, for example, spend more time identifying and evaluating learning processes and are able to state the rules leading to problem solution. Thinking aloud can detract from learning if it interferes with the fundamental processes that must be reported, as in thinking about verbalizations. Neither of these consequences of strategy use implies that strategies identified through self-report are not veridical with strategies that would otherwise have occurred.

Review of research on applications of learning strategies

As we noted in Chapter 2, the literature on learning strategies in second language acquisition emerged largely independent of research and theory developing in cognitive psychology. Rubin's (1975) early suggestion that the "good language learner" has much to teach us about learning strategies was apparently made in awareness of some of the literature in cognitive psychology extant at the time (Rubin, personal communication), namely Bruner, Flavell, and some others, but most of the major developments in what is currently known in cognitive theory were only just emerging when Rubin made this suggestion. The significant work in cognitive psychology on different types of learning (Rumelhart and Norman 1978), automaticity (LaBerge and Samuels 1974), declarative versus procedural knowledge (Anderson 1976), and schema theory (Schank and Abelson 1977) had not filtered into the second language acquisition literature or awareness. There are probably historical reasons why linguists avoided referring to psychological theories, stemming back to the Skinner debate with Chomsky and to Chomsky's (1980) suggestion that language acquisition occurs through processes that are independent of other behaviors and may indeed be linked to different faculties in the mind. Nevertheless, regardless of the reason, none of the more prominent cognitive psychologists of the 1970s or any of their research or theory is cited in the early learning strategies studies in second language acquisition (e.g., Rubin 1975, 1978; Naiman et al. 1978). Furthermore, none of the research on learning strategies, which began to emerge in the mid- to late 1970s in cognitive psychology (e.g., O'Neil 1978), was cited in the early research on learning strategies in second language acquisition.

At least three major contributions of this work in cognitive psychology were emerging by the early 1980s at the time we developed our first studies of strategy applications in second language acquisition:

1. A definition and classification of learning strategies;
2. Descriptive information on strategy application for different types of students and tasks; and
3. Validation of strategy effectiveness through either correlational or experimental work on the effectiveness of strategy training.

The second language acquisition literature was also struggling with each of these topics, but had not reached into the area of strategy training. Interestingly, neither the cognitive literature nor the literature in second language acquisition had developed a full theoretical understanding of why strategies were effective in enhancing learning or of the relationship between strategies and underlying mental processes. At best, the research on strategies was viewed in cognitive psychology as being consistent with emerging views in which learning occurred through active manipulation of information, or generative processing (e.g., Wittrock 1974; Wittrock, Marks, and Doctorow 1975), and in which the superior problem-solving performance of experts as contrasted with novices was due to the use of strategic modes of processing (e.g., Chase and Simon 1973; Larkin et al. 1980).

Definition and classification

One of the principal contributions of the literature in cognitive psychology was to distinguish between metacognitive and cognitive strategies. While the literature is not without difficulties, due to differences in opinion about what constitutes a metacognitive or a cognitive strategy (Brown et al. 1983), the distinction served to sharpen the discussion of how strategies function, who uses them, and the conditions under which they can be taught. In the following discussion, we will review some of the early descriptive work on strategy definitions and classification, and suggest some directions that were important for studying strategies in second language acquisition at the time that we began our own investigations into this area.

Metacognition has been used to refer to knowledge about cognition or the regulation of cognition. Knowledge about cognition may include applying thoughts about the cognitive operations of oneself or others, while regulation of cognition includes planning, monitoring, and evaluating a learning or problem-solving activity (Brown and Palincsar 1982; Brown et al. 1983). Examples of metacognitive strategies are directed attention, or consciously directing one's own attention to the learning task, and self-evaluation, or apraising the successes and difficulties in one's own learning efforts. Cognitive strategies are often specific to distinct learning activities and would include using operations or steps in learning or problem solving that require direct analysis, transformation, or synthesis of learning materials (Brown and Palincsar 1982; Brown et al. 1983; Rigney 1978). Cognitive strategies are exemplified by inferencing, or guessing meaning from context, and elaboration, or relating new information to other concepts in memory. The distinction between metacognitive and cognitive strategies has significance, among other reasons, because effective strategy training requires both types of strategies. Commenting on the failure of strategy training to transfer to new learning activities, Brown (1982) noted that much of this difficulty could be attributed to the failure to combine metacognitive strategies with cognitive strategies during learning. As we have noted elsewhere, "students without metacognitive approaches are essentially learners without direction and ability to review their progress, accomplishments, and future learning directions" (O'Malley et al. 1985a).

Dansereau (1985) has drawn a distinction between *primary strategies,* which are used to operate directly on learning materials (e.g., comprehension and memory strategies), and *support strategies,* which help to establish an appropriate learning attitude and aid in coping with distractions, fatigue, frustration, and so forth (e.g., concentration strategies). He also noted that strategies can differ according to the scope of the task they are intended to influence, as in strategies for general reading comprehension versus strategies for vocabulary learning, and the degree to which the strategy is specialized for particular tasks, as in strategies for learning from general texts versus strategies for learning about scientific theories. Dansereau notes that the theoretical underpinnings of more complicated learning strategies often used in strategy training, such as networking or mapping, may be difficult to analyze because a number of mental processes may be activated by the learner, including increased depth of processing, reorganization of the material, novel schematic representations, and imagery.

The significance we give to the contributions of cognitive psychology is not to suggest that the early studies of learning strategies in second language acquisition were not productive in contributing to the definition and classification of strategies. In fact, the redirection of linguistic thought resulting from Rubin's (1975) introduction of the concept of the good language learner can be seen as all the more important because it occurred independent of the stimulus from cognitive theoretical developments that dominated the late 1970s and continue to influence the 1980s. Rubin's work also ran counter to the main thread of linguistic thought of the time that effective language learners simply had a good "aptitude" for language learning, were more motivated, or had had extensive exposure to natural language learning situations, most preferably in a country where the language was taught. Rubin later (1981) used a variety of procedures to identify learning strategies, including observations and videotapes of classrooms, observations of tutorial situations, student self-reports, strip stories (a reasoning task in which a group of students assembles a complete story when each has been given only a single sentence out of context), and directed diaries (students are given explicit instructions on how to keep the diary). Rubin reported that: (1) the observations were "not very productive," since teachers focused on getting correct answers, not on the process by which students derived the answers; (2) some students were better able to describe strategies than others; and (3) most students needed to be tutored to report on their learning strategies. Most of Rubin's more productive reports were derived from diary accounts of sophisticated second language learners. Rubin noted the strategies that occurred and developed a classification scheme which included two general categories: processes that contribute directly to learning (e.g., clarification/verification, monitoring, memorization) and processes that contribute indirectly to learning (e.g., creating opportunities for practice, production tricks).

Rubin's finding that observations were not productive is consistent with research reported by Cohen and Aphek (1981), in which observations in language classrooms failed to reveal useful information about strategies or about patterns of communication, such as communication success and error corrections, which would signal that a strategy was being used. Part of the problem in conducting these observations was that students did not talk a great deal in the class except when directed or orchestrated by the teacher.

In one of the more extensive early studies of learning strategies to appear in the second language acquisition literature, Naiman et al. (1978) explored Rubin's suggestion that the good language learner has something to teach us and conducted retrospective interviews with thirty-four adults who were considered proficient in a foreign language. Naiman et al.'s list of general strategies used by good language learners sound a bit less like mental processes and more like admonitions for general learning success. These strategies, as noted in Chapter 1, include an active task approach, realization of language as a system, realization of language as a means of communication and interaction, management of affective demands, and monitoring L2 performance.

An interest in examining learning strategies from a number of independent perspectives led Naiman et al. to use classroom observations, interviews, questionnaires, and ability testing to detect the use of strategies. Four populations concurrently studying French were investigated: students in grade 8, those in grade 10, grade 12 pre-university students with at least two years' exposure to French, and grade 12 pre-university students who were specializing in French. Teachers were asked to designate from the seventy-two students participating in the study those whom they would expect to do best and those they would expect to do worst. Naiman et al. found that overtly observable strategies such as student self-correction, student-initiated repetition, student questioning, and self-initiated responding rarely occurred in classrooms and that these strategies did not differentiate effective from less effective students. During interviews, however, students reported using strategies primarily on vocabulary tasks but rarely on other tasks, except for the use of repetition in grammar drills and occasional creation of self-generated opportunities for oral or aural exposure.

More recent work on learning strategies in second language acquisition has been more focused. Wenden (1983) concentrated on self-directed learning among adult foreign language learners. Based on interviews, Wenden explored self-directed language learning activities in a variety of social settings. Wenden concluded that the self-directed activities could be characterized by eight questions learners might pose

TABLE 4.1. SECOND LANGUAGE LEARNING STRATEGIES

Knowing about learning

Question: How does this language work?	Decision: Learners make judgments about the linguistic and sociolinguistic codes.
Question: What's it like to learn a language?	Decision: Learners make judgments about how to learn a language and about what language learning is like.

Planning

Question: What should I learn and how?	Decision: Learners decide on linguistic objectives, resources, and use of resources.
Question: What should I emphasize?	Decision: Learners decide to give priority to special linguistic items.
Question: How should I change?	Decision: Learners decide to change their approach to language learning.

Self-evaluation

Question: How am I doing?	Decision: Learners determine how well they use the language and diagnose their needs.
Question: What am I getting?	Decision: Learners determine if an activity or strategy is useful.
Question: How am I responsible for learning? How is language learning affecting me?	Decision: Learners make judgments about how to learn a language and about what language learning is like.

to themselves that lead to decisions about language learning practices. Table 4.1 lists the questions and the corresponding decisions within three of the four designators – knowing about learning, planning, monitoring, and self-evaluation – Brown and Palincsar (1982) used to describe metacognitive strategies.

The eight questions Wenden used to characterize self-directed learning fit conveniently within the categories Brown used to describe metacognitive strategies. However, Brown's self-monitoring category has no counterpart in Wenden's analysis. Self-monitoring involves on-line analysis of comprehension to detect lapses in attention or understanding, or analysis of production to detect errors that would interfere with communication. The failure of this strategy to appear in Wenden's scheme suggests either that monitoring is not a critical component of self-directed learning or that Wenden's data collection procedures did not elicit self-monitoring. The use of self-monitoring will emerge as an important strategy in some of the studies we discuss later in this chapter. Wenden appeared to be looking for strategies at the macro level, representing general approaches to learning, rather than internal mental processes, as would be true of self-monitoring.

One of the principal questions that continued to be emphasized in the early studies of learning strategies is the definition and classification of strategies. Wenden (1983) recommended using classification schemes like Rubin's in future research and proposed refining the classification based on the results of new data collection. One possibility was to add a specific metacognitive component to the strategies Rubin had already suggested, since some of the strategies she identified (viz., monitoring, creating opportunities for practice) were reflections on the process of learning or a manipulation of learning opportunities. Wenden's own work (1983) and her more recent work (1987a) has focused on meta-cognitive strategies, suggesting that a synthesis of the two approaches could be useful.

Oxford (1985) attempted to build on some of these earlier classifi-cation schemes (including our own, described in Chapter 5 as Study 1) by suggesting two broad categories paralleling Dansereau's (1978, 1985): primary strategies and support strategies. These are similar to the terms Rubin (1981) used to describe her strategy classifications, but the actual definitions and specific strategies are different. In Oxford's classification, primary strategies include nine subcategories (e.g., infer-encing, mnemonics, summarizing, and practice), while support strategies include eight subcategories (e.g., attention enhancers, self-management, affective strategies, planning, and cooperation). Furthermore, within each of these subcategories, additional examples of strategies are men-tioned, producing an extended listing of some sixty-four strategies in all. What Oxford apparently tried to do was to subsume within her classification virtually every strategy that had previously been cited in the literature on learning strategies. The problem with this approach, so far as a taxonomy of strategies is concerned, is that this extended listing is far removed from any underlying cognitive theory, fails to prioritize which strategies are most important to learning, and generates subcategories that appear to overlap.

Oxford's extended classification scheme served another purpose, how-ever, which was to provide the foundation for generating items for a questionnaire designed to assess uses of learning strategies in second language acquisition (Oxford 1986). The Strategy Inventory for Lan-guage Learning (SILL) is based on the primary and support strategies identified in the classification and contains items tapping the sixty-four

individual strategies identified in the literature review but later augmented by linking strategies to specific language tasks (speaking, listening, reading, writing). The SILL underwent successive revisions,
producing a shortened version with 135 items, which still covered the
range of strategies in the taxonomy. This version of the SILL was field-
tested with adults learning foreign languages in military settings. A rotated (promax) factor analysis of responses to the SILL, based on 483
respondents, produced eight factors that seemed to have a reasonably
clear interpretation as well as two others. The eight factors were as
follows:

1. General study habits – previewing lessons, using time well.
2. Functional practice – seeking L2 speakers, initiating L2 conversations, attending L2 events.
3. Seeking and communicating meaning – analyzing words for meaning, using
   cues for meaning, using all the information when reading, guessing meanings
   from context.
4. Studying or practicing independently – listing related words, using a mirror,
   recording words and definitions, elaborating sentences, imitating an L2
   speaker.
5. Use of mnemonic devices – finding cognates, making unusual memory linkages, using rhymes to memorize, using imagery.
6. Reliance on L1 or on another speaker (a negative factor) – translating,
   reverting to L1, asking for slower speech or explanations.
7. Formal practice – applying rules, grammar practice, error analysis.
8. Use of metacognitive strategies – self-encouragement, self-reward, planning,
   and reviewing one's progress.

Oxford and her coworkers have used these dimensions to analyze strategy uses among different populations, as described in the next section.

Descriptions of strategy applications

Extensive research directly on learning strategies or on related mental
processing during cognitive development has led to a general understanding of strategies and the types of individuals who use them. The
significance of strategy use is shown in Brown et al.'s (1983) discussion
of the tetrahedral model they use to describe the factors that must be
considered in describing a learning activity. The model consists of learning strategies, learner characteristics (which includes strategies but also
includes attitudes and prior knowledge), the nature of the materials (the
similarity of elements to be learned, complexity of the materials, sequencing, organization), and the criterion task (e.g., recognition, recall,
transfer, or problem solving). After reviewing research in considerable
depth on the influence of each of these elements on learning, Brown et
al. conclude that the strategies, or the deliberate plans and routines used
in learning, remembering, and problem solving, are the primary deter-

minants of learning outcomes. Because the literature in this area is so extensive, we will only briefly touch on some of the major conclusions drawn thus far.

In their summary of the literature on development, Brown et al. show that older children are consistently revealed as active and strategic learners who gradually acquire a repertoire of strategies as they mature. Strategies in younger children begin as task-specific activities and later may emerge into a broad repertoire of more flexible and generalizable skills. Although young children or developmentally delayed children may not use strategies spontaneously, they may, under direct instruction, employ strategies with specific tasks and as a consequence improve their memory performance. Studies from the early 1970s show that rehearsal, categorization, and elaboration (relating the subject to be learned to existing knowledge) emerge between five and eight years of age. Brown et al. refer to these findings as "robust" and "reliable." Less was known about precursors to these strategies or about the use of strategies after the middle school years, although Brown et al. noted a shift among researchers in attention toward these topics.

Brown et al. also highlight the distinction between cognitive and metacognitive strategies. Two of the cognitive strategies described are rehearsal and summarization. Rehearsal of more mature learners entails "active, systematic, elaborative procedures," as compared to the rote repetition of younger learners. Similarly, whereas summarization performed by more mature learners entails elaboration, restatement, and revision of the goals and subgoals of an activity, summarization performed by younger or novice learners may entail such simple strategies as copy-delete – the deletion of elements of a text considered unessential and the copying of the remainder verbatim. Brown et al. comment that less sophisticated strategies are resistant to retraining, because these strategies are effective in achieving partial success on the task.

Metacognitive strategies involve both knowledge about learning (metacognitive knowledge) and control or regulation over learning (metacognitive strategies). *Metacognitive knowledge* refers to knowledge of one's own cognitive processes and those of others. As Brown et al. point out, this knowledge bears some interesting and important characteristics for applications to learning. Metacognitive knowledge is *stable,* thus it is retrievable for use with learning tasks. It is *statable,* therefore it can be reflected upon and used as the topic of discussion with others. However, this type of knowledge may be *fallible,* so that what one believes about one's cognitive processes may be inaccurate, such as the belief that simple rote repetition is the key that underlies all learning. And finally, it appears *late in development,* since the ability of learners to step back from learning and reflect on their cognitive processes may require prior learning experiences as a point of reference.

Regulation of learning, as distinguished from knowledge about learning, entails the use of metacognitive strategies. These include *planning,* or predicting outcomes, scheduling, and trial and error; *monitoring,* or testing, revising, and rescheduling learning activities; and *checking* outcomes, or evaluating the outcomes of strategic actions for efficiency and effectiveness. Metacognitive strategies do not necessarily share the qualities of being stable and statable with metacognitive knowledge, and may be more task- than age-dependent.

In the developmental literature and more generally in the literature on learning in psychology, there was virtually no attention to listening or speaking skills or to second language acquisition in describing strategy applications. The majority of work on strategies in the developmental literature focused on activities that enhanced rote recall of words or pictures, although there were also studies with complete reading texts, studies of problem solving, and studies with other complex tasks. Strategies analyzed with vocabulary lists and isolated factual information included grouping, rehearsal, and special mnemonic devices (see, e.g., Atkinson and Raugh 1975; Levin 1981). Strategies investigated with reading tasks included study strategies, rating the importance of a passage to a main theme, note taking and summarizing, outlining and mapping, and self-questioning (Brown et al. 1983). Strategies analyzed with writing tasks included advanced planning and elaboration, restatement, and revision of the goals and subgoals of the assignment. The general conclusion from the developmental studies was that learning strategies develop with age, are used spontaneously with increasing sophistication by older students, result in improved task performance, and can be taught. Furthermore, with older children, strategic modes of processing have "coherence" and "stability" even under varying task demands, and have "transsituational applicability," or transfer across different learning contexts (Brown et al. 1983).

Recent efforts to describe strategy applications in second language acquisition by Oxford and her coworkers have identified gender and other differences in strategy use. Research using the Strategy Inventory for Language Learning (SILL) by Oxford and Ehrman (1987) with both students and instructors at the U.S. Foreign Service Institute led to the conclusion that females reported using learning strategies significantly more often than males and used a wider range of strategies. Additionally, professional linguists used more strategies and used them more frequently than untrained instructors or students. Subsequent factor analysis of the SILL with 1,200 university students (Oxford, Nyikos, and Crookall 1987) replicated the first four of the eight factors cited earlier (Oxford, 1986), and repeated the findings with regard to gender (females showed more frequent strategy use than males on three of the first five factors). In addition, students with higher self-rated motivation to learn the language had significantly higher scores on four of the first five factors. Finally, students with at least five years of study in the language used functional practice strategies significantly more frequently than students with four or fewer years. In comparing results from the various studies, Oxford et al. commented that those in the university sample tended to use formal, rule-related practice more than those in the military sample, while memory devices and strategies for seeking and communicating meaning were used more in the military setting.

Validation of strategy effectiveness

The work designed to validate strategy effectiveness has used anecdotal reports, correlational approaches, and experimental training. Experimental strategy training will be discussed in a later chapter. The correlational work has been of two kinds: attempts to correlate strategic behavior with language proficiency, and studies designed to correlate learning strategies with growth in language proficiency associated with instruction. All of the correlational work has been performed in second language acquisition studies, while virtually all of the experimental work has been performed in the field of cognitive psychology.

Cohen and Aphek (1981) used anecdotal reports in asking students to record the associations they made while learning vocabulary lists, with the expectation that certain types of associations would be more productive than others. One important feature of their study is the longitudinal approach to data collection. English-speaking students in an intensive Hebrew program abroad recorded associations to vocabulary lists on 7 occasions distributed over 100 days and indicated the frequency with which they encountered the words outside of class. Cohen and Aphek checked the recall of students for word lists presented in earlier interviews but apparently did not analyze student retention data statistically. The students produced associations based on similarities between the target word and a word or phrase in English or Hebrew; similarities in sound both in English and Hebrew that reminded the learner of the meaning; and similarities between the target word and proper names, signs, and personal images. Cohen and Aphek noted that students who produced associations seemed to retain the words more often than students who did not produce associations, but that success in learning was independent of the frequency with which the students encountered the words outside of class.

Bialystok (1981) analyzed the validity of strategies for second language acquisition using correlational techniques. The study concentrated on strategies used in functional and in formal language learning settings. Functional use was defined as employing language in communicative situations, such as in conversations and exchanging information, while formal use was defined as the study of language as a structured system. Bialystok pointed out that both types of language learning may occur in classrooms. She hypothesized that strategy use would facilitate second language acquisition, and that the type of strategy used would depend on the purpose and the language modality, either oral or written. The students in her study were in grades 10 and 12 and all had been studying French as a second language since grade 6 in the Canadian school system. Data on strategies were collected with a 12-item structured rating scale, which asked questions about the extent to which two strategies in functional settings (practice and inferencing) and two strategies in formal settings (practice and monitoring) were used by respondents on both oral and written tasks. An example given for written tasks on which functional practice was used was engaging in a learning activity (reading newspapers, magazines, books, etc.) "because of the meaning," while an example of formal practice was engaging in the same activity "to learn new words or structures." Inferencing on a written task included ch∋cking to see if an unknown word reminded the learner of a familiar English word, or trying to figure out meaning from context, and monitoring on a written task included checking for and correcting grammar errors and rewriting incorrect parts of assignments. Inferencing and monitoring on the oral tasks were defined in a similar manner. Achievement data were collected on a functional written task (reading for meaning), a functional oral task (listening for comprehension), a formal written task (filling in blanks with an appropriate form on isolated sentences), and a formal oral task (deciding if a spoken sentence is correct or incorrect). Results indicated that functional practice had a stronger relationship with achievement than any other strategy, irrespective of the task, even though inferencing and monitoring were reported to have been used more frequently. The effectiveness of the other strategies depended on the nature of the task and years of exposure to the language (i.e., the grade level). For example, monitoring was more strongly associated with listening for comprehension, reading for meaning, and listening in a grammar task than with writing, but at the twelfth grade only. Virtually none of the associations between strategies and achievement at the tenth-grade level was significant, except for functional practice with reading for comprehension. Inferencing (use of cognates, determining meaning from context, etc.) was unrelated to achievement at any grade level, even though it was used about as much as monitoring. Bialystok (1980) elsewhere provides evidence to indicate that use of inferencing depends on having achieved a threshold level of proficiency in the second language.

In a similar use of questionnaire data to empirically validate strategy use, Politzer and McGroarty (1985) developed a questionnaire to assess a variety of presumed "good learning behaviors," which they related to performance in an eight-week intensive course in English as a foreign language. Whereas the Bialystok (1981) work was concerned with the relationship between strategy use and language achievement, the Politzer and McGroarty study related strategy use to language learning. The English course Politzer and McGroarty used was designed to prepare students at the intermediate level of proficiency for graduate work at the university level in the United States. The 51-item questionnaire they used was based on prior work by Rubin (1981) and Naiman et al. (1978) and was divided into three scales corresponding to the setting in which the strategy occurred: in a classroom, during individual study, or in social interaction outside the classroom. Proficiency measures used in the study assessed pre- and posttest performance, relative to graduate professional study, on aural comprehension (match an oral stimulus with one of four pictures), English grammar (multiple choice), and an individually administered oral communicative competence test based on responses elicited by pictures (scored to produce a holistic rating and three types of discrete-point scores). Gains over the eight-week course were substantial for the aural comprehension test and the English grammar test but not for the communicative competence test, whether scored holistically or with a discrete-point approach. Adjusted gain scores for the proficiency measures were unrelated to the three general categories identified on the learning strategies questionnaire (classroom, individual study, social interaction), but were found to be associated with selected strategies represented by individual questionnaire items. For example, adjusted gains on the aural comprehension test were positively associated with the following items: asking the teacher questions for clarification and saying correct forms silently in response to teacher questions directed toward other students. Adjusted gains for discrete-point scores on the test of communicative competence were also positively associated with various forms of asking questions for clarification, and holistically scored gains were associated with the same forms of question asking plus an item measuring self-monitoring. In contrast, grammatical knowledge was related to use of vocabulary cards and to practicing words or constructions missed in class. Politzer and McGroarty concluded that the types of strategies associated with learning on the test of grammatical competence were different than those that influenced performance on the other measures. There was a notable absence of inferencing as an effective strategy in this study, which could have been due to the fact that virtually all of the respondents indicated that they used the strategy on each item intended to assess it.

Two more recent studies have examined the correspondence between self-reported strategy use and performance on measures of reading comprehension. One of these studies, by Padron and Waxman (1988), employed Hispanic ESL students in grades 3–5, apparently selected to represent both beginning and intermediate levels of English proficiency. The outcome measure consisted of gains in English reading comprehension between January and April on a standardized diagnostic reading test. To prevent lack of reading ability in English from interfering with measures of performance, students were read aloud items from a 14-item reading strategies questionnaire that contained Likert-type items on the extent to which students reported using learning strategies (1 = never, 2 = sometimes, 3 = always). The fourteen items were drawn from prior analysis of this questionnaire and included seven items that were positively related to learning and seven that had negative relationships with learning. The seven positive and seven negative strategies were as follows:

Positive	*Negative*
summarizing in writing	thinking about something else
underlining while reading	writing down every word
self-generating questions	skipping parts not understood
checking while reading	reading as fast as you can
asking questions	saying every word over again
taking notes	looking up words in dictionary
imagining what is read	saying main idea over and over

Padron and Waxman found that six of the seven most frequently used strategies were positive, and six of these seven strategies had average frequencies of 2 or better on the 3-point scale. More important, correlations between strategy use and posttest score revealed that only two strategies were significantly associated with reading outcomes, controlling for pretest score, and this was in the negative direction: thinking about something else while reading, and saying the main idea over and over. Both of these strategies were among the seven lowest strategies in frequency of use. These results indicate that negative strategies may interfere with English reading comprehension for Hispanic students, and suggest that positive strategy use was not associated with learning. As we noted in discussing McLaughlin (1987b), it may be that bilingual students, even those who appear to be fluent in English, have yet to transfer procedural strategies from their native language to English, but it could also be that these students have little familiarity with strategies at all.

A study by Zimmerman and Pons (1986) bears on the issue of the relationship between strategies and reading achievement (as contrasted with learning, as in Padron and Waxman). Zimmerman and Pons administered a "self-regulated" learning strategies interview to tenth-grade students from both high and low achievement tracks. The interview used open-ended questions about "particular methods for preparing" that focused on six different learning contexts: classroom situations, at home, times when completing writing assignments outside class, completing math assignments outside class, preparing for and taking tests, and times when poorly motivated. Once students had indicated use of a strategy, they were asked to rate the frequency with which they used it on a 4-point scale from "seldom" to "most of the time." Probe questions were used to compensate for differences in verbal skills between the two achievement tracks. Interviews were recorded and coded into fourteen strategy categories defined from analyses of prior literature. The categories and definitions were as follows:

Category	*Definitions*
1. Self-evaluation	Evaluating progress of one's own work
2. Organizing and transforming	Rearrangement of instructional materials to improve learning (overt or covert)
3. Goal setting and planning	Setting goals or plans for sequencing, timing, and completing activities
4. Seeking information	Seeking information nonsocially
5. Keeping records and monitoring	Recording events or results
6. Environmental structuring	Arranging physical setting to make learning easier
7. Self-consequences	Arranging or imagining incentives
8. Rehearsing and memorizing	Memorizing by practicing
9– Seeking social 11. assistance	Soliciting help from peers (9), teachers (10), or adults (11)
12– Reviewing 14. records	Rereading texts (12), notes (13), or textbooks (14)
15. Other	Learning initiated by other persons as well as all unclear responses

Zimmerman and Pons used two basic approaches in validating the influence of strategy use on learning. In the first approach, each of the fifteen strategies was found to discriminate significantly between students in the high and low achievement tracks based on findings in a discriminant function analysis. Thus, regardless of learning context, the high achievement track students reported using significantly more strategies than the low track. The three strategies that had the highest canonical correlation coefficients in the discriminant function analysis were seeking information (strategy 4), keeping records and monitoring (strategy 5), and organizing and transforming (strategy 2). The next three highest coefficients consisted of strategies requiring interaction with others: seeking teacher assistance (strategy 10), seeking peer assistance (strategy 9), and seeking adult assistance (strategy 11). The lowest correlations occurred for self-evaluation (strategy 1), which was also the least frequently used strategy among the high-track group.

The second approach to validating the influence of strategy use on learning was to analyze the relationships between the total self-regulated learning strategies score and performance on a standardized test of reading and math achievement, controlling for socioeconomic status (SES) and gender. The self-regulated learning total score was the best predictor of both achievement areas, and improved the prediction of English achievement 41 percent over gender and SES, while self-regulated learning improved the prediction of math achievement 36 percent over gender and SES. Thus, using either criterion in the Zimmerman and Pons study, self-regulated learning (i.e., learning strategy) scores were shown to be valid indicators of achievement. Although this study did not concern second language acquisition, it nevertheless confirms that self-reported strategy use has a meaningful relationship with learning outcomes in reading and math.

Conclusions

This chapter began with a review of data collection procedures based on self-report that have been used to analyze the ways students apply learning strategies to enhance second language acquisition. The procedures varied, depending on the objective of data collection, the language task, the temporal relationship between the task and the report, the degree of informant training required, the elicitation procedure, and the use of individual versus group data collection. We appraised the strengths and limitations of each of these methods and concluded that some of the criticisms of self-report to detect strategic modes of mental processing on second language tasks were unjustified. Nevertheless, the number, type, tasks, and detail with which strategies are reported may well depend on the methodology used. For this reason, researchers should clearly define their purpose in determining the methodology they select.

The research reviewed here on learning strategies in second language acquisition fell into three categories: studies designed to define and classify learning strategies, those intended to describe strategy applications with specific tasks or by certain types of learners, and studies intended to validate strategy effectiveness. These studies provide preliminary evidence that learners can report on their own learning processes, yield an initial definition and classification of strategy types, and suggest that self-reported strategy use is associated with learning outcomes. However, the strength of association between strategy use and learning outcomes depended on the nature of the task and the years of prior exposure to the language. Some of the strategies that emerged as having meaningful relationships with second language acquisition were use of elaborative associations (Cohen and Aphek 1981), monitoring (Bialystok 1981), asking questions for clarification, and self-monitoring (Politzer and McGroarty 1985). Bialystok (1981) noted that functional practice (engaging in a learning activity such as reading magazines or newspapers because of the "meaning") was more consistently related to learning across tasks than any other strategy.

These studies leave a variety of questions concerning the use of learning strategies in second language acquisition unanswered. One question concerns the definition and classification of strategies and the extent to which a classification scheme relying on the distinction between metacognitive and cognitive processing can be useful in second language acquisition. A second question concerns the need to understand in greater detail the types of second language tasks with which strategies are used, the frequency with which different strategies appear with different tasks, the conditions under which they are used, and the characteristics of the individuals who use them. We are particularly interested in determining whether or not individuals who meet independent criteria as "good language learners" in fact use strategies differently or more frequently than individuals identified as less effective learners. We will also see more clearly the differences that emerge in the use of varied data collection methodologies with learning strategies research.

5 *Strategies used by second language learners*

In this chapter, we will build upon the review presented in Chapter 4 and describe a series of studies we performed that elicited both general and specific information about strategies, the students who use them, and the second language tasks with which the strategies are used. The first study attempted to define and classify strategies used in second language acquisition and used retrospective interviews with students learning English as a second language. The second study extended this purpose and again used retrospective interviews to identify strategies in second language acquisition but with native English-speaking students learning foreign languages. The third study was designed to build on the definitions and classifications established with retrospective interviews by using think-aloud data collection to probe in greater depth the ways in which individual strategies are used by ESL students on a listening comprehension task. The final study reports the results of think-aloud interviews conducted longitudinally with students learning foreign languages.

Study 1: learning strategies used by beginning and intermediate ESL students

At the time we began our first study of learning strategies in second language acquisition, we were aware of most of the research discussed in the previous chapter, with the exception of a few specific studies using questionnaires in second language acquisition (e.g., Oxford 1986; Padron and Waxman 1988; Politzer and McGroarty 1985; Zimmerman and Pons 1986), which emerged later. There had been no studies performed of strategies used by students learning English as a second language, and no integration of the separate work performed in cognitive psychology and second language research. Furthermore, in second language acquisition there had been no consensus on the definition and classification of strategies, and there continued to be persistent confusion over the distinction between learning strategies and other types of strategies applied more to language use, such as communication and production strategies. In cognitive psychology, there were questions about the overlap between metacognitive and cognitive strategies and very little interest in how strategies were used with second language learning tasks or at different levels of language proficiency, with the exception of a few studies of the keyword method with students learning a foreign language (e.g., Atkinson and Raugh 1975; Pressley et al. 1981).

Objectives

The primary purposes of this study were: (1) to identify the range of learning strategies used by high school students on language learning tasks that are typical in English as a second language classrooms; (2) to determine if the strategies could be defined and organized within existing strategy classification frameworks; and (3) to determine if the strategies varied depending on the task or the level of English proficiency of the student (O'Malley et al. 1985a).

We preferred not to use a predefined list of strategies, because we were interested in the range of strategies students might identify with specific tasks. An initial literature review had identified some fourteen or so strategies, and we wanted to determine how much the list would be augmented by encouraging a dynamic exchange between students in small groups discussing strategies. No previous investigators had attempted this approach with second language acquisition data. We nevertheless anticipated being able to obtain useful information, because the specific language tasks on which we focused were based on prior observations of the tasks that students actually performed in classrooms. We were also interested in knowing whether or not ESL students would report using strategies in functional language situations outside of the classroom, since a sharp distinction had been drawn in the second language literature between "acquisition" in functional settings, which was said to occur without conscious deliberation, and "learning" in formal settings, where conscious processes are presumably more typical (Krashen 1977, 1982).

A secondary purpose of the investigation was to determine what teachers knew about the strategies their students used while learning on second language tasks. No previous investigators had asked teachers about the strategies their students used. If teachers knew little about the strategies used by their students, we expected that familiarizing teachers with these strategies and how to teach them would be productive. This study was the first phase of a two-part investigation that also contained an experimental analysis of the effectiveness of training people to use learning strategies. The experimental training study is described in the next chapter.

Procedures

The study was designed to provide retrospective interview data from high school ESL students and their teachers on the uses of learning strategies in second language acquisition activities occurring both within and outside the classroom. We were particularly interested in better-performing students at both the beginning and intermediate levels of English proficiency, because we expected these students to have more strategies. We identified seven oral language activities that were typical in the classrooms of these students based on prior observations; we then added to this two language tasks that were expected to represent functional demands in their nonclassroom activities. The seven classroom tasks were pronunciation, oral drills and grammar exercises, vocabulary, following directions, listening for main ideas and facts, inferencing while listening (obtaining meaning from context and using predicting skills), and making an oral presentation or report. The two nonclassroom activities consisted of social interactions outside of the ESL classroom, and any functional communication activity, such as language used at work, in commercial transactions, obtaining information, and so forth.

PARTICIPANTS

The participants in this study were seventy high-school-age students enrolled in ESL classes during the 1983 Spring semester and twenty-two teachers providing instruction in the classes. The study was performed in three high schools in two suburban school districts in a mid-Atlantic state. Both school districts categorized ESL students into the beginning, intermediate, and advanced levels of English proficiency for instructional purposes. The students participating in this study were either beginning or intermediate level and, except for one group of five Vietnamese students, were all native speakers of Spanish from Central America, South America, or Puerto Rico. Beginning level students in both school districts were described as those with little or no proficiency in English and in need of intensive English instruction, while intermediate level students were described as having little or no skill in reading and writing English, but with some proficiency in understanding or speaking English. Schools were asked to assign ESL students with higher academic ability to the interviews, regardless of English proficiency level, along with a smaller percentage of·lower ability students. Although most of the teachers interviewed taught ESL classes, one biology and one English language arts teacher were included to determine whether different types of strategies were used once the students began to make the transition to all-English classes.

METHODS

We used three data collection instruments in gathering information on strategies used by students. The first was a student interview guide, which contained questions concerning strategy use with each of the seven classroom tasks and two nonclassroom language tasks. Students were asked to describe the "special things they did" or the "tricks they used" to study each task. Prompt questions were used to clarify strategy definitions or to elicit strategies when the interview was not being productive (which was rare). The second data collection instrument was a teacher interview guide that was parallel to the student interview guide in focusing on specific language tasks and asking about strategies used by the ESL students of the teachers interviewed. The third approach was classroom observation. The observation form was designed to detect learning strategy use in classroom settings. Observers, using an event sampling approach, scanned an entire classroom (typically fifteen students) for evidence of learning strategies that had been identified in an earlier literature review. For example, a student who spontaneously corrected his or her pronunciation would be monitoring, and one who requested additional information from a teacher would be questioning for clarification. We used an observation approach despite the lack of success of previous investigators in doing so because we thought that having a precise definition of the tasks used in the classes and a prior classification scheme for the strategies might help in the data collection.

The seventy students were interviewed in nineteen small groups, with three to five in each group. Interviews with beginning level Hispanic students were conducted in Spanish while interviews with intermediate level students were conducted in English. All interviews were tape-recorded and rated afterwards for the occurrence of strategies, based on an abbreviated transcript prepared by the the person conducting the interview. The abbreviated transcript consisted only of verbatim descriptions of each strategy mentioned by students and the task on which it was used. The strategy was labeled at the time the transcript was prepared if the classification was known. A type of strategy was counted as having occurred once each new time it was mentioned in the interview, except if one student simply affirmed what another student had already indicated. Group consensus among the four interviewers was used to resolve uncertainties in strategy definitions. Multiple strategies or new strategy definitions were recorded whenever no single strategy from the prior literature review adequately described the approach students reported using.

The interrater reliability of the data coding was determined by having independent raters listen to the tape, develop an abbreviated transcript, and compare the coding with the initial transcript. Instances where specific strategies were classified the same or differently were noted and tallied. The average interobserver agreement was 79 percent for four raters, each measured against a common standard. Interobserver agreement in classroom observations was determined through parallel observations. The interobserver agreement was low, in part due to low frequencies but also due to the difficulty of reaching agreement on what was observed.

Results

Generally we had considerable success in identifying learning strategies through interviews with students, but less success in interviews with teachers and negligible success in conducting observations. A total of 638 independent strategy occurrences was identified across the nineteen student interviews, indicating that students had no difficulty in identifying the "special tricks" they used in learning on the tasks identified for the study. There were 33.6 strategies per student interview, and 25.4 individual strategies per teacher interview. The smaller number of strategies among teachers is probably due in part to the use of small group sessions for student interviews and individual interviews for teachers. However, even this number is inflated because the teachers often mentioned teaching strategies when asked about the learning strategies used by their students. There were only 3.7 strategies per classroom observation of a full hour, clearly a low return given the investment of effort, considering that the student and teacher interviews each took about the same amount of time. Because the student interviews were more reliable and more productive than the other sources of data, all analyses were based on self-reports from students.

DEFINITION AND CLASSIFICATION

The basic classification scheme proposed by Brown and Palinesar (1982) consisting of metacognitive and cognitive strategies was used in the initial definition of strategies. However, a third classification, consisting of strategies requiring social mediation, was added, and an initial list of fourteen or so strategies that had been identified in the literature review was nearly doubled to twenty-five independent strategy types that were actually used by students. The three classifications of strategies and the definitions of the individual strategy types are shown in Table 5.1. As can be seen from inspection of the Table, there were seven metacognitive strategies, fourteen cognitive strategies, and two social strategies. The metacognitive strategies are differentiated to show those that illustrate planning, monitoring, and evaluating a learning activity.

STRATEGY USE BY TYPE OF STUDENT

We also found that beginning level students were able to identify more strategies than intermediate level students. Students with beginning level proficiency in English identified almost twice as many cognitive strategies as students with intermediate level proficiency, and identified 40 percent more metacognitive strategies. The reason why beginning level students reported using strategies more frequently is unclear, but could have been due to the use of their native language in the interviews or the nature and difficulty of the tasks to which they were exposed. Overall, both begin-

TABLE 5.1. ESL DESCRIPTIVE STUDY: LEARNING STRATEGY DEFINITIONS
AND CLASSIFICATIONS

Learning strategy	Definition
A. Metacognitive Strategies	
Planning	
Advance organizers	Previewing the main ideas and concepts of the material to be learned, often by skimming the text for the organizing principle.
Directed attention	Deciding in advance to attend in general to a learning task and to ignore irrelevant distractors.
Functional planning	Planning for and rehearsing linguistic components necessary to carry out an upcoming language task.
Selective attention	Deciding in advance to attend to specific aspects of input, often by scanning for key words, concepts, and/or linguistic markers.
Self-management	Understanding the conditions that help one learn and arranging for the presence of those conditions.
Monitoring	
Self-monitoring	Checking one's comprehension during listening or reading or checking the accuracy and/or appropriateness of one's oral or written production while it is taking place.
Evaluation	
Self-evaluation	Checking the outcomes of one's own language learning against a standard after it has been completed.
B. Cognitive Strategies	
Resourcing	Using target language reference materials such as dictionaries, encyclopedias, or textbooks.
Repetition	Imitating a language model, including overt practice and silent rehearsal.
Grouping	Classifying words, terminology, or concepts according to their attributes or meaning.
Deduction	Applying rules to understand or produce the second language or making up rules based on language analysis.
Imagery	Using visual images (either mental or actual) to understand or remember new information.
Auditory representation	Planning back in one's mind the sound of a word, phrase, or longer language sequence.

TABLE 5.I. *(continued)*

Learning strategy	Definition
Keyword method	Remembering a new word in the second language by: (1) identifying a familiar word in the first language that sounds like or otherwise resembles the new word, and (2) generating easily recalled images of some relationship with the first language homonym and the new word in the second language.
Elaboration	Relating new information to prior knowledge, relating different parts of new information to each other, or making meaningful personal associations with the new information.
Transfer	Using previous linguistic knowledge or prior skills to assist comprehension or production.
Inferencing	Using available information to guess meanings of new items, predict outcomes, or fill in missing information.
Note taking	Writing down key words or concepts in abbreviated verbal, graphic, or numerical form while listening or reading.
Summarizing	Making a mental, oral, or written summary of new information gained through listening or reading.
Recombination	Constructing a meaningful sentence or larger language sequence by combining known elements in a new way.
Translation	Using the first language as a base for understanding and/or producing the second language.
C. Social Mediation	
Question for clarification	Eliciting from a teacher or peer additional explanations, rephrasing, examples, or verification.
Cooperation	Working together with one or more peers to solve a problem, pool information, check a learning task, model a language activity, or get feedback on oral or written performance.

Source: Adapted from O'Malley, Chamot, Stewner-Manzanares, Küpper, and Russo (1985a).

ning and intermediate level students used far more cognitive strategies. About 73 percent of strategy uses by beginning students were cognitive, as were about 65 percent of strategy uses for intermediate level students.

RANGE AND TYPES OF STRATEGIES

The various types of planning shown in Table 5.1 accounted for 85 percent of all metacognitive strategies, with selective attention (22.3 percent of metacognitive strategies), advance preparation (21.4 percent), and self-management (19.6) assuming predominant roles. In contrast, no single cognitive strategy seemed to emerge as dominant, with the highest use mentioned for repetition (19.6 percent of all cognitive strategies), notetaking (18.8 percent), imagery (12.5 percent), and translation (11.3 percent). Two strategies that require little conceptual processing – repetition and translation – accounted for over 30 percent of all strategy uses. We had no evidence on the extent to which note taking as used by this group of students entailed active manipulation of ideas, but we noticed instances in which students attempted to replicate what the teacher stated without appearing to filter or actively process the information. The social/affective strategies – cooperation and questioning for clarification – were used infrequently relative to the cognitive and metacognitive strategies. The pattern of use for the different types of strategies among beginning and intermediate level students was highly similar.

In order to represent the complexity of strategy use by students, we sometimes coded double uses of strategies. This occurred with 20.9 percent of all strategies reported. There were virtually no differences between beginning and intermediate level students in this regard, and multiple strategies were reported with all language tasks. Metacognitive strategies occurred in combination with cognitive strategies in only 7 percent of all strategies identified.

One incidental finding of interest was the overall degree of metacognitive knowledge of language as a system exhibited by many of the students interviewed, suggesting a high level of metalinguistic awareness. *Metalinguistic knowledge* is the ability to reflect on the forms and structures of a language independently from its informational or social functions (Ryan 1975) and to analyze language structures overtly or "to think and talk *about* language" (Gass 1983, p. 277). Some of the students in our study, even those with beginning level skills in English, were aware of their strengths and weaknesses as language learners and deliberately capitalized on their strengths in social interactions through such communication strategies as choosing or changing topics of conversation to include words and structures with which they were familiar. Some students reflected on the similarities and differences between Spanish and English, and used their knowledge of Spanish to infer meanings from context, while others commented on style and register differences between classroom uses of English and the informal language of their English-speaking peers.

TYPE OF TASK

Among the language learning tasks, the highest frequencies of strategy use were for vocabulary learning (16.6 percent of all strategies reported), pronunciation (13.8 percent), and oral drills (11.4 percent), for a total of over 40 percent. The lowest frequencies of strategy use were for listening comprehension with inferencing (7.2 percent), making an oral presentation (8.2 percent), and engaging in operational communication (9.9 percent). One of the reasons why a task might have been represented with infrequent strategies is the infrequent occurrence of the task itself in the student's experience. Nevertheless, the highest reported strategy uses were for isolated language learning tasks and the lowest were for integrative language tasks.

Discussion

One of the primary purposes for conducting this study was to determine if a strategy classification scheme based on the distinction between meta-cognitive and cognitive strategies would be useful with second language acquisition. Not only did we confirm the importance of this distinction but we were able to add a considerable amount of information about the types of tasks with which strategies are used and the students who use them.

At least four important implications emerged from the study. First, although students reported using strategies, they rarely used them on integrative tasks and often relied upon strategies that did not demand elaborative or active mental processing. Some of these strategies were used in combination with other strategies and in some cases were combinations of metacognitive and cognitive strategies. Second, although the teachers of these students had little awareness of the types of strategies their students actually used and little familiarity with processes by which strategy use could be encouraged, they expressed interest in strategy uses and inquired how they could find out more about the topic. These first two points suggest that a strategy training approach could be useful for both students and teachers. Third, the strategies did not appear to be different from those reported in the cognitive literature, suggesting that strategic processing is a generic activity applied to all areas of learning. And fourth, strategy use and conscious analysis of learning occur with both classroom and nonclassroom learning. Two implications of this conclusion are that the learning versus acquisition distinction drawn in the second language acquisition literature may be misleading, and that students can profit from learning about strategies outside as well as inside the classroom.

Study 2: learning strategies used by foreign language students

After completing our initial studies with ESL students, we became interested in extending our research to students studying a foreign language in high school and college settings. We attempted to determine if the same methodological approaches used successfully in the ESL studies would be equally effective in discovering the strategies used by native English-speaking students learning a foreign language. A three-year project was conducted (1985–88) to investigate learning strategies in foreign language instruction (Chamot et al. 1987; Chamot, Küpper, and Impink-Hernandez 1988a, b). This project consisted of three separate studies – a descriptive study, a longitudinal study, and a course development study. The first two studies, which are discussed in this chapter, sought to identify the learning strategies used by high school students of Spanish and college students of Russian at different levels of language proficiency. The third study identified the learning strategies taught by Spanish and Russian instructors; this is described in Chapter 6, along with other strategy training studies.

Objectives

The major purposes of the descriptive study were: (1) to determine if students of Spanish and Russian use similar strategies and if these strategies can be defined using the classification framework developed in the ESL descriptive study presented in the preceding section (O'Malley et al. 1985a); (2) to determine differences in strategy use between beginning level and intermediate or advanced level students; and (3) to identify the range and variety of strategies used by high school and college foreign language students for the types of language tasks they encounter in formal language study. Thus, this study replicated the ESL descriptive study in most of its objectives except for the relation of strategy use to type of task. This question was investigated in the following longitudinal foreign language study, in which students actually worked on different types of foreign language tasks instead of only reporting on them retrospectively.

Procedures

In the descriptive phase of the study we were interested in identifying learning strategies used by typical foreign language students at the high school and college level. Therefore we interviewed as many students in intact classes as were willing to participate in the study, rather than gather information about the more effective students only. Classroom observations took place prior to interviewing students in order to ascertain the types of language tasks typically occurring in the different classrooms. These observations allowed us to identify seven different types of language learning activities that foreign language students encountered in class, and we added two types of activities that they might encounter outside of class in communicative situations. The seven classroom activities were: vocabulary learning, oral or written grammar drills, listening comprehension, reading comprehension, written composition, and oral presentations. The two activities outside of class were identical to those included in the ESL study, that is, operational or functional communication such as ordering a meal in a Spanish (or Russian) restaurant, and social communication, such as engaging in a conversation with native speakers of Russian (or Spanish).

PARTICIPANTS

The participants in this study were sixty-seven high school Spanish students and thirty-four college Russian students. Of the Spanish students, thirty-one were in first-year Spanish, twenty-one were in third-year Spanish, and fifteen were in a combined fifth- and sixth-year Spanish class. Nineteen of the Russian students participating in the study were in first-year Russian and fifteen were in third- and fourth-year Russian courses. As mentioned earlier, all levels of ability were included in the sample of students. However, less effective overall students were concentrated at the beginning level of language study for both languages.

METHODS

The instrument used to collect data on strategy use reported by students was the General Interview Guide. The same instrument was used for each language group, the only difference being references to the specific language in question. The General Interview Guide described the nine types of learning tasks and contained questions after each task description. In these interviews students were asked about any special tricks or techniques they normally applied to the particular task. Probing questions elicited information about what students did to prepare for the task, how they managed the task while engaged in it, and, where appropriate, how they recalled or checked the task after completion.

The group interviews consisted for the most part of three to five students, though some Russian interviews were with individual students because of scheduling difficulties. Students were asked how they approached each of the nine language tasks included in the General Interview Guide, and the interviews were tape-recorded. Abbreviated transcripts were made of the tapes, which noted the learning strategies identified by students as well as identified the class level, number of students in the group, and language task to which the strategy was applied. As in the ESL study, a strategy was counted each time it was mentioned for a particular learning task. However, when students merely affirmed that they also used a strategy just mentioned, it was not counted. Multiple or combination strategies were recorded when a single strategy did not adequately describe a student's approach to a language task. Reliability on strategy identification and classification was established by having an independent rater listen to, transcribe, and identify the strategies from a taped interview; this second transcription was then compared to the original one. Areas of confusion were marked for resolution through joint discussions. The interrater reliability established was .86 for the Spanish interviews and .88 for the Russian interviews.

Results

The average number of strategies used at different levels of language study were computed for each language, but direct comparisons between strategy use for the two languages were not made because of differences in the interview situation for each language group. Interviews with Spanish students were restricted to a class period of 50 minutes and the groups consisted of three to five students. The Russian interviews, on the other hand, took place during students' free time and lasted an hour or longer, and the groups were smaller, ranging from one to three students. For these reasons, there was more time and opportunity for Russian students to contribute more strategies and to discuss more different types of language tasks than was possible for the Spanish students.

DEFINITION AND CLASSIFICATION

The classification scheme developed for the ESL study (see Table 5.1) was used with some modifications to classify strategies reported by Spanish and Russian students. Strategies not reported were eliminated and additional strategies reported were added, resulting in the augmented list of strategies shown in Table 5.2. One of the cognitive strategies (key word) that had been reported in the ESL study was not reported at all in the foreign language study, and one new metacognitive strategy (delayed production) was reported in the foreign language study, but it represented less than 1 percent of all metacognitive strategy occurrences. Additional strategies mentioned by foreign language students consisted of five cognitive strategies (rehearsal, translation, note taking, substitution, and contextualization), and one social/affective strategy (self-talk). The name of the metacognitive strategy identified in Table 5.1 as functional planning was changed to organizational planning in order to

TABLE 5.2. FOREIGN LANGUAGE DESCRIPTIVE STUDY: LEARNING STRATEGY
DEFINITIONS AND CLASSIFICATIONS

Learning strategy	Definition
A. Metacognitive Strategies	
Planning	
Organizational planning	Planning the parts, sequence, main ideas, or language functions to be expressed orally or in writing.
Delayed production	Consciously deciding to postpone speaking to learn initially through listening comprehension.
B. Cognitive Strategies	
Rehearsal	Rehearsing the language needed, with attention to meaning, for an oral or written task.
Translation	Using the first language as a base for understanding and/or producing the second language.
Note taking	Writing down key words and concepts in abbreviated verbal, graphic, or numerical form during a listening or reading activity.
Substitution	Using a replacement target language word or phrase when the intended word or phrase is not available.
Contextualization	Assisting comprehension or recall by placing a word or phrase in a meaningful language sequence or situational context.
C. Social/Affective Strategies	
Self-talk	Reducing anxiety by using mental techniques that make one feel competent to do the learning task.

capture the ordering and sequencing aspects of this planning strategy. The addition of reading and writing tasks to the general group interview also required modifications of strategy definitions, which for the ESL study had concerned only oral language activities.

RANGE AND TYPES OF STRATEGIES

Foreign language students show similar patterns of metacognitive and cognitive strategy use as compared to those reported by ESL students. Both Russian and Spanish students at all levels of study reported using far more cognitive strategies than metacognitive ones, though the differences were not as great as those reported by ESL students. Cognitive strategy use was about 59 percent for Spanish students and about 58 percent for Russian students, whereas ESL students reported using cognitive strategies between 65 and 73 percent of the time.

Patterns emerged in analyses of each of the three major categories (metacognitive, cognitive, and social/affective). In metacognitive strategy use, both Spanish and Russian students predominantly reported using planning strategies, such as selective attention, organizational planning, and self-management. In cognitive strategy use, students at all levels of Spanish instruction reported using translation most frequently, whereas beginning level Russian students reported using repetition and translation most often, and intermediate/advanced Russian students reported greater use of note taking. In both language groups, students at the beginning levels of language study relied most on repetition, translation, and transfer, whereas more advanced students relied most on inferencing, though without abandoning familiar strategies such as repetition and translation. These students reported using relatively few instances of more cognitively active strategies such as rehearsal, grouping, substitution, imagery, elaboration, and summarizing. Use of social and affective strategies was reported much less frequently than use of metacognitive and cognitive strategies by Russian and Spanish students, accounting for less than 1 percent of all strategies.

STRATEGY USE BY LEVEL OF STUDY

Both Spanish and Russian students at higher levels of study reported using more strategies than did beginning level students. Beginning level Spanish students reported an average of 12.4 strategies per interview while intermediate/advanced students reported an average of 16.9 strategies. Beginning level Russian students reported an average of 26.9 strategies per interview, while intermediate/advanced students reported an average of 30.0 strategies. This was in contrast to the ESL study, in which beginning level students reported more strategies on the average than did intermediate level students.

STRATEGIES ASSOCIATED WITH INSTRUCTIONAL TASKS

Strategies appeared in the foreign language study that may have been used as a result of direct instruction by a specific teacher. For example, only Russian students reported using rehearsal and summarizing strategies, which may have been encouraged by their instructors. For the most part, however, major strategies were used by students of all three of the languages under study, so that the basic classification scheme proved useful for describing and categorizing the learning strategies of both foreign and second language students.

EFFECTIVE VERSUS INEFFECTIVE LEARNERS

The foreign language descriptive study also examined the range of learning strategies for all ability levels of students, rather than concentrating on the strategies of "good" language learners, as in the ESL study. In the foreign language study, students of all ability levels were found to use learning strategies. More effective students used learning strategies more often and had a wider repertoire of learning strategies than did less effective students. But the fact that the less effective students were at least acquainted with some learning strategies and, more important, were able to report on their own mental processes related to foreign language study provides a starting point for instruction of learning strategy that may benefit those students who are not yet encountering significant success in their learning of a new language.

Discussion

An important objective of the foreign language descriptive study was to discover whether the classification scheme developed to describe learning strategies reported by ESL students would be applicable to English-speaking students learning a foreign language. We found that the learning strategies of foreign language students could also be classified as metacognitive, cognitive, or social/affective. Some modifications of strategy definitions were made to accommodate strategies for reading and writing as well as oral tasks in the foreign language. Because cognitive strategies are directly related to specific learning tasks, the types of tasks required in a particular classroom can be expected to influence the cognitive strategies used to accomplish them. For example, in a classroom in which grammar is emphasized, successful students would use deduction as a strategy in applying rules to formulate correct sentences, and in a classroom in which vocabulary acquisition or reading for details is emphasized, students would find translation as a strategy to be effective.

Study 3: listening comprehension strategies used by ESL students

In this descriptive study of learning strategies in second language acquisition, we depart from the broader focus of the prior work and concentrate on language skills and data collection procedures that are more appropriate for an in-depth understanding of learning strategies (O'Malley, Chamot, and Küpper 1989). First, we specifically focus on listening comprehension in this study, not only because of the salience that listening skills have taken in a number of instructional approaches, but also because there has been little research that clarifies what listeners actually do while listening to oral texts in academic settings (Richards 1983). Second, we adopt a different methodology for this study, a think-aloud procedure that attempts to identify concurrent strategies used as a language task is being performed instead of identifying retrospectively strategies that were used with tasks performed in the past. One of the features of the concurrent analysis of an ongoing task is that the mental processing in short-term memory, which is lost in retrospection, can be described and reported (Ericsson and Simon 1980; Garner 1988). While the advantage of this data collection technique is that it provides different kinds of information than may be provided through retrospective analyses, the possibility exists that a more limited range of strategies will emerge from informant reports. Third, in this study we collected information from both effective and ineffective listeners to examine differences in the degree and character of learning strategy use by different types of learners. And fourth, we were particularly concerned about the acquisition of what Cummins (1981) called academic language skills, or the ability to manipulate concepts in a second language rather than simply comprehend meaning. This type of language is what ESL students are exposed to after they exit from bilingual or ESL programs, and the types of strategies they use to deal with these complicated language demands are critical in understanding how to improve the students' performance.

Research and theoretical background

Listening comprehension has become the foundation of a number of theories of second language acquisition that focus on the beginning levels of second language proficiency (e.g., Asher 1969; James 1984; Krashen et al. 1984; Winitz 1978; Wipf 1984). The primary assumption underlying these theories is that language acquisition is an implicit process in which linguistic rules are internalized by extensive exposure to authentic texts and particularly to comprehensible input that provides an appropriate level of challenge to the listener. When applied in instructional settings, these theories suggest that modified teacher input will enhance comprehension, and enhanced comprehension will in turn promote acquisition (Long 1985). The focus in these discussions is exclusively on adaptations of teacher input to enhance comprehension instead of on the ways in which learners process the input. In fact, the learner's conscious processing is often de-emphasized during instruction, because language is believed to be an implicit process (Brown 1984). This exclusive focus on teacher behaviors fails to take into consideration deliberate learner strategies for comprehending language texts, for processing new information, and for learning and retaining concepts related to academic language and content.

In parallel with but independent of the emphasis on comprehension-based approaches to second language instruction, there has been an equal degree of theoretical interest in the mental processes involved in listening. Listening to spoken language has been acknowledged in second language theory to consist of active and complex processes that determine the content and level of what is comprehended (Byrnes 1984; Call 1985; Richards 1983). These processes take utterances as input for constructing meaning-based propositional representations that are identified initially in short-term memory and stored in long-term memory. In Chapter 2, we discussed the cognitive theory underlying these processes and suggested that comprehension could be differentiated into three distinct phases: perceptual processing, parsing, and utilization. In *perceptual processing* the listener focuses attention on the oral text and the sounds are retained in echoic memory. In *parsing*, words and messages are used to construct meaningful mental representations by forming propositional representations that are abstractions of the original message. The size of the unit or segment (or "chunk") of information processed depends on the learner's knowledge of the language, general knowledge of the topic, and how the information is processed (Richards 1983). The third phase, *utilization*, consists of relating a mental representation of the text meaning to existing knowledge, thereby enhancing comprehension and, most likely, retention of the information presented.

Objectives

The questions addressed in this study concern the comprehension processing of ESL students while listening to academic texts. We wanted to know if the strategies students used paralleled the three theoretically derived phases of the comprehension process and if there were differences in the strategies reported by effective and ineffective listeners.

Procedures

PARTICIPANTS

Eleven high-school-age students enrolled in ESL classes in two suburban public high schools served as participants in this study. All students were classified by the school district at the intermediate level of English proficiency, which the district defined as limited proficiency in understanding and speaking English, and little or no skill in reading and writing English. All participants were from Spanish-speaking countries in Central or South America. Students were nominated for participation in the study by their ESL teachers, who designated students as effective or ineffective listeners based on a common set of criteria on which they had previously reached agreement. The criteria included attentiveness in class, ability to follow directions without asking for clarification, ability and willingness to comprehend the general meaning of a difficult listening passage, ability to respond appropriately in a conversation, and ability and willingness to guess at the meaning of unfamiliar words and phrases. Application of these criteria and subsequent selection narrowed the sample to five effective and three ineffective listeners.

METHODS

Data collection was entirely conducted through individual interviews and consisted of two phases of approximately one hour each: a training phase, in which students were pretrained on thinking aloud; and a reporting phase, which consisted of a warm-up, transition, and think-aloud verbal report on a listening comprehension task. Students were given the option to think aloud in either Spanish or English, although most students chose to think aloud in Spanish and make occasional remarks in English. The interviewer asked probe questions in Spanish when necessary to stimulate the verbal reports, such as "What are you thinking?" and "What didn't you understand?"

In the reporting phase, students were presented with three listening activities selected from among the following: a history lecture (the story of the American Indian Massasoit), a science lecture (the invention of the diving bell or a description of a major volcanic eruption), a short story ("The Baboon and the Tortoise"), and a dictation passage (a brief narrative about life span expectations). Each listening passage had been previously taped and contained short pauses during which the interviewer stopped the tape and asked the students to relate as much as they could about their thoughts while listening. The students' think-aloud reports were taped and later transcribed and coded for strategy use, with an intercoder reliability of 85 percent. Neither interviewers nor data coders had previous knowledge concerning the identity of effective and ineffective listeners.

Results

Statistical analyses of strategy uses indicated that there were significant differences between effective and ineffective listeners on self-monitoring, or checking one's comprehension while it is taking place; elaboration, or relating new information to prior knowledge or to other ideas in the text; and inferencing, or using information in the text to guess at meaning or complete missing ideas (Mann-Whitney U test, $p < .05$).

Qualitative analyses of the transcripts indicated that strategies used by students could be differentiated in terms of the phase of the listening comprehension process. For example, during perceptual processing students reported using attentional strategies that maintained their concentration on the task. One condition that distracted ineffective listeners was encountering an unknown word or phrase. They typically would stop listening, fail to be aware of their inattention, and not attempt to redirect their attention to the oral text. Effective listeners seemed to be more aware when they stopped attending and made an effort to redirect their attention to the task. Other factors that detracted from attending to the task included the length and difficulty of a passage, which led some students to translate earlier portions of a passage and miss subsequent portions; occasional extraneous stimuli, such as custodians walking into the room and other students making noise outside; and fatigue (some of the students worked evenings).

During the parsing phase, students segmented portions of the oral text based on cues to meaning or on structural characteristics. Effective listeners reported listening to larger chunks than ineffective listeners, shifting their attention to individual words only when their comprehension failed altogether. Effective listeners also inferred meaning from context for unfamiliar words, unlike the less effective listeners. One of the students reported listening for segments to parse and concatenating segments to produce overall meaning. Ineffective listeners appeared to approach the listening as a task primarily requiring comprehension on a word-by-word basis. Thus, whereas the effective listeners used both a top-down and a bottom-up approach, the ineffective listeners used only a bottom-up approach to comprehension.

In the utilization phase, effective listeners appeared to make use of three types of elaborations to assist comprehension and recall: world knowledge, which may have been acquired in either an academic or nonacademic context; personal experiences, which may entail making a judgment about the correspondence between the new information and the experience; and self-questioning, or asking oneself questions about the new information and trying to answer them from existing knowledge. Effective listeners also used elaborations to support inferencing with unfamiliar words, in some cases by using a personal experience and in others by using prior knowledge about the topic. Inferencing therefore could be based on prior knowledge, as when it occurs in combination with elaboration, as well as based on structural characteristics of the text.

Discussion

The picture of listening comprehension for ESL students that emerged in this study was consistent with the depiction of general comprehension processes in the cognitive and second language acquisition literature. Listening comprehension entails active and conscious processes in which the listener constructs meaning by using cues from contextual information and from existing knowledge, while relying upon multiple strategic resources to fulfill the task requirements. The task requirements and the strategies used could be seen to vary depending on the phase in the listening comprehension process:

Phase	Strategy
Perceptual processing	Selective attention
	Self-monitoring
Parsing	Grouping (listening for larger chunks)
	Inferencing from context
Utilization	Elaboration from world knowledge, personal experiences, or self-questioning

The fact that students nominated as effective listeners used strategies more successfully than those nominated as less effective listeners suggests that the less successful students may need assistance in becoming more strategic learners. One implication of these findings is that instructional approaches that rely exclusively upon teacher input or other teacher techniques that function independently of how students process information are failing to draw upon what the students can contribute to the learning process. By failing to draw upon the students as a resource in instruction, these techniques diminish the chances of student success and exclude them from opportunities to gain independent control over the learning process.

Study 4: longitudinal study of learning strategies used by foreign language students for different language tasks

The fourth study investigating the identification of learning strategies in second language acquisition was conducted longitudinally with a sample of the same foreign language students who had participated in the descriptive foreign language study (Study 2) (Chamot et al. 1988a, b). This strategy identification study differed from our previous research in a number of ways. Participating students were drawn from beginning, intermediate, and advanced levels of language study and were followed longitudinally for four semesters, allowing us to note any changes occurring in strategy use over time. We used the same think-aloud methodology that was used for the ESL listening comprehension study, but provided students with a variety of different tasks calling upon additional language skills. This allowed us to identify specific strategies used most frequently for particular language tasks. Students identified as effective or ineffective by their teachers participated in the study, making it possible to describe differences in their strategic approaches to language learning. What we discovered from this longitudinal study has direct applications to instruction, as will be discussed in Chapter 6.

Objectives

The objectives of the foreign language longitudinal study were to: (1) investigate the cognitive processes revealed by students of Spanish and Russian as they worked on different foreign language tasks; (2) describe the range and frequency of strategies used for the different tasks; (3) identify differences in strategy use between effective and less effective students; and (4) discover if the strategy use of individual students changed over time.

Procedures

The general procedure followed in the longitudinal foreign language study was to elicit from students accounts of their cognitive processes as they engaged in a variety of language tasks. The tasks students undertook during the think-aloud sessions included: filling in the blank with appropriate vocabulary items; writing about a picture; speaking in a descriptive or role-playing activity; listening to a dialogue, monologue, or narrative; completing a cloze exercise; and reading for comprehension. Due to time limitations, not all activities were completed by each student interviewed.

PARTICIPANTS

The subjects of the longitudinal study included both effective and ineffective language learners and students at different levels of language study. Instructors ranked students in their classes, and those ranked as most and least effective at each level of study were invited to participate in the study. For the first semester of the study, participants in the study included forty Spanish students (twenty-seven effective and thirteen ineffective) and thirteen Russian students (eight effective and five ineffective). In subsequent semesters, graduation and attrition reduced the numbers of students, particularly ineffective students, so that only thirteen Spanish students (eleven effective and two ineffective) and six Russian students (all effective) remained for longitudinal comparisons by the end of the study.

METHODS

Student workbooks and interview guides were developed for each level of study for both Spanish and Russian students. The workbooks contained various language tasks based on the types of activities included in the curriculum that the students were currently studying. Workbooks for the first semester of the study contained more tasks than students were able to complete in the allotted time, so in subsequent semesters workbooks contained only three to four tasks: listening, reading, writing, and a cloze activity. The interview guides provided a script for the interviewer to introduce each activity, copies of the student tasks, and probe questions (e.g., "What are you thinking ?" or "How did you figure that out?").

Small group training sessions were held with students one to two weeks before the initial interviews. In the training sessions students were acquainted with the concept of thinking aloud about their mental processes and practiced thinking aloud with English and target language materials.

Think-aloud interviews were conducted with participating students on an individual basis. Spanish students were interviewed during 50-minute class periods, while interviews with Russian students were conducted during their free time and lasted from one to one and a half hours each. Think-aloud interviews began with a warm-up session during which the interviewer gathered general information about the student's background and motivation concerning the language under study. Next came a transition stage during which students were reminded of the training session and were provided practice in thinking aloud with a task presented in English. Finally, students began working on the target language tasks in their workbooks and were reminded by interviewers to tell what they were thinking. The complete interview sessions were tape-recorded, with verbatim transcripts made of students' verbal reports as they worked on the foreign language tasks. Selected tasks at each level and semester were analyzed for evidence of strategic processes used by students. Criteria for selecting a task for analysis included availability of good quality recording for most of the students interviewed at a given level, and appropriate level of difficulty of the task. For example, tasks that were too easy for the students' level were completed rapidly and nearly automatically, without eliciting many learning strategies. Similarly, tasks that were too difficult merely elicited a string of "I didn't understand that" or "I don't know" remarks.

Transcripts were coded by underlining student remarks that revealed cognitive processes, numbering the underlined remarks and transferring them to a coding sheet, and writing the name of the strategies thus revealed on the coding sheets as well as any comments or insights developed by the researchers as a result of the detailed analysis of the transcripts. Agreement between coders was established by comparing independent scoring of the same transcripts and discussing any differences until consensus was reached. In the event that coders could not reach agreement on problematic strategies, the strategies were not counted. Strategies thus identified and coded were counted for each student, and average use of strategies by level of study and task was computed. A qualitative analysis of the data was undertaken to identify different ways in which strategies were used by different students at varying levels of study and for the different types of language tasks. The qualitative analyses consisted of descriptions and examples of how students approached and worked on the different tasks.

Results

The results of the longitudinal foreign language study include a refinement of our definitions of learning strategies, a greater understanding of the factors affecting performance on foreign language tasks, an analysis of strategic differences between effective and less effective students, longitudinal comparisons of students, and a description of preferred strategies for different types of foreign language tasks.

DEFINITIONS OF LEARNING STRATEGIES

The think-aloud interviews revealed a variety of complex strategy applications, some of which are identified as separate strategies and some of which are integrated into our existing strategy classifications. Table 5.3 lists the new strategies identified and the definitions or expanded definitions of previously listed strategies (see Tables 5.1 and 5.2).

Advance organization, which we had previously viewed as a reading strategy with potential applications for listening comprehension, was found to have definite applications in this task. Some students prepared for a listening task by first making a general review of their knowledge of the topic and then generating some of the language that they expected to hear in the listening passage. Production tasks like writing elicited **organizational planning** strategies, such as planning to compose something, planning the total product at the discourse level, planning for goals, planning particular sentences, and planning to use specific known language items. The examples we found of these planning strategies (advance organization and organizational planning) illustrate Anderson's (1985) model of language comprehension and production (see Chapter 2).

Students sometimes used directed attention to focus on a task while they were actively engaged in completing it rather than before starting it. Similarly, **selective attention** was also used as a regulatory on-line strategy. **Self-monitoring** was used in a variety of ways for both comprehension and production. In comprehension, students monitored visually presented information as well as monitoring auditorially. In language production, students monitored at different levels, as in monitoring at the word, phrase, or sentence level, and also monitored for style, for their writing plan, and for the effectiveness of their choice of

TABLE 5.3. FOREIGN LANGUAGE LONGITUDINAL STUDY: LEARNING STRATEGIES AND THEIR DEFINITIONS

Metacognitive strategies involve thinking about the learning process, planning for learning, monitoring the learning task, and evaluating how well one has learned.

1. *Planning*: Previewing the organizing concept or principle of an anticipated learning task (*advance organization*); proposing strategies for handling an upcoming task; generating a plan for the parts, sequence, main ideas, or language functions to be used in handling a task (*organizational planning*).
2. *Directed attention*: Deciding in advance to attend in general to a learning task and to ignore irrelevant distractors; maintaining attention during task execution.
3. *Selective attention*: Deciding in advance to attend to specific aspects of language input or situational details that assist in performance of a task; attending to specific aspects of language input during task execution.
4. *Self-management*: Understanding the conditions that help one successfully accomplish language tasks and arranging for the presence of those conditions; controlling one's language performance to maximize use of what is already known.
5. *Self-monitoring*: Checking, verifying, or correcting one's comprehension or performance in the course of a language task. This has been coded in the think-alouds in the following ways:
   a. *Comprehension* monitoring: checking, verifying, or correcting one's understanding.
   b. *Production* monitoring: checking, verifying, or correcting one's language production.
   c. *Auditory* monitoring: using one's "ear" for the language (how something sounds) to make decisions.
   d. *Visual* monitoring: using one's "eye" for the language (how something looks) to make decisions.
   e. *Style* monitoring: checking, verifying, or correcting based upon an internal stylistic register.
   f. *Strategy* monitoring: tracking use of how well a strategy is working.
   g. *Plan* monitoring: tracking how well a plan is working.
   h. *Double-check* monitoring: tracking, across the task, previously undertaken acts or possibilities considered.
6. *Problem identification*: Explicitly identifying the central point needing resolution in a task or identifying an aspect of the task that hinders its successful completion.
7. *Self-evaluation*: Checking the outcomes of one's own language performance against an internal measure of completeness and accuracy; checking one's language repertoire, strategy use, or ability to perform the task at hand. This has been coded in the think-alouds as:
   a. *Production* evaluation: checking one's work when the task is finished.
   b. *Performance* evaluation: judging one's overall execution of the task.
   c. *Ability* evaluation: judging one's ability to perform the task.
   d. *Strategy* evaluation: judging one's strategy use when the task is completed.

TABLE 5.3. *(continued)*

   e. *Language repertoire* evaluation: judging how much one knows of the L2, at the word, phrase, sentence, or concept level.

Cognitive strategies involve interacting with the material to be learned, manipulating the material mentally or physically, or applying a specific technique to a learning task.

1. *Repetition*: Repeating a chunk of language (a word or phrase) in the course of performing a language task.
2. *Resourcing*: Using available reference sources of information about the target language, including dictionaries, textbooks, and prior work.
3. *Grouping*: Ordering, classifying, or labeling material used in a language task based on common attributes; recalling information based on grouping previously done.
4. *Note taking*: Writing down key words and concepts in abbreviated verbal, graphic, or numerical form to assist performance of a language task.
5. *Deduction/Induction*: Consciously applying learned or self-developed rules to produce or understand the target language.
6. *Substitution*: Selecting alternative approaches, revised plans, or different words or phrases to accomplish a language task.
7. *Elaboration*: Relating new information to prior knowledge; relating different parts of new information to each other; making meaningful personal associations to information presented. This has been coded in the think-aloud data in the following ways:
   a. *Personal* elaboration: Making judgments about or reacting personally to the material presented.
   b. *World* elaboration: Using knowledge gained from experience in the world.
   c. *Academic* elaboration: Using knowledge gained in academic situations.
   d. *Between parts* elaboration: Relating parts of the task to each other.
   e. *Questioning* elaboration: Using a combination of questions and world knowledge to brainstorm logical solutions to a task.
   f. *Self-evaluative* elaboration: Judging self in relation to materials.
   g. *Creative* elaboration: Making up a story line, or adopting a clever perspective.
   h. *Imagery*: Using mental or actual pictures or visuals to represent information; coded as a separate category, but viewed as a form of elaboration.
8. *Summarization*: Making a mental or written summary of language and information presented in a task.
9. *Translation*: Rendering ideas from one language to another in a relatively verbatim manner.
10. *Transfer*: Using previously acquired linguistic knowledge to facilitate a language task.
11. *Inferencing*: Using available information to guess the meanings or usage of unfamiliar language items associated with a language task, to predict outcomes, or to fill in missing information.

TABLE 5.3. *(continued)*

Social and affective strategies involve interacting with another person to assist learning or using affective control to assist a learning task.

1. *Questioning for clarification*: Asking for explanation, verification, rephrasing, or examples about the material; asking for clarification or verification about the task; posing questions to the self.
2. *Cooperation*: Working together with peers to solve a problem, pool information, check a learning task, model a language activity, or get feedback on oral or written performance.
3. *Self-talk*: Reducing anxiety by using mental techniques that make one feel competent to do the learning task.
4. *Self-reinforcement*: Providing personal motivation by arranging rewards for oneself when a language learning activity has been successfully completed.

Source: From Chamot, Küpper, and Impink-Hernandez (1988b, pp. 17–19).

strategy. Another type of monitoring that was applied to both language comprehension and production tasks was checking previous textual items to determine whether or not personal learning or performance goals were realized.

A new strategy category identified in this study was **problem identification**, which is similar to Brown et al.'s (1983) metacognitive knowledge. Students (especially effective ones) explicitly identified the central problem of a task or identified an aspect of a task that needed to be resolved. We also found that students used **self-evaluation** to review their own performance in relation to their actual production, their own ability, their strategy use, and their language repertoire at the word, phrase, or concept level.

Among the cognitive strategies, elaboration emerged as a major learning strategy that was used in a variety of ways, sometimes in combination with other strategies. Elaboration co-occurred with strategies such as **imagery**, inferencing, and **transfer** with sufficient regularity to suggest that these strategies may be so closely related as to be inseparable at times.

Social and affective strategies were mentioned infrequently in this study, perhaps because of the inhibiting influence of the adult–student interview situation, which may have prevented the occurrence of strategies such as cooperation and self-talk. However, **questioning for clarification** did occur when students asked questions of the interviewer about the task, or addressed questions to themselves as they worked through a language activity.

FACTORS AFFECTING LANGUAGE PERFORMANCE

A number of factors were found to influence the strategies students chose to employ and whether or not they used strategies at all. For example, the objectives of a particular language course determined to a large degree the types of strategies students learned to use. A classroom emphasizing the grammatical structure of the foreign language and an analytical comparison of the target to the native language fosters strategies such as **deduction** and translation. On the other hand, a classroom focusing on proficiency fosters strategies such as inferencing and **substitution.**

Another factor found to influence strategy use was the degree of language learning expertise of the students interviewed. Novice foreign language learners at the high school level sometimes panicked when they realized that they lacked procedural skills for solving language problems, whereas expert learners (e.g., those who had already studied another foreign language) approached new language tasks calmly and were able to deploy procedural skills developed in other language learning situations.

Another critical factor in strategy use was the task itself. At all levels of study, the demands of the task heavily influenced the strategies selected. This was evidenced in activities such as cloze, which encouraged the use of translation and deduction, and listening comprehension, which encouraged selective attention and note taking.

In all interviews, students' motivation for learning and studying the language emerged as a primary influence. Ineffective students generally displayed low motivation to learn the language. Effective students tended to be highly motivated, but they also displayed variations in motivational level during the four semesters of study. One conclusion from this study was that factors such as program objectives, prior foreign language study, task demands, and student motivation must be taken into account in understanding the use of learning strategies.

EFFECTIVE VERSUS INEFFECTIVE STUDENTS

Differences between effective and ineffective students in both the Russian and the Spanish substudies were reflected in the range of strategies used and the way in which individual strategies were used. In general, more effective students used a greater variety of strategies and used them in ways that helped the students complete the language task successfully. Less effective students not only had fewer strategy types in their repertoires but also frequently used strategies that were inappropriate to the task or that did not lead to successful task completion. The qualitative analyses revealed that effective foreign language students, much more than less effective ones, were purposeful in their approach to a task, monitored their comprehension and production for overall meaning-fulness rather than only for individual components, and effectively used their prior general knowledge as well as their linguistic knowledge while working on a task.

LONGITUDINAL COMPARISONS

No clear pattern emerged in the longitudinal comparisons of strategy use, possibly due to differences in the tasks students worked on from one year to the next and/or to the limited number of students for whom longitudinal data were available. However, some differences in strategy use by individual students were apparent. Strategies used for the writing task by an effective and a less effective student were compared for their first and second year of Russian study. While the effective student used nearly the same types and numbers of strategies in the second year of study, the less effective student showed a dramatic increase in numbers of metacognitive, cognitive, and social/affective strategies used for the task.

Data from the writing task were available longitudinally for seven effective students at the beginning level in Spanish. Spanish students moving from first- to second-year Spanish showed large increases in their use of strategies for the writing task, more than doubling the average number of strategies used. Ways in which certain strategies were used also changed from one year to the next. For example, in Spanish II, students began to plan more at the phrase level than predominantly at the sentence level, and they were more concerned with monitoring the comprehensibility of their production than they had been the previous year. Considerably more personal and academic elaborations of prior knowledge were used by second-year Spanish students.

Data for four effective intermediate level Spanish students were available longitudinally for the listening and writing tasks. The pattern of strategy use differed in the two years on both tasks. In listening, Spanish IV students planned less and monitored more, and used more elaboration and summarizing strategies than they had in the prior year. In writing, Spanish IV students planned more and monitored their style instead of focusing only on the selection of individual words. In cognitive strategy use for writing, students substantially increased their use of elaboration and summarizing at the fourth year of Spanish study.

Data from writing and cloze tasks were available for longitudinal comparisons of two effective students at the advanced level of Spanish. In writing, these students greatly increased their strategy use between Spanish V and Spanish VI. Strategies showing the greatest increase were planning for the written product, monitoring the writing as it was taking place, and cognitive strategies such as elaborating on personal and creative prior knowledge, deduction of grammar rules, and substitution of alternative words or phrases. In addition,

TABLE 5.4. FOREIGN LANGUAGE LONGITUDINAL STUDY: STRATEGIES
PREFERRED FOR DIFFERENT LANGUAGE TASKS

Task	Metacognitive strategies	Cognitive strategies
Vocabulary	Self-monitoring Self-evaluation	Resourcing Elaboration
Listening	Selective attention Self-monitoring Problem identification	Note taking Elaboration Inferencing Summarizing
Cloze	Self-monitoring Self-evaluation	Translation Deduction Inferencing Elaboration
Writing	Organizational planning Self-monitoring Self-evaluation	Resourcing Translation Deduction Substitution Elaboration Summarizing

the writing samples produced by these students in their sixth year of Spanish study were qualitatively superior to those produced the year before. For the cloze task, the data indicate that both students used a similar general approach in completing the task. They paid attention to understanding the meaning of the sentence or paragraph instead of being satisfied with finding a correct grammatical form, as had novice learners at lower levels of study.

In general, the longitudinal analysis of students moving from one level of foreign language study to a more advanced level revealed stability over time with some strategies and increases in the use of other strategies for specific tasks.

STRATEGIES USED FOR DIFFERENT TASKS

The importance of the specific language task in eliciting particular types of strategies became increasingly apparent as we analyzed data from the foreign language longitudinal study. Table 5.4 identifies favored strategies for different types of language tasks. The metacognitive and cognitive strategies that students used most frequently for different language tasks are interesting for two major reasons. First, the matching of a strategy to a task by students provides a rationale for teachers to show students how to use that strategy for the same type of task. Second, strategies that are used for many different language tasks appear to be of primary importance and should become the instructional focus of strategy teaching. For example, self-monitoring and elaboration were important strategies for all language tasks analyzed – vocabulary, listening, cloze, and writing. Self-evaluation was used for three different tasks, and resourcing, inferencing, summarizing (see Table 5.1), translation, and deduction were used for two different tasks each. Metacognitive strategies and cognitive strategies such as elaboration were used in a variety of ways, suggesting that task demands and student proficiency level affect the level of complexity with which a given strategy can be employed.

Discussion

The longitudinal study of strategy use in foreign language acquisition revealed that no clear pattern of strategy shift appeared for students interviewed over a period of one school year (Spring to Spring), although there were both increases and decreases of individual strategies. Changes in strategy use appeared to be limited to the type of task on which students were assigned to work by their teachers, which was related to the stated instructional objectives of the class. Students nominated as more effective language learners not only used a greater variety of strategies and used them more often, but they appeared to be more adept at problem identification, or the recognition and articulation of obstacles to language comprehension. Elaboration not only co-occurred frequently with inferencing, as in Study 3, but also with imagery and transfer. Affective factors appeared to influence language performance, as when inexperienced learners became disconcerted about a difficult task, while more experienced learners deployed strategic modes of processing that had been successful in the past. Finally, nomination as a successful language learner appeared to be associated with greater motivation for learning the second language as well as with more frequent and varied use of learning strategies.

Summary

The primary conclusion drawn from these four studies was that second language acquisition entails active and dynamic mental processes that can be broadly grouped into three categories: metacognitive strategies, cognitive strategies, and social/affective strategies. This and other conclusions drawn from these studies have direct implications for the theoretical analysis of second language acquisition developed earlier (see Chapters 2 and 3). We have already described the implications of the findings for a theoretical analysis of listening comprehension as part of the discussion of Study 3. Four additional aspects of the theory will be discussed here: the differentiation between metacognitive and cognitive strategies, the distinction in long-term memory between declarative and procedural knowledge, the description of stages entailed in acquiring a complex cognitive skill, and the distinction between experts and novices.

Metacognitive and cognitive strategies

The distinction between metacognitive and cognitive strategies has been described as difficult to circumscribe with precise boundaries (Brown et al. 1983). What is metacognitive to one analyst is sometimes cognitive to another. Brown et al. note that the difficulty in classification is more obvious with metacognitive strategies than it is with metacognitive knowledge. We address here whether or not we also had difficulty with these distinctions and, if so, what implications the presence of diffuse boundaries has for additional work in this area.

Although the approach is not without problems, the classification scheme based on a division of learning strategies into three categories – metacognitive, cognitive, and social/affective strategies – is useful in describing the strategies derived from both retrospective and think-aloud interviews. Our experience in collecting these data is consistent with the description by Brown et al. (1983) of metacognitive strategies as involving planning, monitoring, and checking the outcomes of learning. We also found indications of metacognitive knowledge, which we called problem identification. As Brown et al. note, strategy use is highly task-dependent. Although we were able to define occurrences of a strategy from transcripts of a taped interview with acceptable reliability, it nevertheless became evident that the depth and frequency with which students reported using any strategy might depend on the data collection procedure employed. Thus we needed to define for what purpose we wanted to collect data prior to initiating any of the studies.

We also experienced the same difficulties as did other investigators in precisely classifying any one strategy as being metacognitive in all instances where it occurred. We particularly found this to be true in analyzing our think-aloud transcripts in Study 3, where it was evident that strategies classified initially as metacognitive may at times appear to function as cognitive strategies. One example of this was *directed attention,* or orienting one's own attention to the learning task, which we had classified initially as a metacognitive strategy and which was presumed to occur prior to the onset of a task. However, we encountered instances where students directed their attention to the task while it was ongoing, and the boundary between using the strategy as an executive thinking skill and using it as an integral aspect of task performance became somewhat obscure. A second example was with selective attention, which also at times took on the feature of being an integral aspect of task performance rather than the type of skill that seems more readily portrayed as an executive function.

While these examples suggest that the distinction between metacognitive and cognitive strategies may be less precise than we would wish, we do not suggest abandoning the distinction. However, for the purposes of conducting research, we agree with Brown et al. that specific strategy terms and operational definitions to describe strategic processing should be used. But in describing learning strategies for teachers and other practitioners, we find the three-way distinction between metacognitive, cognitive, and social/affective strategies to be useful for describing how one integrates strategies into instruction, as will be discussed in the following chapters.

Declarative versus procedural knowledge

The necessity of having distinct processes for storing declarative and procedural knowledge in long-term memory has been questioned by a number of investigators (e.g., Rabinowitz, personal communication), while other investigators have constructed memory systems that have no reference to procedural knowledge at all (e.g., Rumelhart and Norman 1978). The importance of procedural knowledge has been discussed in previous chapters, where we asserted that both learning strategies and language skills such as communicative competence can be represented through production systems. In this section we discuss the ways in which declarative information is used in language comprehension and production, and point out the correspondence between production systems and the strategic processing we have observed in our research with second language learners.

We found clear evidence that students understand language through accessing declarative knowledge, tapping into schemata related to the language topic, and calling upon that information to assist in their comprehension or production. Students faced with a second language text in Studies 3 and 4 (both of which employed think-aloud techniques) discussed what they knew about the topic and used that information to find the most meaningful interpretation of the text, using inferencing or other skills to fill in information needed for comprehension. The comprehension of a second language was in a sense a problem-solving activity in which all pieces of information available from the text, from knowledge of vocabulary and grammar, and from prior knowledge of the topic needed to be brought into correspondence in the construction of meaning.

It is through procedural knowledge as represented in production systems (interrelated IF-THEN contingencies) that the goal-oriented nature of learning is illustrated. Some of the key elements in production systems are goal directedness, adaptability, and contingent planning. To the extent that these are evident in learning strategies and in language, we believe that production systems can be a useful device for describing underlying processes.

The think-aloud interviews we performed have produced a number of examples of goal directedness, adaptability, and contingency planning that apply to second language acquisition. In Study 4, we commented on planning strategies such as advance organization and organizational planning, which have goal directedness as an essential feature. Second language learners who use advance organization in either reading or listening comprehension may make a general preview of their prior (declarative) knowledge of the topic and generate some of the language they anticipate will occur in the task. The adaptability of this strategy is shown when students encounter language that is inconsistent with their expectations and revise the language content they previously had anticipated would occur. Thus, second language comprehension is recursive in nature as students revise their understanding of a text based on new information made available throughout the passage.

Second language learners who use organizational planning with a writing task develop a general plan to compose a text, formulate a framework for the overall product at the discourse level, and then plan individual goals that will result in completion of particular sentences and other language items. As the product emerges, the student can revise some of the initial goals or revise the structure of the product, illustrating adaptability. Students may also develop contingency plans for alternative ways in which to formulate the product or to treat individual parts of the overall composition. An important point concerning the use of contingency planning among effective learners is the manner in which control for one production system appears to shift, depending on the outcomes of prior decisions, and progresses onward in a fluid manner as if the learner had used these same processes on numerous previous occasions.

We find this evidence of goal formulations, adaptability, and contingency planning to be consistent with the original description we provided of IF-THEN contingencies as represented in production systems. We noted that experienced second language learners seem to have a repertoire of strategies and approach language learning problems systematically as contrasted with novices at the task, who may experience distress at the uncertainty of the task requirements. This indicates that there is at least some positive transfer in the procedural knowledge experts bring to the language task. McLaughlin and Nayak (in press) report that there may be "metaprocedural" gains from learning languages in that procedures for language learning may become automatic. One of the functions of transfer of procedural strategies that have become automatic is to free attention for more demanding aspects of the task that are required in either comprehension or production.

Stages of skill acquisition

In describing the acquisition of a complex cognitive skill, Anderson (1985) has suggested that skilled performance comes about in a progression through three stages of learning: a cognitive stage, in which individuals develop a declarative understanding of the steps required in skill performance; an associative stage, in which errors in understanding or performance are reduced and execution of the skill becomes more fluid; and an autonomous stage, where the skill becomes increasingly automatic. It is in the associative stage that production systems emerge to represent skilled performance and may co-exist with declarative knowledge of the skill. The question that needs to be addressed is how second language acquisition and strategic modes of processing interact throughout these stages of learning.

We have questioned earlier the notion that language begins with a set of rules for learning, as it may with some other complex cognitive skills, and have suggested that individuals use a combination of factors to assist their increasing acquaintance with the new language. We know that individuals learn a language in nonclassroom as well as classroom settings and may develop their own implicit or explicit rules for how the language functions, as has been described for interlanguage (Selinker 1972, 1984). We have referred to second language learners as "opportunistic" in this respect. Even in classroom settings, individuals may rely upon their own constructions of the rules governing how the second language functions, or may operate initially by modeling words or phrases until some of the underlying rules become apparent or are provided in a way that can be retained. In most psychological studies of the development of a complex cognitive skill, the context, the task, and the outcome are specified by the investigator. With second language acquisition, the learner must often analyze the language demands of the setting, determine what kinds of language skills are required, and proceed to devise ways of acquiring the information and levels of skilled performance that will enable satisfactory functioning in the second language at the level required in that setting. Thus, second language acquisition has parallels with problem solving in both classroom and nonclassroom settings.

This issue also bears on whether it is an effective learning procedure in second language acquisition to learn the rules associated with a component of the complete skill, exercise the component, and then concatenate the components to produce the complete skill. As Anderson (1985) points out, in the area of motor skills, the answer depends on the extent to which the subskills to be practiced are truly independent or require careful integration. Whole learning is superior to part learning when the skills require integration, as in playing the piano. One could argue that the same should be true of language, which is an integrative skill rather than the sum of a series of subcomponents (Oller 1979). However, the complexity of the complete language skill on which performance is expected or desired will inevitably influence the individual's decision to select subskills for learning. Nevertheless, as McLaughlin (1988) suggests, learning a second language involves "a process whereby controlled, attention-demanding operations become automatic through practice" and "an increasing number of information chunks are compiled into an automatic procedure" (p. 14).

Another related issue concerns the applicability of language transfer throughout these stages of learning. Faerch and Kasper (1987) define transfer as the process by which L2 learners activate L1 knowledge in developing or using their interlanguage, and point out that the process may either support (positive transfer) or detract (negative transfer) from learning. The focus in recent research has been on positive transfer. Learners may activate L1 knowledge in either language without retaining specific rules in memory, and may do so for purposes of either communication or learning. There are strong elements of inferencing and hypothesis testing involved in transfer insofar as learners use linguistic knowledge to build a representation of the second language skills. As Faerch and Kasper point out, there are parallels in transfer processes with the distinction Anderson makes between declarative and procedural knowledge. While linguistic knowledge in either L1 or L2 is represented as declarative knowledge, the transfer process by which rules and elements from L1 are combined with L2 knowledge in L2 comprehension and production is more accurately described as procedural. The Bialystok and Ryan (1985) notion of analyzed and nonanalyzed knowledge leads to the implication that analyzed L1 information is more accessible for transfer than other types of information. This is consistent with the notion in cognitive psychology that accessible domain-specific knowledge is essential for learning (Chi, Glaser, and Rees 1982; Gagné 1985).

This analysis of the stages of skill learning and the type of information used in transfer suggests that different strategies may be used, depending on the students' level of proficiency. Our own research confirms that second language learners may use a variety of types of information in order to comprehend either aural or written texts or to produce language. As we noted in Study 2, beginning level Spanish and Russian students used transfer as a major strategy, but intermediate and advanced level students used transfer somewhat less. Thus, whereas less proficient learners rely upon declarative knowledge about L1, more proficient learners may rely upon other types of information. At the more proficient levels of Spanish and Russian, inferencing was used to a greater degree. This suggests that more proficient learners were relying upon information from the text to predict or guess at meaning. Inferencing was often combined with elaboration or the use of declarative information about the topic identified in the text.

Thus, not only is the type of information selected for use different depending on the stage of learning, but the strategies may differ as well.

Experts versus novices

Some of the major discoveries in understanding cognition are based on differences in the mental processing of experts and novices. The mental processing of experts is learned, however, and results from persistence with a task rather than from innate differences in ability or skill. As Anderson (1985) notes, experts learn to *perceive recurring patterns* in a problem and to link their solution to these patterns. They learn to represent the problem in terms of *abstract features,* which may be predictive of the problem solution as contrasted with surface features of the problem. Experts also *reorganize their approach to the problem* in terms of the features of the domain. And finally, experts *develop better memories* for information that is involved in the problem solution. Gagné (1985) notes also that experts differ from novices in terms of the *domain-specific knowledge* they possess. While these conclusions regarding the differences between experts and novices were originally developed on studies of mathematical problem solving and similar areas such as physics, we have found at least some parallels in the study of second language acquisition.

We have noted that students experienced at language learning and effective language learners brought strategies to the task which they deployed in a problem-solving fashion. In order to do so, they must have recognized recurring patterns in the language tasks that were not evident to less experienced or less effective learners. More effective learners also understood language tasks in terms of the meaning-based intent of the communication rather than in terms of the linguistic elements or surface language features of the text. We have noted how effective language learners reorganize their approach to the problem and apply a variety of strategies, depending on the task demands. Also, more effective language learners know when and how to call up information that is related to the text in order to analyze the intended meaning, which suggests that they have better retrieval of information important for learning, whether that information consists of story schemata, schemata representing natural categories, event schemata (see Anderson 1985), or problem-solving and strategy application schemata. This bears again on the issue of the availability of domain-specific knowledge in second language acquisition. It has been suggested that experts have better organized long-term memory structures for their area of expertise. With language learners, the accessibility of domain-specific knowledge that is related to the text content gives the learner a clear advantage in being able to use elaborative and inferencing strategies to detect meaning.

Conclusions

While these studies have given some clear evidence about the ways in which strategic processing influences second language acquisition, questions remain about the specific connection between language learning and the contents of memory as well as the processes that assist learning. Furthermore, our own studies did not use correlational data to establish the relationship between individual strategies or total strategy scores and measures of second language learning, and we believe that more work of this kind should be performed. Neither did we investigate the relationship between strategy use in L1 and in L2 to determine which strategies transfer most readily and which ones do not for which kinds of language tasks. We find it difficult to reconcile totally our finding that second language learners are active, dynamic processors of information with the reported difficulty that balanced bilinguals have in L2 reading comprehension (McLaughlin 1987b) and presumably in the application of comprehension strategies. The brief description we provide of transfer processes in second language acquisition should be augmented with additional work, as should the more lofty ambition for second language theory Spolsky (1988) has suggested, of determining "who learns how much of what language under what conditions" (p. 380).

6 *Instruction in learning strategies*

Most learning strategy research in second language acquisition has concentrated on the identification, description, and classification of learning strategies used by second language learners. One of the principal concerns in this research has been the description of strategies used by more effective versus less effective language learners. Once strategies used by good language learners are identified and the strategy use of effective and less effective learners are compared, the questions arise of whether less effective learners can learn to use strategies to assist their learning and, if so, what strategies can and should be taught, and what instructional approach can be used to teach the strategies selected.

Instruction in learning strategies has been done with strategies that facilitate the acquisition of declarative knowledge (generally referred to as memory training) and of procedural knowledge (such as reading comprehension and problem solving). Considerable research on training learning strategies has been conducted outside the second language field in various areas of the curriculum, including reading comprehension, memory training (e.g., recall of vocabulary, facts, definitions), and problem solving. Noticeably absent from learning strategy training research in first language contexts is training in oral language production (Derry and Murphy 1986). Relatively little research has been completed on instruction in writing strategies compared to the substantial body of research on direct instruction in reading strategies (see, for example, Pearson and Dole 1987). Although much recent research interest in first language written composition has concentrated on identification of the writing process and analysis of discourse (Scardamalia and Bereiter 1986), some investigations of instruction in learning strategies for composition have been reported. Graham and coworkers (1987), for example, have conducted composition strategy training with learning-disabled upper elementary school students. The inquiry approach to writing (which involves direct training of writing strategies) has also been found to be an effective instructional approach to improving composition in first language contexts (Hillocks 1987).

In second language learning contexts, language production skills are particularly important because students' acquisition of speaking and writing competence is crucial to their success in academic settings. Although the small number of second language learning strategy training studies does include memory training, listening, and reading comprehension, few studies have examined how strategies for productive language can be trained.

In this chapter we first discuss some of the major issues that need to be addressed in training learning strategies. Next we describe representative training studies conducted with second language learners and with learners in first language settings that may have applications to second language learning. Following this are descriptions of training studies we have conducted with ESL students and with foreign language students. The chapter ends with a summary of the findings and conclusions of the studies reviewed, and a suggested area for future research.

Issues in instruction

Separate versus integrated instruction

An unresolved issue in instruction in learning strategies is whether instruction should focus only on learning strategy instruction or should be integrated with classroom instruction in the language or content subject. Arguments in favor of separate training programs advance the notion that strategies are generalizable to many contexts (Derry and Murphy 1986; Jones et al. 1987) and that students will learn strategies better if they can focus all their attention on developing strategic processing skills rather than try to learn content at the same time (Jones et al. 1987). Examples of separate strategy training are Dansereau's (1985) Computer-Assisted Cooperative Learning (CACL) Program, designed to train pairs of students to use a sequence of reading comprehension strategies, which are presented and practiced by computer, and his learning strategy system (identified by its acronym MURDER), which trains primary strategies for comprehension/retention and for retrieval/utilization, and support strategies for planning, monitoring, and concentration management.

Those in favor of integrated strategy instruction programs, on the other hand, argue that learning in context is more effective than learning separate skills whose immediate applicability may not be evident to the learner (Wenden 1987b) and that practicing strategies on authentic academic and language tasks facilitates the transfer of strategies to similar tasks encountered in other classes (Campione and Armbruster 1985; Chamot and O'Malley 1987). Dansereau (1985), finding that students encountered difficulty in adapting the strategies they had learned in the

MURDER learning strategy system to particular kinds of text materials, developed a strategy training program in which the strategies were designed for specific types of science texts. Instruction in developing an organizational schema for science theories and using headings to facilitate comprehension of scientific text were both effective aids for college students' recall of material read in science textbooks.

Dansereau (1985) suggests that future studies evaluate a learning strategy system that integrates both content-independent strategies and content-dependent ones. This type of integration is also suggested by Derry's (1984) incidental learning model, in which students receive short periods of separate strategy training followed by reminders to use the strategies in content classrooms. Weinstein (1982) and her coworkers (Weinstein and Underwood 1985) have developed and implemented both separate and integrated instruction in learning strategies. The separate training consists of a special university course designed to teach students how to use learning strategies effectively. Practice is provided by applying these strategies to students' other courses. The integrated training consists of teaching content teachers how to incorporate learning strategy instruction into their regular classrooms.

Direct versus embedded instruction

The arguments for separate and integrated learning strategy training programs are similar to the question of whether the actual training (whether separate or integrated) should be direct or embedded. In *direct instruction,* students are informed of the value and purpose of strategy training, whereas in *embedded instruction,* students are presented with activities and materials structured to elicit the use of the strategies being taught but are not informed of the reasons why this approach to learning is being practiced. Early research on training learning strategies following the embedded approach found little transfer of training to new tasks (Brown, Armbruster, and Baker 1986). More recent studies have added a metacognitive component to training by informing students about the purpose and importance of the strategies to be trained and providing instruction on the regulation and monitoring of strategies. The addition of this metacognitive component has been helpful in maintaining strategy use over time and in transferring strategies to new tasks (Brown et al. 1986; Palincsar and Brown 1986).

An advantage cited for strategy training embedded in instructional materials is that little teacher training is required (Jones 1983). As students work on exercises and activities, they learn to use the strategies that are cued by the textbook. An example of uninformed strategy training in a second language context is Barnett's (1988) study of college students of French. The purpose of the study was to see if reading strategy instruction in the first year of French would result in higher reading achievement at the end of the first semester of second-year French. Beginning level students in the experimental groups were provided with special reading comprehension exercises designed to teach students to recognize cognates, make inferences to guess at meanings, use titles and illustrations, and make predictions about the text. However, students were not told the rationale or intent of this strategy instruction because the researchers wanted to "avoid as much as possible the impact of enthusiasm sometimes generated by an experimental situation" (p. 111). Students in the experimental group showed somewhat greater improvement in reading comprehension than did control group students, but the differences were not statistically significant. A criticism of uninformed strategy training of this type is that students who are not aware of the strategies they are using do not develop independent learning strategies and have little opportunity of becoming autonomous learners (Wenden 1987b).

Many researchers, therefore, recommend that instruction in learning strategies be direct rather than embedded (Brown et al. 1986; Palincsar and Brown 1984; Wenden 1987b; Weinstein and Mayer 1986; Winograd and Hare 1988) or that direct instruction be added to a curriculum or instructional materials designed with embedded strategies (Derry and Murphy 1986).

Instructional implementation

A number of issues related to actual implementation of learning strategy instruction can be identified. Probably the most important issue is developing in teachers the understanding and techniques for delivering effective learning strategy instruction to students. A second and related issue is the development and adaptation of instructional materials that provide learning strategy instruction, either as a supplement to the core second language textbooks or as an integrated system included in core textbooks. Third, the specific scope, sequence, and methods of training activities to meet the needs of particular students need to be considered. Finally, the level of language proficiency at which strategy training can and should be started has to be determined.

TEACHER TRAINING

Very little attention has been given to training in which teachers are familiarized with techniques for learning strategy instruction. Virtually all learning strategy training in both first and second language contexts has been conducted by researchers. In their comprehensive review of systems developed to train learning ability, Derry and Murphy (1986) discuss a number of strategy training studies conducted in four learning domains – memory training, reading strategies training, problem-solving training, and affective support training. In each domain, issues such as instructional materials, curriculum, and training procedures are described, but no mention is made of how teachers have been or can be trained to teach learning strategies to their students. Yet there is a need not only to train teachers in methods of incorporating strategy instruction in their classrooms but also to convince teachers that learning strategies can be effective for their students (Wilson 1988). One pilot study to train teachers to use a learning strategy curriculum in high schools and community colleges was conducted by Weinstein and Underwood (1985), who reported student performance gains six months after the conclusion of the teacher training sessions.

In the second language field, the role of teacher training is equally unclear. Holec (1987), for example, reported a series of investigations in which students who elected to self-direct their own language learning worked with a teacher who "functions as counsellor in the context of individual non-directive interviews" (p. 147). How the teacher learns to function as a counsellor is not mentioned. In other second language training studies, researchers and their associates work directly with students, with teachers involved mainly as observers (e.g., Cohen and Aphek 1981; Hosenfeld et al. 1981; O'Malley et al. 1985a). In our own teacher training efforts, we discovered that teachers need considerable exposure to the concept of learning strategies as opposed to teaching strategies, and repeated practice in designing and providing learning strategy instruction before they feel comfortable with incorporating strategy training in their classrooms.

A recent synthesis of research on staff development over the last thirty years has identified the features of training design that have the greatest effect in terms of teachers incorporating new concepts and skills into their classrooms (Showers, Joyce, and Bennett 1987). This synthesis found that effective training includes both presentation of theory and demonstration of the new approach, followed by immediate practice and feedback in the training setting. Development of a basic level of knowledge and skills with the new approach is a necessary though time-consuming requirement for successful training. In addition, this synthesis found that teachers are more likely to use the new approach in their own classrooms if they receive coaching during their implementation efforts. A staff development model that provides for ongoing training, practice, and feedback is the coaching model developed by Joyce and Showers (1987). In this model, teachers participate in training activities that extend over one or more school years and include frequent workshops, collaborative planning, and classroom observation with a peer.

The coaching model has three main stages for staff development activities. These stages are recursive in nature, that is, each stage is continually recycled to provide for review and internalization of new concepts and skills. In the first stage, new information is presented to the participants. The rationale for the value of the new information is emphasized, and the classroom applications are demonstrated so that teachers can see how the theory works in practice. The second stage consists of practice and feedback opportunities. Participants practice the new techniques during the training session and receive feedback from each other and from the trainer. This is followed by immediate practice in the classroom. The third stage consists of consolidation of the new information. In this stage, teachers observe each other's approaches to using the new information in the classroom, plan together, and encourage each other. To facilitate the coaching process, videotapes are made of teachers as they try out the new techniques. These videotapes are shown during debriefing sessions and teachers think aloud about what was going through their minds as they were delivering instruction. This latter technique can be helpful in providing ways for teachers to share their instructional procedures and to coach each other when joint classroom observation cannot be arranged.

This type of intensive and ongoing staff development may be essential in developing what Jones and her colleagues (Jones et al. 1987) have termed a "strategic teacher." In their view, a strategic teacher first spends considerable time thinking and making decisions about the variables of the instructional process, content to be learned, assessment, and development of strategy instruction, then draws on an extensive knowledge base in both the content of the curriculum and teaching and learning strategies to develop lessons, and finally engages in interactive instruction in which he or she models learning processes and mediates instruction by helping students organize and interpret what they are learning. Because the focus is on the learner and the learning process instead of on the teacher as information provider, this model is quite different from more familiar ones and can be expected to require a considerable investment in teacher training.

Ogle (1988) reports on a three-year approach to staff development on the strategic teaching model that has many elements of the coaching model. In the first year, in-service workshops on strategic teaching principles and practice were provided by expert consultants to participating teachers. In the second year, the consultants demonstrated the concepts developed in the first year by teaching lessons in the teachers' classrooms. By the third year, teachers were working collaboratively to develop, implement, and demonstrate to each other lessons designed on the strategic teaching model. In spite of the extended time allocated to these staff development activities, teachers still encountered difficulty with some of the techniques they were learning, notably in analyzing and evaluating students' prior knowledge of the lesson topic.

MATERIALS AND CURRICULUM DEVELOPMENT

A number of instructional materials have been developed for strategy training for native English-speaking students, including, for example, the Chicago Mastery Learning Reading Program with Learning Strategies (Jones 1983; Jones, Amiran, and Katims 1985), the Job Skills Educational Program developed for the Army (Derry 1984; Murphy and Derry 1984), and the Computer-Assisted Cooperative Learning Program (Dansereau 1984).

There are few readily available materials to teach learning strategies in the second language classroom. This makes it even more difficult for potential "strategic" teachers to incorporate learning strategy instruction into their classrooms, because they must develop materials as well as carry out the instructional techniques that will familiarize their students with learning strategy applications. The few easily available training materials that have been developed for teaching learning strategies to second language learners are described in Chapter 7.

Procedures for planning the scope and sequence of strategy training activities have been suggested by a number of researchers. In all of these, the teacher identifies and assesses the strategies students are already using, then explains the strategy and provides opportunities to practice it (Hosenfeld et al. 1981; Jones et al. 1987; O'Malley and Chamot 1988; Weinstein and Underwood 1985). Table 6.1 summarizes several suggested learning strategy instructional sequences. The Jones et al. (1987) sequence is a component of their strategic teaching model and is intended for use in all content areas in mainstream classrooms. The Weinstein and Underwood (1985) sequence was developed for a university course designed for students who need or wish to improve their academic learning skills. Our sequence (O'Malley and Chamot 1988) was developed as part of a content-based elementary and secondary ESL program, the Cognitive Academic Language Learning Approach (CALLA), which is described in Chapter 7. The Hosenfeld et al. (1981) sequence was designed to improve the reading comprehension skills of high school students of French as a foreign language. Similar sequences have been developed for reading comprehension strategy training (Pearson and Dole 1987) and for written composition strategy training (Graham, Harris, and Sawyer 1987).

The four sequences described in Table 6.1 share a basic structure, in which the teacher first identifies or shows students how to identify their current learning strategies, explains the rationale and application for using additional learning strategies, provides opportunities

TABLE 6.1. SCOPE AND SEQUENCE FRAMEWORKS FOR
LEARNING STRATEGY INSTRUCTION

First language contexts	Second language contexts

Jones et al. (1987)
 general guidelines (all subjects)
 1. Assess strategy use with:
   – think-aloud
   – interviews
   – questionnaire
 2. Explain strategy by:
   – naming it
   – telling how to use it, step by
    step
 3. Model strategy by:
   – demonstrating it
   – verbalizing own thought
    processes while doing task
 4. Scaffold instruction by:
   – providing support while
    students practice
   – adjusting support to student
    needs
   – phasing out support to
    encourage autonomous
    strategy use
 5. Develop motivation by:
   – providing successful
    experiences
   – relating strategy use to
    improved performance
	O'Malley and Chamot (1988)
	 general guidelines (content-based ESL)
	 1. Preparation: Develop student
	   awareness of different strategies
	   through:
	   – small group retrospective
	    interviews about school tasks
	   – modeling think-aloud, then
	    having students think aloud in
	    small groups
	   – discussion of interviews and
	    think-alouds
	 2. Presentation: develop student
	   knowledge about strategies by:
	   – providing rationale for strategy
	    use
	   – describing and naming strategy
	   – modeling strategy
	 3. Practice: Develop student skills in
	   using strategies for academic
	   learning through:
	   – cooperative learning tasks
	   – think-alouds while problem
	    solving
	   – peer tutoring in academic tasks
	   – group discussions
	 4. Evaluation: Develop student ability
	   to evaluate own strategy use
	   through:
	   – writing strategies used
	    immediately after task
	   – discussing strategy use in class
	   – keeping dialogue journals (with
	    teacher) on strategy use
	 5. Expansion: Develop transfer of
	   strategies to new tasks by:
	   – discussions on metacognitive and
	    motivational aspects of strategy
	    use
	   – additional practice on similar
	    academic tasks
	   – assignments to use learning
	    strategies on tasks related to
	    cultural backgrounds of students

TABLE 6.1. *(continued)*

First language contexts	Second language contexts
Weinstein and Underwood (1985)	*Hosenfeld et al. (1981)*
college course	reading comprehension
(individual learning skills)	(French)
1. Identify academic and strategy needs through:	1. Provide think-aloud training
– Learning and Study Skills Inventory (LASSI)	2. Identify current reading strategies
– other self-report measures	3. Explain importance of strategies
– reading comprehension test	4. Help students analyze own strategies in L1 (English)
– individual interviews	5. Have students practice L1 strategies in L2 (French)
– group discussions	6. Provide direct instruction on reading comprehension strategies by:
2. Develop goals for strategy use and affective control for:	– explanation
– individuals	– practice
– entire class	– application to reading assignments
3. Provide background information on:	– evaluation of success of strategies
– motivation	7. Evaluate success of strategy training by repeating Step 2
– cognition	
– strategies and study skills	
– transfer	
4. Provide different practice opportunities with varied content:	
– discussion	
– role playing	
– peer tutoring	
5. Evaluate strategy acquisition by:	
– providing both individual and group feedback	
– administering same instruments as in Step 1	
– developing self-evaluation with student journals and papers	

and materials for practice, and evaluates or assists students to evaluate their degree of success with the new learning strategies. In other words, all the sequences are examples of direct rather than embedded training.

A learning strategy scope and sequence is the first step toward developing a curriculum that integrates learning strategies with other instructional objectives. Research is needed on the development, implementation, and evaluation of such a curriculum. Our current learning strategy projects focus on this need.

LANGUAGE PROFICIENCY

Another important implementation issue in second language education concerns the language proficiency level at which learning strategy instruction can most effectively be initiated. In a monolingual setting, learning strategy instruction can be given from the beginning, because the instruction is provided in a language that students understand. In a second language setting, however, students at the initial level of language proficiency may not be able to understand the language associated with learning strategy instruction. In this situation, the options are either to delay introduction of learning strategy instruction until students have developed sufficient proficiency to understand and talk about learning strategies, or provide initial learning strategy instruction in the native language. In a bilingual setting this may be not only possible but the best way to deliver instruction about the importance and application of learning strategies. However, in a multilingual setting the teacher must either explain and practice learning strategies with extremely simple language (which may not be adequate to express metacognitive analysis and understanding), or else postpone learning strategy instruction until students have developed a basic proficiency in the second language. This dilemma has yet to be resolved. Wenden (personal communication, 1987) suggests that teaching beginning level students the language of metacognition be given high priority in order to provide the language needed to talk about and receive instruction in learning strategies.

Student characteristics

The effect of student characteristics on instruction in learning strategies cannot be overemphasized. Characteristics such as motivation, aptitude or effectiveness as a learner, age, sex, prior education and cultural background, and learning style may play an important role in the receptiveness of students to learning strategy training and in their ability to acquire new learning strategies. For instance, in our own work with strategy training (O'Malley et al. 1985b), we found that acceptance of new strategies during training was related to prior success with alternative strategies, and this overlapped with ethnicity (or prior educational background).

Motivation is probably the most important characteristic that students bring to a learning task. Motivation, or the will to learn, can be considered a component of metacognition insofar as it plays a self-regulatory role in learning (Jones et al. 1987). Students who have experienced success in learning have developed confidence in their own ability to learn. They are therefore likely to approach new learning tasks with a higher degree of motivation than students who, because they have not been successful in the past, may have developed a negative attitude toward their ability to learn. Learning strategy instruction would be most valuable for students who are not successful learners, yet these are the very students who may be least motivated to try new strategies, since they may not have confidence that they are able to learn successfully anyway. In the case of second language learners, some students may indicate that they are "not good at languages" or do not "have an ear for languages," and therefore may not consider it worthwhile to make an effort to improve their own language learning. Strategy training programs could benefit from a motivation component to help get reluctant students over the initial hurdle of learning to use new strategies. Once students begin to experience some success in using strategies, their attitudes about their own abilities may change, thus increasing their motivation. Jones et al. (1987) indicate that a major objective of strategy training should be to change students' attitudes about their own abilities by "teaching them that their failures can be attributed to the lack of effective strategies rather than to the lack of ability or to laziness" (p. 56).

Paris (1988a) agrees that informed training in the use of strategies is not sufficient, but that a motivational training component needs to be added to learning strategy instructional programs. He identifies the following four instructional techniques that lend themselves to the integration of motivational and cognitive strategy instruction:

Modeling, in which the expert (the teacher) demonstrates to the novice (the student) how to use the strategy, often by thinking aloud about the goals and mental processes involved;

Direct explanation, in which the teacher provides a persuasive rationale and benefits expected from use of strategies, so that students become convinced of their own potential success;

Scaffolding instruction, in which the teacher provides temporary support to students as they try out the new strategies (e.g., as in reciprocal teaching), and

Cooperative learning, in which heterogeneous student teams work together to solve a problem or complete a task.

As we will discuss in Chapter 7, these instructional techniques are not mutually exclusive and have considerable potential for use with second language learners.

In second language learning, the importance of attitude and motivation is illustrated in Wenden's (1987b) account of the strategy training she conducted at the American Language Program at Columbia University. ESL students in this intensive program were given, in addition to the regular ESL course, instruction and practice on the nature of language learning in order to develop metacognitive awareness. A questionnaire to evaluate the learner training component was administered at the end of the course, and the responses indicated that for the most part, students did not perceive any value in the learner training. Wenden attributes these negative results to the fact that the learner training was not closely linked to the language learning objectives of the course, so students did not clearly understand why and how the use of metacognitive strategies could improve their English.

There is a long history of research regarding the notion of specific aptitude for foreign or second language learning (Carroll 1981). In Carroll's (1981) review of research in this area during the last twenty-five years, he offers a number of definitions of foreign language aptitude, including the following:

- a knack for learning a foreign language (p. 86)
- aptitude, as defined in terms of prediction of rate of learning (p. 91)
- some special cognitive talent or group of talents that is largely independent of intelligence and operates independently of the motivations and attitudes of the learner (p. 94)

Each of these definitions is congruent with our understanding of effective learning strategies. In fact, individuals with a special aptitude for learning foreign languages may simply be learners who have found on their own the strategies that are particularly effective for efficient language learning. The parallels are even more striking when Carroll's four major components of foreign language aptitude are examined from a cognitive and learning strategies perspective, as the following examples illustrate:

1. Phonetic coding ability: An ability to identify distinct sounds, to form associations between those sounds and symbols representing them, and to retain these associations. (Carroll 1981, p. 105)

This ability seems to operate largely at the perceptual processing stage (Anderson 1985). As discussed in Chapter 5, effective listeners in a second or foreign language know how to make use of strategies such as directed attention and selective attention to assist their perceptual processing (Chamot et al. 1988a, b; O'Malley et al. 1988).

2. Grammatical sensitivity: The ability to recognize the grammatical functions of words (or other linguistic entities) in sentence structures. (Carroll 1981, p. 105)

This grammatical aptitude appears to correspond to Anderson's (1985) parsing stage of comprehension, in which incoming language is segmented into constituents, and structural and semantic clues are used to assign meaning to the oral or written text. In our own work, recognition of grammar rules was assisted particularly through the use of deductive strategies, and interpretation of the language functions of words and phrases was assisted through self-monitoring of comprehension, elaboration of prior knowledge, inferencing, and linguistic transfer.

3. Rote learning ability for foreign language materials: The ability to learn associations between sounds and meanings rapidly and efficiently, and to retain these associations. (Carroll 1981, p. 105)

Learning of declarative knowledge is illustrated in this component of Carroll's model of foreign language aptitude. As we discussed in Chapter 2, this type of knowledge is most efficiently and effectively learned through making elaborative associations with prior knowledge by activating relevant schemata in long-term memory. Associations between sounds and meanings can be facilitated by strategies such as the keyword method, which has had considerable success in the acquisition of foreign language vocabulary (Atkinson and Raugh 1975; Levin 1981; Pressley et al. 1980, 1981).

4. Inductive language learning ability: The ability to infer or induce the rules governing a set of language materials, given samples of language materials that permit such inferences. (Carroll 1981, p. 105)

This ability clearly calls for inferencing and may operate both at the parsing stage and at the utilization stage of Anderson's (1985) comprehension model. Our own research in listening comprehension indicates that students at the utilization stage use elaboration, summarizing, and self-monitoring as well as inferencing to comprehend and recall information presented in the second or foreign language (Chamot et al. 1988b; O'Malley et al. 1988).

From these examples, it seems entirely possible that the link between aptitude and effective learning strategy use is a strong one. If this is the case, then aptitude should not be seen as an innate trait but as a strategic ability that can be learned.

Another student characteristic sharing common elements with aptitude is learning style, or the way in which an individual prefers to learn (Kolb 1984). Learning style comprises both a person's cognitive approach to learning and his or her attitudes toward the task. A number of models have been developed to describe learning style dimensions (Guild and Gerger 1985). Among these are field independence versus field dependence, visual versus auditory learning preference, and reflective versus impulsive learners. An individual's learning style may predispose that person to adopt particular learning strategies. For example, a visual learner may naturally use imagery as a preferred strategy, and a field-independent or analytic learner may naturally gravitate toward strategies such as **grouping** (see Table 5.1) and deduction. Research in this area is sparse, but a number of instructional programs recommend that teachers include activities in their lessons that address the needs of students' different learning styles (McCarthy 1987). Although teaching to different learning styles certainly seems educationally sound, we would like to suggest that in learning strategy instruction, students probably need assistance and additional practice in those learning strategies that may not be closely allied to their natural learning styles but which nevertheless are valuable in successfully completing language learning tasks. Examples of such strategies are those requiring focusing of attention, monitoring of comprehension, elaboration of prior knowledge, making use of inferences, using deduction to apply language rules, taking notes on listening and reading materials, asking questions for clarification, and cooperating with peers to accomplish a learning task. Not all of these strategies may fall into the natural learning style preferences of a second or foreign language student, yet all are of potential value in increasing language learning effectiveness. The thoughtful use of strategies such as these may in fact be characteristics of learners with an aptitude for foreign and second language learning.

Other student characteristics that need to be considered in designing learning strategy instruction, especially for second language learners, are age, sex, and prior educational experiences and cultural background.

Most second language learning strategy instruction has been conducted with adolescent or adult learners, whereas a number of successful training interventions have been conducted in first language contexts to teach elementary and secondary school children reading comprehension strategies, mathematics problem-solving strategies, and vocabulary learning (Carpenter et al. 1988; Gagné 1985; Pressley, Levin, and Ghatala 1984; Weinstein 1978). Pressley (1988) argues that because rudimentary learning strategies are used by children as young as two to four years of age, learning strategy training should begin before the first grade. Although some research has been conducted on the identification of learning strategies of elementary school bilingual students (e.g., Chesterfield and Chesterfield 1985; Padron and Waxman 1988), research is needed on the design and effects of second language learning strategy instruction for younger students.

A student characteristic that has received scant attention in second language learning strategy research is differential strategy use of males and females. In their review of gender differences in language learning strategy use, Oxford and her associates found only four studies in which this question was addressed (Oxford, Nyikos, and Ehrman 1988). Three were strategy identification studies, and all showed differences in strategy use favoring women. The other study provided strategy training and showed mixed results, favoring men for some skills tested and women for others. All four studies were conducted with university or adult students, so that gender differences of younger language students remain unexplored.

In the second language learning arena, cultural background can be expected to play a part in both identifying the set of learning strategies students bring to a task and the ease or difficulty with which new strategies can be trained. Part of the cultural background of students is their prior educational experiences. For example, students whose initial educational training emphasized rote memorization of curriculum content may have developed quite effective memory strategies but be rather inexperienced with comprehension or problem-solving strategies. O'Malley et al. (1985b) found resistance from Asian students to using strategies for imagery and grouping to learn vocabulary definitions. Asian students in the control group applied rote memorization strategies to the vocabulary task so successfully that they outperformed the experimental groups who had been trained in what we perceived as more sophisticated strategies. On the other hand, Hispanic students appeared to enjoy the training of new learning strategies and performed better on the posttest than did Hispanic students in the control group. Although these differences in strategy approach and application could be attributed to cultural differences, they could in fact be due merely to differences in prior schooling (which of course is embedded in a cultural context). Additional research in this area is certainly called for.

Review of representative studies

In this section we describe a sample of studies conducted on learning strategy instruction in second language contexts, as well as in first language contexts that have applications for the second language classroom. Most of the monolingual studies have been experimental in nature, with objective measures of learning outcomes, and were often conducted outside of the regular classroom in individual student-researcher settings. In contrast, most of the second language studies have been nonexperimental, include data based on measures such as interviews, questionnaires, and teacher comments, and have been conducted in classroom settings. After reviewing a representative sample of training studies in both second language learning and in first language memory and skill training, we will describe our own work in training second language learning strategies.

Instruction in learning strategies for second language acquisition

Memory training in second language learning has focused on mnemonic techniques that facilitate vocabulary learning (Thompson 1987). Training procedures that use paired associate techniques include the *peg-word method*, in which second language learners use a list of memorized cue words to learn vocabulary or grammatical categories in the second language (Desrochers 1980; Paivio and Desrochers 1979), and the key-word method, in which students learn sets of words through the combination of an auditory and imagery link (Atkinson and Raugh 1975; Pressley, Levin, and Delaney 1982). In reviewing the various mnemonic techniques for memory training, Thompson (1987) identifies a number of constraints that can limit the usefulness of these techniques for strategy training, including the additional effort required to learn the associated relationships, the lack of meaningful relationships between the items to be learned, potential difficulties with pronunciation, individual differences such as age, prior educational experiences and cultural background, learning style predilections, task difficulty, and proficiency level of students.

Cohen and Aphek (1980) trained students of Hebrew to recall new vocabulary words through paired associations. First, students were given brief instructions on how to use associations to assist in vocabulary recall, then they selected their own new words from a reading text and made their own associations for them. The students practiced using the new words in a variety of cloze activities over a period of several weeks. At the time of the posttest, students most often used the initial association they had made in order to recall the new word, and this led to better performance than using a different association or none at all.

Training studies on comprehension strategies in second language learning have investigated reading comprehension more frequently than listening comprehension. Hosenfeld and her associates (1981) taught a series of reading strategies to high school French students following the curricular sequence described in Table 6.1. As Wenden (1987b) points out, this is an example of informed or direct training, because students were apprised of the nature and value of the strategies taught and had to determine the relative personal usefulness of the strategies. However, information about the effectiveness of the strategies taught for improving reading comprehension or even the gain of strategy use from pretest (Step 2) to posttest (Step 7) is not provided.

A number of second language learning strategy studies have been undertaken in France and elsewhere under the auspices of CRAPEL (Centre de Recherches et d'Applications Pedagogiques en Langues) at the University of Nancy, France. These studies are guided by an approach in which second language learners are provided with an option for self-directed rather than traditional classroom courses (Holec 1987). Improving comprehension skills (listening and reading) and oral production skills were objectives of these studies. Students choosing the self-directed learning option meet with a counselor on an on-going basis to decide upon course objectives, discuss learning techniques, and select instructional materials. A striking feature of the CRAPEL model is the degree of autonomy, unusual in a university or other formal educational entity, provided to the learner. Learners decide what to learn, how they will learn it (with suggestions from the helper, who is carefully not cast in the role of teacher), and what materials they will use. Adult students, both beginning as well as more advanced second language learners, have been successful in this type of learning environment. The success of autonomous learning with the CRAPEL model was reported through evaluations conducted by means of informal summaries by researchers, interviews with students, and questionnaires (Holec 1987; Moulden 1978, 1980; Wenden 1987b).

Oral production skills were the focus of a training project conducted at a Eurocentre language training institute in England. Wenden (1987b) summarizes the objectives of this project as the development of students' ability to assess their own oral language through activities such as using a checklist to evaluate their own taped language samples. Teachers reported that students were successful in learning to use the criteria for self-evaluation and enjoyed the activities.

Learning strategy instruction in first language contexts

While second language learning strategy instruction studies have been relatively few in number, such is not the case in first language settings, where a variety of training studies have been conducted in the last fifteen years (see Derry and Murphy 1986 for a comprehensive review of learning strategy training studies). In this section we discuss a representative sample of these training studies, limiting our discussion to those studies that appear to have the greatest potential for applications to the second language classroom, particularly for the development of integrative language skills (e.g., listening and reading comprehension, and oral and written production).

Several studies have sought to improve students' reading comprehension through training in the use of elaboration, or meaningful association of new information with prior knowledge. The ability to use elaboration successfully allows a reader to construct meaning by making explicit connections between the written text and individual schemata, or knowledge frameworks. These schemata can consist of general or academic knowledge about the topic and of knowledge about the organization of the type of discourse being read, such as knowledge about specific story grammars. Expert readers' use of elaboration leads to top-down, or meaning-based, reading, whereas novice readers tend to use bottom-up processing as they read, assigning meaning to individual words but not relating larger chunks of language to their own prior knowledge. In our strategy identification research, we have found elaboration to be a frequently used strategy for listening, reading, writing, and grammar activities (Chamot et al. 1988b; O'Malley et al. 1987).

In second language learning, elaboration is of particular interest to researchers studying transfer in bilingual individuals who learn to use the body of prior knowledge originally acquired in the first language to comprehend new information presented in the second language. Our own strategy identification research seems to indicate that such cross-lingual elaboration is much more likely to be used by more effective language learners than by less effective ones, who may believe that knowledge acquired in the first language is not accessible in the second language. For these reasons, training second language learners to use appropriate elaborations to enhance comprehension could be extremely effective in improving both listening and reading skills.

Two elaboration training studies conducted in first language settings could be adapted fairly easily for second language students. Weinstein (1978) conducted a study in which ninth-grade students were taught to use a variety of elaborations, including sentences, images, analogies, implications, relationships, and paraphrases, and to apply them to both memory tasks and reading comprehension passages. The materials on which the strategies were practiced were taken from different content areas in the ninth-grade curriculum. Cues to use the strategies were reduced during later training sessions so that students could begin to use the strategies autonomously. The delayed reading comprehension posttest showed that the students trained to use the strategies significantly outperformed those in the control groups. Having shown that students could be taught to use elaboration strategies effectively, Weinstein and her colleagues went on to develop the Individual Learning Skills university course (described in Table 6.1), in which students significantly increased their learning ability, particularly in reading comprehension (Weinstein and Underwood 1985).

A second elaboration training approach that can be used with second language learners was investigated by Gagné (1985). Seventh graders were taught how to recognize, generate, and evaluate elaboration strategies for a text they wanted to remember. The training sequence began with students deciding on the value of the material to be read; an important point communicated was that not every type of text is or should be necessarily remembered. Once students made the decision that they wanted to remember a text, they engaged in a variety of training activities. First, students had to determine whether they understood the material. If there were comprehension difficulties, students were directed to use strategies such as using resources or asking for clarification to understand the text. Once comprehension was perceived to be satisfactory, students had to generate elaborations on the new information that would help establish links between prior knowledge and the information to be recalled. At the conclusion of the study, students who had been trained to make appropriate elaborations were able to recall significantly more from the reading passages than were control group students.

Another type of learning strategy that has been successfully used for training in first language contexts is cooperation or cooperative learning. *Cooperative learning* involves social strategies in which students work together in heterogeneous small groups toward a common goal. Extensive research on cooperative learning indicates that it is effective in increasing achievement on school tasks as well as fostering positive attitudes of students toward themselves and each other (Slavin 1980). The extension of cooperative learning strategies to the second language classroom has been advocated as a way of achieving these same benefits for second language learners, with the additional benefit of increasing opportunities for meaningful language practice (Chamot and O'Malley 1987; Kagan 1988).

Good language learners have a wide repertoire of learning strategies and use a series of strategies rather than a single one when engaged in a learning task. Therefore, a training system in which multiple strategies are taught within a single package would appear to be beneficial. Such a multiple-strategy training program is Reciprocal Teaching, developed by Palincsar and Brown (1984) for improving reading comprehension. This instructional strategy embodies cooperative learning techniques in which students work in small groups to develop comprehension of a written text. At first the teacher models the strategies to be used; later each student in the group acts as the teacher and goes through the strategies in turn. Group members first read a portion of the text (one paragraph or more) silently, then the person acting as teacher summarizes what has been read, identifies and clarifies difficult parts, asks group members comprehension questions, and then predicts what information the next paragraph or section will present. As this sequence is repeated, students become more adept at using the four comprehension strategies and also improve their performance on reading comprehension tests (Brown et al. 1986). By using Reciprocal Teaching in a second language classroom, students also practice using the new language for academic purposes as they develop the four learning strategies taught in this program. The general framework of cooperative learning, with group members sharing the responsibility for developing competence in a task, could be developed for language skills other than reading comprehension.

Another promising teaching technique with clear application to the second language classroom is K-W-L (Ogle 1987), in which students first identify what they already *K*now about a topic, then state what they *W*ant to learn about the topic, and, after interacting with the new information, what they have *L*earned about the topic. This sequence of strategies involves first elaboration (activation of prior knowledge), then selective attention to the particular content that they want to learn, and finally, summarizing the main points learned. The final phase also serves as a self-evaluation activity in which the student identifies the personal learning outcomes of the task. This sequence of strategies is obviously useful for any content area, including second language learning and learning of content in a second language.

Graham et al. (1987) have conducted a number of studies in which learning-disabled English-speaking upper elementary students received explicit instruction in composition strategies to improve their written production. These studies included training on vocabulary enrichment, use of advanced planning to generate content to be included, and techniques for revising and editing what students had written (Graham et al. 1987; Harris and Graham 1985, in press). In the vocabulary study, students developed their ability to conduct memory searches for lexical items by generating words from a picture stimulus. In other studies, students were taught how to use advance planning to generate content for a composition by responding to a series of information questions. In another study, students were taught specific techniques for revising and editing essays written on a microcomputer. The results indicate that strategy training techniques can be used for various aspects of the writing process and that students weak in writing skills can improve the quality of their writing through the application of specific composition strategies.

These brief summaries of learning strategy instruction studies recently conducted in first language contexts provide only a sampling of the innovative research being conducted with students educated in their native language. The studies are waiting to be replicated and adapted to students learning a second language for academic purposes.

Study 1: learning strategy instruction with students of English as a second language

Research on instruction in learning strategies in first language contexts left a number of important questions concerning strategies in second language acquisition unanswered. First, no studies in second language acquisition in which strategies had been trained with integrative language skills had been done. All previous work had focused on strategies for vocabulary learning, while ignoring altogether more complicated language tasks such as listening and speaking. Second, there were very few studies of the effects of strategy instruction using an experimental approach that would permit the independent effects of the training to be isolated. What few experimental studies existed concentrated on vocabulary learning. Third, little of the second language acquisition research had been performed in classroom settings with typical class-size groups. The instruction was usually performed in individual sessions with a researcher-trainer. Fourth, the strategy instruction tended to concentrate on isolated strategies instead of on combinations of strategies, as might be represented by combining metacognitive with cognitive strategies. Fifth, there was little effort in the second language acquisition literature to determine if strategies transferred across similar tasks. Most of the instruction had been administered in single sessions and concentrated on a single set of tasks presented immediately following training. And finally, none of the learning strategy training research in second language acquisition had been performed with students studying English as a second language but was performed with students studying foreign languages or studying non-English languages abroad.

Objectives

The primary objective of this study (O'Malley et al. 1985b) was to determine whether strategy instruction in a natural classroom setting would result in improved learning for varied types of second language tasks with students of English as a second language. We were particularly interested in the effectiveness of strategy instruction with integrative language tasks such as listening and speaking as well as with vocabulary learning, on which there had been a reasonable amount of work previously done. The listening and speaking tasks used would have to be representative of the types of academic tasks that students are expected to perform in the ESL curriculum. Representativeness also extended to the strategy combinations we selected, since we felt that most teachers would not present isolated strategies but would look for combinations that seemed appropriate for the types of tasks students were performing. We felt that demonstrating strategy training would be convincing in the second language acquisition field only if it was performed with the usual ESL classroom tasks and group sizes and by teachers who were presenting the strategy training in the context of a typical ESL curriculum. This study represents the second phase of the descriptive ESL study reported in Chapter 5.

Method

The overall approach taken in this study was to randomly assign students to receive strategy instruction in one of three groups that were differentiated by the combination of strategies they received. In the metacognitive group, students received combined instruction on metacognitive, cognitive, and social/affective strategies; the cognitive group received instruction on cognitive and social/affective strategies alone; and the control group was asked to work on the language learning tasks using whatever procedures they typically used in performing classroom assignments. The control group also received some special reading instruction intended to support the school program.

PARTICIPANTS

The students in this study were seventy-five enrollees in ESL programs at the secondary level in three mid-Atlantic suburban high schools. The students were all at the intermediate level of English proficiency, defined as limited proficiency in speaking and understanding English and little or no skill in reading or writing English. About a third were from Spanish-speaking countries, another third from Asian countries, and a third from other language backgrounds.

PROCEDURE

The students were randomly assigned to one of the three groups in proportion to the overall ethnic and gender mix within each school. The size of the instructional groups varied from eight to ten students, depending on the school. To control for teacher effects, each of three project staff members presented a different treatment condition at the three participating schools.

Students received instruction and practice in the use of learning strategies for fifty minutes daily for eight days. One additional period was reserved at the beginning and end of the eight instructional sessions for pretesting and posttesting. On any single day, the students typically performed on two of the following three language activities: vocabulary, listening, or speaking. The same learning strategies were always presented with each language task, although the materials varied on each occasion the task was presented. Students could therefore practice strategy applications with new materials over a period of time. Explicit directions and cues for strategy use were faded on successive days of treatment, until by the posttest only a reminder was given to use the same strategies they had used before. Tests for the vocabulary and listening tasks were also given each day on which those tasks occurred.

Table 6.2 illustrates the way in which strategies were combined with the different language tasks for the metacognitive group and shows that three strategies were used with vocabulary, three with listening, and two with speaking. The cognitive group received all the same strategies except the metacognitive strategies, and the control group received no direction to use special strategies with learning. Table 6.2 also indicates that the vocabulary task consisted of word lists, the listening task consisted of listening to a 5-minute lecture on an academic topic (which included personal-interest topics, geography, and science), and the speaking task

TABLE 6.2. ESL INSTRUCTION STUDY: LANGUAGE ACTIVITIES AND
ACCOMPANYING LEARNING STRATEGIES FOR THE METACOGNITIVE GROUP

Language task	Strategy type	Strategy
Vocabulary (word lists)	Metacognitive	Self-evaluation
	Cognitive	Imagery and grouping
	Social/affective	None
Listening (5-minute	Metacognitive	Selective attention
lecture on an academic	Cognitive	Note taking
topic)	Social/affective	Cooperation
Speaking (2-minute	Metacognitive	Functional planning
presentation on a familiar	Cognitive	None
topic)	Social/affective	Cooperation

consisted of making a brief presentation on a familiar topic (e.g., differences between people in my country and people here, my favorite things to do, my first day in this country, etc.).

Some indication of the way in which the strategies and tasks were combined can be seen in the following description of instruction for the metacognitive group:

Vocabulary
Students were presented with ten-item word lists comprised of tangible items and encouraged to *group* the words based on meaningful classifications as they studied them and to *imagine* themselves interacting with the object while using its name. After a 5-minute study period, students were tested for recall. Students were then given the opportunity to review their tests and were encouraged to analyze which strategies worked, which didn't work, and why.

Listening
Before hearing a listening passage, students were instructed to *selectively attend* to linguistic markers (key words) in a listening passage that signal a main idea (e.g., "today I will talk about," "the most important point," "one major idea," or "in summary") or a detail ("for example," "for instance"). They were also given directions in *note taking* using a *T list,* in which the main ideas of a listening passage are noted on the left side of a page and the corresponding details are listed on the right. After hearing the listening passage and taking notes, students had the opportunity to interact using *cooperative learning,* where they exchanged information on what they considered to be the main ideas and details of the passage. They were then tested for recall.

Speaking
Before presenting their 2-minute talk, students were reminded about the use of linguistic markers, were encouraged to use them in their talk to signal important points or details, and were told about the major sections (overview, body, conclusions) that usually are included in an oral presentation (*functional planning*). Students then selected their topic, wrote a draft of the oral presentation, tried it out with a small group (*cooperative learning*), rewrote it

if necessary, and then made the presentation to the group while it was tape-recorded. Students received feedback from peers in the small group on the same criteria against which their speeches were later rated.

The technique for fading cues for strategy use on the listening comprehension task included presenting *T* lists that were partially completed early in training and gradually eliminating the number of words on the page over the course of training. The pretest and posttest audiotapes for the speaking task were scored blind by raters who were only generally introduced to the purpose of the study. The rating system was on a 1–5 scale of criteria similar to those used by the Foreign Service Institute and reflected delivery (volume and pace), accuracy (phonological, syntactic, and semantic), and organization (coherence and cohesion). Interjudge reliability was about 85 percent.

Results

The strategy instruction for listening and speaking was implemented without major difficulties, although the instruction for vocabulary was found to require substantial modification despite a successful pilot test of the approach. Despite these mid-instructional modifications, the results of the vocabulary instruction are discussed here because they reveal some interesting findings. There was substantial evidence that students in the metacognitive and cognitive groups used the strategies in which they had been trained, including teacher observations, student work sheets, and student interactions, during cooperative learning sessions.

Results of statistical analyses on the speaking task indicate that differences among the three groups were statistically significant on the posttest, as adjusted for initial differences at the pretest. The metacognitive group scored higher than the cognitive group, which in turn scored higher than the control group. The differences between groups were also practically significant, as shown by differences on the FSI scale of about half a scale point between the metacognitive group and the control group. The metacognitive group scored about 2 + whereas the control group scores were just below 2, reflecting differences in organization, sequencing, and comprehensibility.

Results of statistical analyses for the listening task were not significant at the posttest as adjusted for initial differences, although some of the daily tests were significant. The tasks where significance was found tended to be the human interest stories, the more interesting (to this group of students) and less demanding of the tasks, whereas significance was not found for the geography or science lessons. There are three possibilities why significance was not found on the listening task at the posttest: the greater difficulty of the posttest materials, the lower interest level of the materials, or the advanced rate at which the cues for strategy use were faded.

On the vocabulary test, there were no significant differences overall among the treatment groups. However, when the results were disaggregated by ethnic group, it was clear that the Asian control group outperformed the Asian training groups, while the Hispanic training groups outperformed the Hispanic control groups. This effectively nullified the overall findings. Reflecting on these results, the teachers indicated that the Asian students had resisted using the strategies during training and had preferred to use rote repetition, which is what the control group used, while the Hispanic students had been more interested in alternatives to the usual processes they used to learn.

Discussion

This study demonstrated that strategy training can be effective in a natural classroom environment with integrative language tasks such as speaking and listening, although it suggests that training effectiveness depends on the difficulty of the materials or the rate at which cues for strategy use are faded over time. The fact that the language tasks on which the strategies proved effective were academic language skills suggests that this type of training has promise for improving the learning ability of minority language students both in their higher level ESL classes and after they exit from ESL or bilingual programs.

Study 2: learning strategies taught by foreign language instructors

The ESL training study (O'Malley et al. 1985b) demonstrated that learning strategies instruction can be effectively implemented in real classroom settings. However, the instruction was conducted by researchers who, although experienced language teachers themselves, were nevertheless not the regular classroom teachers of the students involved. This left open the question of whether classroom teachers would and could provide learning strategy instruction as part of their regular classes.

The Foreign Language Course Development Study, which was conducted as part of the study of learning strategies in foreign language instruction (Chamot et al. 1987, 1988a, b), sought to answer this and other practical implementation questions.

Objectives

The Foreign Language Course Development Study (Chamot et al. 1988b) had three main objectives. The principal objective was to discover whether and how foreign language instructors would incorporate learning strategy instruction in their classrooms. A second objective was to use the instructors' in-depth knowledge about their students and their course objectives to select for instruction those strategies which they believed would be most effective in promoting student achievement in specific language skills. Finally, we wished to discover how instructors would integrate the strategy instruction into other class activities and whether they would opt for direct or embedded instruction.

Method

The main approach taken in this study was to gain the cooperation of the foreign language instructors whose students we had been working with in the strategy identification studies. We wanted to add some instruction in learning strategies to these teachers' classes. A number of classes of participating instructors were then observed when learning strategy instruction was taking place, and narrative descriptions were developed of the instructional context, individual class activities, learning strategies taught and practiced, and any difficulties encountered.

PARTICIPANTS

The instructors who were asked to participate in this study were the regular classroom teachers or professors of high school students of Spanish and college students of Russian who had been involved in the foreign language strategy identification studies (see Chapter 5 for descriptions of these studies). Of the seven instructors of these students invited to collaborate in the study, two Spanish teachers and three Russian instructors expressed interest in participating. Of these five, one Spanish instructor subsequently withdrew from the study. Of those remaining, three (two Russian professors, one Spanish teacher) were highly experienced language teachers who said they had already integrated learning strategy instruction in their courses, and one less experienced Russian instructor who was nevertheless convinced of the utility of learning strategy instruction and interested in incorporating it into her teaching.

PROCEDURE

Meetings were set up with the Spanish teachers and Russian instructors in order to acquaint them with the results of the Descriptive Study of Foreign Language Learning Strategies (Chamot et al. 1987) and to ask for their participation in the Course Development Study. Separate meetings were held for the Spanish and the Russian instructors.

After a discussion of their students' learning strategies, as revealed in the Descriptive Study, instructors were asked if they would be willing to allow members of the research team to observe classes in which the teachers would either introduce learning strategy instruction or continue with the strategy instruction they were already presenting. As stated earlier, of the three Spanish teachers and four Russian instructors present at these initial meetings, one Spanish teacher and three Russian instructors eventually agreed to participate in the study.

Nine classroom observations were then conducted during the Spring and Fall 1987 semesters. The classes observed were: third-year Spanish, in which the instructional focus was on strategies for listening comprehension; nonintensive (e.g., four hours per week) first-year Russian focusing on speaking skills; intensive (e.g., eight hours per week) first-year Russian, also focusing on strategies for speaking skills; and another intensive first-year Russian class, in which strategies for reading comprehension were developed.

For each observation, the researcher met for a short time with the instructor before the class and was briefed on lesson objectives, student needs, and instructional concerns. During the class, the researcher sat in the back of the classroom and took notes on teaching procedures, materials, student responses, learning strategies introduced and practiced, and reminders to use previously introduced strategies.

When time permitted, a debriefing session took place after the class between the researcher and the instructor, in which the instructor explained the reasons for specific procedures or activities and commented on students' reactions and behaviors.

Notes made by researchers on the class observations and briefing and debriefing sessions with instructors were transcribed immediately following the observations. These transcriptions provide detailed descriptions of the directions, cues, and activities used by these instructors in training their students to apply learning strategies to various types of foreign language tasks. Content analyses of these detailed descriptions were conducted in order to find evidence of the questions we were interested in answering, namely, the relative ease of strategy instruction implementation, the degree to which direct or embedded instruction was provided, and the specific strategies selected for instruction for different language tasks.

Results

We expected that by sharing the results of the first strategy identification study with the instructors whose students had provided the strategy data we would be able to enlist support and enthusiasm for the Course Development Study. This plan was only partially successful, for only one of the three Spanish teachers and three of the four Russian instructors agreed to participate. Typical reasons for teachers' nonparticipation were: lack of interest in teaching learning strategies and lack of time for either planning or implementing the instruction. Of the participating Russian instructors, one encountered difficulties related to student apathy for doing even routine classwork, and finally abandoned the attempt to teach learning strategies to that class (but not to other classes).

These results indicate that not all teachers may be willing to add a strategy instruction component to their second language classrooms, and that even those that do may become discouraged if students do not respond appropriately. Instructors who did agree had some degree of prior knowledge about and experience in teaching learning strategies, and were already employing a number of teaching techniques that encouraged student strategy use.

The transcripts of class observations were analyzed to identify the types of strategies taught for different language tasks and the manner in which individual instructors delivered instruction designed to pro 1ote student use of learning strategies.

Table 6.3 indicates the major strategies taught and practiced for listening comprehension, reading comprehension, and speaking practice. (None of the participating instructors elected to provide strategy instruction for writing.) Each of the three activities selected was taught by a different instructor. As mentioned earlier, the fourth instructor participating in the study had to cancel his plans for learning strategy instruction.

The principal strategies taught for listening comprehension were:

Selective attention: The instructor told students to focus on specific items, such as nouns, unknown words that they can ask for clarification about, numbers, important words that carry meaning, intonation contours and stressed words, language function of the word or phrase, while listening.

Elaboration: The instructor pointed out what students already knew and suggested how they could use this academic or world knowledge to make an inference about the meaning of an unknown word.

Inferencing: The instructor first focused on strategies such as selective attention, elaboration, transfer, or deduction, and then suggested that students make inferences based on information elicited from these strategies.

Transfer: The instructor called attention to similar English words and cognates to suggest meanings of new words; she also pointed out similarities in the root of a new word with that of a known word in the L2.

The principal strategies taught for reading comprehension were:

Inferencing: The instructor identified and named the strategy based on students' descriptions of ways in which they used context both at the sentence and discourse levels to guess at meanings of unknown words.

Deduction: The instructor elicited from students their application of grammatical rules to identify the form of unknown words in the text (in both L1 and L2), which led to guesses about the type of word it would be (e.g., adverb, place noun, etc.).

Elaboration: The instructor recognized and encouraged student use of prior

TABLE 6.3. FOREIGN LANGUAGE COURSE DEVELOPMENT STUDY: MAJOR
LEARNING STRATEGIES TAUGHT FOR DIFFERENT TASKS

Task	Description	Strategies	How used
Listening comprehension	Students listened to tape of authentic dialogues between shoppers and salesperson, then completed comprehension exercise.	Selective attention	Focus on specific items while listening
		Elaboration	Use what you know
		Inferencing	Make logical guesses
		Transfer	Recognize cognates
Reading comprehension	Students identified reading strategies in L1, then applied same strategies to L2 paragraph with new words underlined.	Inferencing	Use immediate and extended context to guess new words
		Deduction	Use grammar rules to identify word forms
		Elaboration	Use prior knowledge
		Transfer	Recognize, use cognates
Speaking	Students worked in groups to prepare sections of difficult reading text to retell to class so that all would understand it.	Substitution	Use synonyms, paraphrases, and gestures to communicate meaning
		Cooperation	Work in pairs or groups to plan and evaluate task
		Self-evaluation	Check own ability to communicate successfully

knowledge, both academic and real world, to make decisions about probable meanings.

Transfer: The instructor elicited from students recognition of cognates and similar-sounding words in the L1 that could be applied to understanding the new words in the L2.

The principal strategies taught for the speaking task were:

Substitution: The instructor told students to use synonyms, paraphrases, and gestures to get across their meaning in the text retelling task.

Cooperation: The instructor had students work in small groups on the speaking assignment and encouraged them to help each other with this task.

Self-evaluation: The instructor provided opportunities for students to check how well they had made themselves understood and to discuss their communicative effectiveness.

In addition to the major strategies identified, instructors also taught or encouraged the use of a number of other strategies that supported the main strategies when used in combination with them. For example, students were reminded to self-monitor comprehension, to decide if an inference made sense in the context, to ask questions for clarification when they did not understand, to make mental images to assist comprehension, to use what they already knew in the speaking activity (elaboration), and to self-monitor their oral production for errors that would impede comprehensibility. The following summary of the general approach followed for each classroom illustrates the differences and similarities of the approach used by each teacher.

LISTENING COMPREHENSION

The materials used in this class were authentic tape recordings of shopping exchanges taking place against the normal background noise of people and traffic. Comprehension questions in English were provided before the tape was played, and students listened to one section of the tape at a time, answering the questions and discussing that section before listening to the next section. The instructor told or reminded students of what and how to listen before playing each tape segment. For example, students were reminded to listen for specific items, such as nouns or the answers to the comprehension questions, and to tune out irrelevant background noise. After playing a section, the instructor would identify new words, remind students of what they already knew, and tell them to use that knowledge to make guesses about new items. Cognates were identified and students were encouraged to use them in clarifying the total meaning of a phrase. The sequence of instruction – listening–discussion–instruction – was repeated at a rapid and enthusiastic pace throughout the classes observed. Strategies were not identified by name; instead, the instructor focused on specific hints and techniques for functional communication in the foreign language. Students were alert, and most seemed to enjoy the pace and concentration required, though some students revealed in interviews that they had felt considerable anxiety when first being exposed to this type of class.

READING COMPREHENSION

The materials used were an English text containing nonsense words and a foreign language text with new words underlined. The instructor provided an introduction about how inferencing is used to guess at meanings of new words in English, but that most people do not carry over this strategy to reading in a second language. Then students read over the English text and individually wrote their guesses for the nonsense words and described how they had arrived at each guess. A general class discussion followed in which students described their mental processes in making the guesses, and the instructor identified each process and wrote a brief description on the board, reminding students of the ways in which they had used inferencing. Students next were given a foreign language text and asked to analyze the new words in the same way. A class discussion elicited different guesses and types of strategies for each of the underlined words in the foreign language text. These included the use of grammatical cues, semantic clues, knowledge of the world, and transfer of linguistic knowledge, especially the use of cognates. The instructor continually named the processes students described, wrote them on the board, and explained how and why these processes were helpful in guessing at meanings of new words. The class ended with students encouraged to use these strategies when reading in the foreign language. Afterward, students were heard to comment favorably on the class and to indicate that they planned to use inferencing strategies in future reading assignments.

SPEAKING

A difficult text was assigned in sections to groups of students, who then prepared it as an oral presentation for the next class. Since the text was challenging, each group had to utilize a number of resources to comprehend it themselves, then had to find ways to retell it to their classmates so that they would understand it. This required that synonyms, paraphrases, and gestures be used to clarify the intended meaning. The instructor provided specific instruction in the use of three strategies for this exercise: *substitution* (finding a different way of saying something), *cooperation* (working with a group to prepare and make a presentation), and *self-evaluation* (checking how well they were able to communicate with the rest of the class). Since the observations of this class, unlike those for listening and reading, took place at weekly intervals, it was possible to trace the types of practice opportunities provided for the three strategies introduced with the original text retelling assignment. One week later, a similar task was undertaken in which students had to read a new text aloud, retell it with substitutions for difficult parts, assist each other when difficulties were encountered, and evaluate the quality of the story retelling. Additional practice sessions included a vocabulary game using the strategies of substitution and cooperation, further practice with text retelling, and finally the development of role plays requiring the use of the three strategies. With each new activity, the instructor reminded students of the strategies and explained how they could be applied to the new task as well as to communicative situations in real life, thus providing direct instruction in transfer of the strategies. Feedback by the instructor and through students' own self-evaluations was continual. Students performed the original task with marked enthusiasm and interest, but appeared somewhat less enthusiastic though still engaged for follow-up activities in subsequent classes.

The fourth instructor participating in the study had planned to provide instruction on inferencing and self-monitoring as aids in developing speaking skills for second-semester beginning level students. However, the attitude and lack of motivation exhibited by students in this class indicated that they were either not interested in or were unable to assume any responsibility for their own learning. In view of this, the instructor reluctantly reverted to what he termed a "mean" stance, requiring students to do extensive drill and practice exercises in order to memorize the basic grammatical elements covered by the course. The instructor indicated that students could benefit from strategy instruction (which he had been accustomed to providing in other classes) only if they were willing to assume some responsibility for their own learning, and he had found that this particular group expected the teacher to direct their learning.

Discussion

A major objective of the study was to find out whether foreign language instructors would be able and willing to integrate learning strategy instruction into their language classes. In earlier second language learning strategy training studies, the training was provided by the researchers (e.g., Hosenfeld et al. 1981; O'Malley et al. 1985b). In order for learning strategy instruction to become an integral part of second language teaching, classroom teachers need not only to see the value of such instruction but also develop the skills for its implementation. In this study only one workshop on learning strategies was provided to the foreign language instructors, and instructors who eventually decided to participate in the study were those who had previous experience with learning strategy instruction. What this appears to indicate is that not all teachers have the necessary motivation or skills to add learning strategy instruction to their classes, and that substantial training may be necessary both to convince teachers of the utility of learning strategy training and to develop the instructional techniques that will help students become more autonomous language learners.

A second objective of the study was to discover the strategies selected for different language learning activities by foreign language instructors. As could be expected, the strategies selected for listening and reading comprehension were quite similar. In both cases instructors encouraged students to use inferencing to make logical guesses from context, elaboration of prior knowledge, and transfer of cognates from the first language. In addition, the use of deduction, which led to the application of grammar rules, was used in reading comprehension. The four strategies identified and practiced for reading were described by the instructor as different forms of inferencing. In the listening comprehension class, the instructor encouraged students to use the metacognitive strategy of selective attention to specific items while listening in addition to the other strategies.

The strategies taught for speaking included a metacognitive strategy (self-evaluation), a cognitive strategy (substitution), and a social/affective strategy (cooperation). Although none of the participating instructors elected to provide strategy instruction for writing, it is likely that the strategies taught for speaking could be equally useful in writing.

Elaboration, which in earlier studies (Chamot et al. 1987; 1988a; O'Malley et al. 1987) emerged as a significant strategy characteristic of more effective language learners, was selected by instructors participating in this study to be taught for receptive language tasks, that is, listening and reading. Elaboration was not selected as a strategy to be taught for speaking, yet speaking (and writing) obviously draws on the student's prior knowledge and schemata in order to deliver a meaningful message.

The third objective of this study was to document the way in which different instructors actually implement instruction in different types of learning strategies. Each participating instructor had an individual way of providing learning strategy instruction. All of them provided direct rather than embedded strategy training by informing students of the purpose and value of the techniques students were asked to try. The instructors for reading comprehension and speaking identified the strategies by name, whereas the listening comprehension instructor described the behavior recommended without giving it a specific name. All strategy instruction and discussion was provided in English, which was probably necessary given the fact that students were still limited in their proficiency in the foreign language. How learning strategy instruction can be provided to limited proficiency students with many different language backgrounds or by a nonbilingual teacher are areas of research that need to be investigated. Only one of the participating instructors had students identify the strategies they were already using in their native language as a springboard to transferring the same strategies to the foreign language.

The importance of motivation in learning strategy instruction was clearly shown in this study. Students in the classrooms of the three instructors who were successful in implementing learning strategy training engaged in the activities with apparent enthusiasm, tempered in some cases by apprehension or diminution of the original level of enthusiasm in subsequent classes. The fourth instructor, however, encountered apathy and indifference to language learning in his class and felt forced to abandon the attempt to train learning strategies. The will to learn appears to be essential for developing the skill to learn (Paris 1988a).

A major instructional implication emerging from this study is that while learning strategy instruction *can* be implemented successfully in second language classrooms, the success of such training is dependent on a number of factors, including teacher interest, development of techniques for instructing students in the effective use of learning strategies, and the ability to provide a motivational framework that can convince students of the value of learning strategies.

Conclusions

In this chapter we first identified some of the major issues involved in training of learning strategies such as whether strategy training should be a separate course or integrated with a regular class. We concluded that strategy training should probably be integrated with regular instruction in order to demonstrate to students the specific applications of the strategies and to promote the transfer of strategies to new tasks. Furthermore, evidence indicates that strategy training should be direct in addition to being embedded. In other words, students should be apprised of the goals of strategy instruction and should be made aware of the strategies they are being taught. It is believed that this metacognitive knowledge will facilitate transfer of the strategies to new tasks and will assist students toward autonomous use of the strategies.

Issues related to implementation of strategy training programs raised questions about the amount of teacher training required to implement innovations successfully such as strategy training. Coaching has been suggested (Joyce and Showers 1987) as a model to facilitate the acquisition of methodological innovations.

The need for materials and curriculum development for learning strategy instruction in second language classrooms was seen as the next critical step in bringing learning strategy instruction to the classroom. Several learning instructional sequences from both first and second language contexts were described as possible starting points for curriculum development. Features of most instructional sequences for explicit learning strategy instruction include initial modeling of the strategy by the teacher, with direct explanation of the strategy's use and importance; guided practice with the strategy; consolidation, in which teachers help students identify the strategy and decide where it might be used; independent practice of the strategy; and finally, application of the strategy to new tasks (Pearson and Dole 1987). As Pearson and Dole (1987) have pointed out, this type of instructional sequence is completely different from a traditional skills approach in which components of a task are practiced separately. Instead, in a learning strategy instructional sequence, the complete task is performed each time, with the teacher providing extensive initial support and students gradually assuming control over a larger portion of the complete task.

The problem of providing learning strategy instruction through the medium of the second language was addressed, but no simple solution was found. One possibility is to teach the language associated with metacognition to beginning level students so that they have the vocabulary with which to discuss learning strategies early in their second language study.

The effect of student characteristics on learning strategy training was discussed in relation to a number of different characteristics, including motivation, aptitude or learner effectiveness, and education and cultural background. All are important factors in learning strategy instruction. Of particular importance is the inclusion of motivational training with learning strategy instruction in order to develop will as well as skill for learning (Paris 1988a).

In the first study we conducted, we taught high school ESL students metacognitive, cognitive, and social strategies to use for vocabulary development, listening comprehension, and oral production. One of the most important findings of this study was that strategy training could be effective in a classroom setting for integrative language tasks such as listening and speaking. Although the results of our training study were statistically significant favoring the group trained in strategies, the size of the effect with listening comprehension was nevertheless modest. A number of factors may have influenced the degree of effectiveness, among them training design, including difficulty of materials and frequency of cues for using the strategies, and the effect on strategy preferences of students' cultural and educational background.

In our second strategy training study we worked with foreign language instructors instead of directly with students. Classroom observations revealed how the instructors integrated learning strategy training into their regular foreign language classes. We identified the particular strategies taught for listening comprehension, reading, and speaking, and also described the somewhat different instructional approaches taken by each instructor. The most important finding from this study was that while learning strategies can be taught in the language classroom, the endeavor is neither simple nor always successful. Factors such as teacher interest and willingness to commit additional time to the instruction and the ability to maintain a high level of student motivation are critical to the success of learning strategy instruction.

Research on strategy training with second and foreign language students is in its infancy, as most studies to date have concentrated on identifying and describing strategies students have either developed on their own or in classes conducted in their first language. In our view, the major obstacle to be overcome in future research on strategy training is to discover how second language teachers can be trained to provide learning strategy instruction to their students. In most second language strategy training studies, researchers, not teachers, have provided direct strategy instruction to students. Because researchers typically have limited amounts of time to spend with students, we have little information about the effects of extended strategy training. As learning strategies are a part of procedural knowledge, we would expect that their acquisition would require a considerable investment of time for cued practice, feedback, and discussion activities. The only way to provide for such extended instruction and practice in learning strategies is to involve regular classroom teachers over a semester or year in the teaching of learning strategies. For this to take place, extensive staff development activities are needed, and neophyte strategic teachers would probably need extensive support from researchers, staff developers, and coaching partners in order to successfully implement a program of learning strategy instruction.

7 Learning strategies: models and materials

Research on the learning strategies that second language students generate and strategies that can be taught is of great significance in understanding the operation of cognitive processes during second language acquisition. Nevertheless, as educators, we are also interested in extending the information gained from research to the improvement of both learning and teaching second languages. To this end, instructional models and materials are helpful in illustrating the ways in which research findings can be converted into practical classroom activities.

This chapter first examines a recent instructional model utilizing learning strategy instruction in first language contexts. Then we discuss the model we designed to teach learning strategies in English as a second language instruction as well as a sample of second language instructional materials that incorporate learning strategies. Finally, we suggest some needed areas of research on applications of learning strategies to second and foreign language classrooms.

Instructional models in first language contexts: strategic teaching

Jones et al. (1987) have developed a framework for instruction in all content areas based on cognitive learning theory and its applications to instruction in mainstream native English-language classroom settings. The Strategic Teaching Model is based on the following six research-based assumptions about learning (Jones et al. 1987):

1. Learning is goal oriented. Expert learners have two major goals during the learning process: to understand the meaning of the task and to regulate their own learning. In other words, learners have both declarative knowledge, or content goals, and procedural knowledge, or strategic goals for a learning task.
2. In learning, new information is linked to prior knowledge. Prior knowledge is stored in memory in the form of knowledge frameworks or schemata, and new information is understood and stored by calling up the appropriate

187

schema and integrating the new information with it. Knowing how and when to access prior knowledge is a characteristic of effective learners.

3. Learning requires knowledge organization. Knowledge is organized in recognizable frameworks such as story grammars, problem/solution structures, comparison/contrast patterns, and description sequences, among others. Skilled learners recognize these organizational structures and use them to assist learning and recall.

4. Learning is strategic. Good learners are aware of the learning process and of themselves as learners, and seek to control their own learning through the use of appropriate learning strategies. Strategies can be taught, but many do not transfer to new tasks. Although each content area may require a particular set of strategies and skills, a number of core skills underlies all subject areas. Examples of these core skills are using prior knowledge, making a representation of the information, self-monitoring, and summarizing.

5. Learning occurs in recursive phases. All types of learning are initiated with a planning phase, followed by on-line processing, and ending with consolidation and extension of the new information. In the planning phase, the problem is identified, goals are set, and prior knowledge is activated. During on-line processing new information is integrated, assimilated, and used to clarify or modify existing ideas. During consolidation and extension the learner summarizes and organizes the new information, assesses achievement of the goal established in the first phase, and extends learning by applying it to new situations. During each phase the learner may return to a previous phase to rework one or more of its aspects.

6. Learning is influenced by development. Differences between older and younger students and between more and less proficient learners are due in large part to differences in prior knowledge and learning strategy use. These differences may be present when children begin school or may develop over time, but in either case they tend to persist unless intervention is undertaken.

In the Strategic Teaching Model these six assumptions guide every aspect of planning and implementing instruction. Teaching therefore becomes an active thinking and decision-making process in which the teacher is constantly assessing what students already know, what they need to know, and how to provide for successful learning. This requires that teachers not only be good managers but also have an extensive knowledge base about their subject and about teaching and learning strategies. In the classroom, teachers act as models and demonstrate mental processes and learning strategies by thinking aloud to their students. They also act as mediators by helping students use strategies to understand and organize information and by showing them how to become autonomous learners.

Instruction and practice in using learning strategies pervades the Strategic Teaching model. The specific sequence recommended for strategy instruction begins with assessing current student strategy use, explaining the new strategy, modeling the strategy, and finally providing "scaffolding," or extensive support for students when they first try out the new strategies, followed by a gradual diminution of support and prompting so that eventually students learn to use the strategies independently. (See Table 6.1 in Chapter 6 for a summary of this sequence for strategy instruction.)

The Strategic Teaching Model identifies three recursive phases for instruction: preparation, presentation, and application/integration. In the preparation phase the teacher activates students' prior knowledge of the lesson topic through questioning, evaluating the relevance of the prior knowledge, and refining that knowledge. During this phase students can also preview the new information to be learned, develop new vocabulary, and identify concepts or beliefs that may be changed or replaced after instruction.

In the presentation phase of the lesson, students interact with the new information presented by the teacher or text through selecting, comparing, organizing, and integrating activities. Reciprocal teaching, in which students and teacher cooperate to understand a text by taking turns to apply a sequence of comprehension strategies, is an illustration of the type of instructional activity that takes place during this phase (see Chapter 6 for a fuller description of reciprocal teaching).

The application and integration phase of the strategic lesson serves the dual purposes of evaluating and consolidating the learning task. To evaluate their learning, students refer back to their original goals that were established during the preparation phase. In doing so they consolidate the new information by using it to restructure their prior knowledge, identified in the preparation phase. Thus the three phases of strategic instruction are recursive, which in the view of the developers of the model reflects the nonlinear character of most thinking and problem-solving processes.

To illustrate how a teacher might plan these three phases of instruction, Jones et al. (1987) provide an example of the thought processes of a strategic teacher as she or he engages in instructional planning. First, the teacher analyzes the textbook coverage of the topic and identifies major ideas and areas that have to be supplemented. Next, the instructor anticipates problems students may have in identifying the most important concepts and assesses strategies students are already familiar with and those that will require extensive guidance. In other words, the teacher identifies the students' prior knowledge so as to relate it to the new information to be taught. Next, the teacher goes back to the textbook to check for vocabulary that may be difficult for students and decides on a vocabulary development activity that will stimulate student thinking about the concepts to be presented. After thinking through the various factors to be considered, the teacher prepares a lesson plan for the three phases of the lesson, preparing for learning, presentation of content, and application and integration of new knowledge. This description of the thinking processes of a strategic teacher reveals the complexity and depth of knowledge such a teacher needs about both subject matter and learning theory. Whether it is devising activities to elicit prior knowledge that students may not at first realize they have, or developing graphic organizers that guide students in structuring and integrating the new information, strategic teachers apply the full range of their own knowledge and experience to the instructional planning process.

The Strategic Teaching Model has been applied to science (Anderson 1987), social studies (Alvermann 1987), mathematics (Lindquist 1987), and literature (Beach 1987) so as to see if the model's underlying assumptions and instructional framework had practical applications in different subject areas. Descriptions of the planning and implementation of the Strategic Teaching Model for each of these content areas provide numerous examples of the thinking processes of strategic teachers, activities that develop students' ability to comprehend and interact with the concepts presented, and ways in which both direct and embedded learning strategy instruction can be integrated into the four content areas.

In sum, the Strategic Teaching Model is an instructional framework designed for teachers of native language speakers. It is based on cognitive learning theory and seeks to develop autonomous learners through scaffolding instruction, in which the teacher at first provides extensive support in showing students the learning strategies that will help them learn more efficiently, and then gradually reduces the support so that students learn to be independent learners. The focus of the model is on the acquisition of the declarative knowledge required in content areas such as social studies, science, and literature. In addition, the procedural (as well as the declarative) knowledge required by mathematics is addressed, and procedures for interpreting literary texts are explained. Since the model is intended for use in first language contexts, language skill development is not addressed directly, except in discussions of explicit strategies for reading comprehension.

Instructional models in second language contexts: the Cognitive Academic Language Learning Approach [1]

The ESL instructional model we developed (Chamot and O'Malley 1986, 1987, in press; O'Malley 1988) is based on cognitive theory and on our own research with second language learning strategies. The Cognitive Academic Language Learning Approach (CALLA) is designed to develop the academic language skills of limited English proficient (LEP) students

---

1 CALLA is a registered trademark of Second Language Learning, Inc.

in upper elementary and secondary schools. CALLA (pronounced kalá) is intended to meet the academic needs of three types of LEP students (Chamot and O'Malley 1987):

1. Students who have developed social communicative skills through beginning level ESL classes or through exposure to an English-speaking environment, but have not yet developed academic language skills appropriate to their grade level;
2. Students who have acquired academic language skills in their native language and initial proficiency in English, but who need assistance in transferring concepts and skills learned in the first language to English; and
3. Bilingual English-dominant students who have not yet developed academic language skills in either language.

CALLA integrates grade-appropriate content topics, academic language development, and direct instruction and practice in using learning strategies to acquire both procedural and declarative knowledge. Although CALLA is intended as a transitional program for students at intermediate and advanced levels of English proficiency, aspects of the model can be implemented with beginning level ESL students and with students from special language programs who have transferred into mainstream classrooms.

Theoretical framework of CALLA

The theoretical model on which CALLA is based suggests that language is a complex cognitive skill, developing through a series of stages, which requires extensive practice and feedback in order to operate at an autonomous level. In this section we describe how the major constructs of cognitive learning theory have been applied to the CALLA instructional model.

Because language proficiency can best be described as procedural knowledge (though constantly fed by declarative knowledge) and the use of learning strategies is also a part of procedural knowledge, the focus of CALLA is on the acquisition and use of procedural skills that facilitate academic language and content learning. At the initial stages of L2 acquisition, the focus is (or should be) almost completely on the acquisition of procedural skills, or how to use the language. Attentional processes are concentrated on learning to understand and communicate in the new language, and limited attention is free for acquiring new nonlinguistic declarative knowledge. As students gradually become more proficient in the language, some attentional processes become available to focus on new declarative knowledge, whether of a general nature or specifically related to content areas of the curriculum. The CALLA instructional program is designed to begin at this point, because it is only at this point that students have a sufficient general proficiency in the new language (including both oral and written skills) to begin to use the language as a learning tool.

As discussed in Chapter 5, an important concern in our understanding of second language acquisition is the operation of transfer of both declarative and procedural knowledge from the first to the second language. There is substantial research indicating that such transfer should not be assumed to happen automatically, for many students do not necessarily transfer either concepts or skills known in the first language to their new language (McLaughlin 1987a; O'Malley et al. 1988). Another concern related to transfer is the effect of cultural experiences on the development of various types of schemata, and the ease or difficulty with which a culturally influenced story grammar, event structure, or discourse organization schema might accommodate new information of this type learned in the second language. The CALLA instructional framework addresses these transfer issues in a number of ways. We distinguish between linguistic transfer and elaboration of prior nonlinguistic knowledge, and teach both as important strategies that students can use to assist their own learning. Students' existing schemata are activated in each instructional sequence, and direct comparisons are made of similarities and differences between new information and previous cultural knowledge and experience.

Anderson's (1985) discussion of the stages of skill acquisition and of the processes underlying language comprehension and production provide useful insights into the academic language needs of LEP students, which CALLA is intended to meet. For example, a student who has been in an ESL program for one or two years may seem superficially to operate at nearly the autonomous stage of language skills acquisition when social interactive language skills are observed. However, such a student often encounters serious difficulties in mainstream academic classrooms. These difficulties are thought to be attributable in large part to lack of development of academic language skills, which have been found to lag behind social language skills by as much as five to eight years (Collier 1987; Cummins 1981). In terms of the Anderson model, such students may be operating at the autonomous stage of social language acquisition, but still be at the cognitive or associative stages of academic language acquisition. The CALLA model is designed for this type of student, as opposed to the student who is at the cognitive stage for both types of language skill.

In language comprehension and production, Anderson (1985) identifies three recursive phases for each type of process. For comprehension, the phases are perceptual processing, parsing, and utilization. An important aspect of perceptual processing included in the CALLA model is training in attentional processes, such as selective attention to specific linguistic or content information and self-monitoring of comprehension during listening and reading. Utilization is also a major focus of CALLA, as students are taught a number of reading and listening comprehension strategies that will enable them to utilize their prior knowledge to understand oral and written texts. In language production, Anderson's three processes are construction, transformation, and execution. CALLA emphasizes the construction of the meaning to be expressed by using strategies to elaborate prior knowledge and existing schemata. Parsing of constituents during comprehension and transformation of ideas into sentences during language production are addressed in CALLA through direct instruction in learning strategies to assist these two processes. The execution phase of language production, which involves the physical aspects of speech and writing, is addressed in CALLA in a completely functional way through small group activities in which students focus on the comprehensibility (rather than complete accuracy) of their oral communications to each other, and work collaboratively on revising their written production so that it communicates their intended meaning.

The most critical feature in cognitive theory incorporated in the CALLA model is the identification and training of learning strategies. In our view, use of effective learning strategies is of even greater importance to students who need to learn through the medium of a second language than for students receiving instruction through their first language. Using the classification system described in Chapter 2, we have selected metacognitive, cognitive, and social/affective learning strategies to be taught and practiced during CALLA instruction. Since learning strategies, like language, are cognitive skills, they require extensive practice to become proceduralized. For this reason learning strategy instruction and practice are an important part of every CALLA lesson.

In this section we have discussed the major aspects of cognitive theory, which form the framework for the CALLA model. The academic and language needs of LEP students at the intermediate level of English proficiency can be understood through an analysis of the distinction between declarative and procedural knowledge and the three stages of skill acquisition. To meet these needs, we have developed an instructional system that teaches LEP students how to apply learning strategies to both academic language and content tasks. The CALLA approach shows students how to capitalize on their own prior knowledge of concepts and skills acquired in the native language as they seek to become successful learners in English mainstream classrooms.

The components of CALLA

The CALLA model includes three components in its curricular and instructional design: topics from the major content subjects, development of academic language skills, and direct instruction in learning strategies for both content and language. Although these three components are not separated during instruction, we will discuss each in turn before describing how they are integrated in CALLA lessons.

THE CONTENT-BASED CURRICULUM

The content topics taught in CALLA are aligned with an all-English curriculum so that practice is provided with a selection of the actual topics students will encounter in the mainstream.

We recommend beginning with science as the first content area, because by using a discovery approach to science, teachers can provide hands-on learning activities that provide both contextual support and academic language development. The next subject that can be introduced in a CALLA program is mathematics, which in the upper grades especially is highly abstract and has a more restricted language register than science. Social studies is the third subject introduced in the CALLA model because of its reading and writing demands and potentially unfamiliar cultural information. Finally, the fourth area to be introduced in CALLA is language arts. Grade-appropriate literature and composition activities are difficult for LEP students not only because of the high level of English proficiency in academic language skills required, but also because of underlying cultural assumptions. In a CALLA classroom, content topics are carefully selected to represent both authentic topics for the grade level concerned and high-priority topics within the curriculum. The intent is for ESL and bilingual teachers to prepare LEP students for what they will encounter in the mainstream, not to duplicate the mainstream curriculum.

A common reaction to the less-than-fluent English of a student is to teach content from a lower grade level and to expect from LEP students only lower-level cognitive skills such as simple recall. CALLA demands the opposite. LEP students need to learn content appropriate to their developmental level and previous educational experience; higher-level thinking skills are as much to be expected from them as from any other student. Instead of watering down content for LEP students, CALLA teachers make challenging content comprehensible by providing additional contextual support in the form of demonstrations, visuals, and hands-on experiences, and by teaching students how to apply learning strategies to understand and remember the content presented. When asking LEP students higher-order questions, CALLA teachers evaluate responses on the basis of the ideas expressed rather than on the correctness of the language used.

ACADEMIC LANGUAGE DEVELOPMENT

In CALLA, language is used functionally as a tool for learning academic subject matter. Academic language skills, such as listening and reading for information and speaking and writing about new knowledge, may or may not have been developed in the first language. Students may either need instruction on how to transfer previously learned language skills to English or may need to learn academic language skills for the first time.

The reasons why academic language may be particularly difficult for LEP students to acquire can most easily be understood by examining the language model developed by Cummins (1982; 1983). This model indicates that two dimensions can be used to describe the language demands encountered by both LEP and native English-speaking students. The first dimension concerns the context in which language takes place, and the second concerns the cognitive complexity of the task. Language that is most comprehensible takes place in a here-and-now context rich in nonverbal and paralinguistic cues such as concrete objects, gestures, facial expressions, visual aids, and vocal intonation and stress markings. Language is least comprehensible when these context clues have been reduced, so that comprehension depends entirely on the listener's or reader's ability to construct the meaning of an oral or written text with little contextual assistance. Cummins's second dimension, task complexity, suggests that when the cognitive demands of a task are high, comprehension is more difficult. Language tasks such as concrete vocabulary learning, following oral directions, and classroom discussions about events and topics in the students' own experience are thought to be low in cognitive demand, whereas tasks such as acquiring new information through reading and listening, or speaking or writing about academic topics, are believed to be high in cognitive demand. In a typical classroom, both contextualized and decontextualized language are present to some degree, and, as teachers are aware, not all of class time is spent on cognitively demanding tasks. However, teachers and tests generally base assessment of students' progress on their ability to perform cognitively demanding tasks in a linguistically decontextualized setting.

Context-reduced language is generally associated with literacy skills, but oral language can also vary along the context-embedded to context-reduced continuum. Davidson, Kline, and Snow (1986) define contextualized oral language as conversational, interactive, and supported by shared knowledge and experiences. Decontextualized oral language, on the other hand, is characterized as language that is not interactive and concerns a topic on which no shared knowledge exists. For example, a secondary level teacher presenting information on an academic topic to a class typically uses mainly decontextualized oral language.

LEP students can begin developing academic language skills in English through cognitively demanding activities in which comprehension is assisted by contextual support. Content-based language activities provide opportunities for LEP students to develop the academic language proficiency in English that will help them be more successful in mainstream classrooms. CALLA teachers assist this development by including in their classes materials and concepts drawn from the content areas. For example, some reading exercises might include skimming a scientific article, scanning a mathematics word problem, and taking notes on a chapter in a social studies textbook. Writing activities could include additional expository writing related to content areas so that students learn how to organize a science laboratory report and how to do library research for a history paper. In CALLA, academic language is developed through a whole language approach in which all language skills are applied and integrated for all content areas of the curriculum.

LEARNING STRATEGY INSTRUCTION

The third and central component in the CALLA system is instruction in learning strategies. The use of learning strategy instruction as a methodological approach in CALLA is based on four important propositions (Chamot and O'Malley 1987, p. 240):

1. Mentally active learners are better learners. Students who organize new information and consciously relate it to existing knowledge have more cognitive linkages to assist comprehension and recall than do students who approach each new task as something to be memorized by rote learning.
2. Strategies can be taught. Students who are taught to use strategies and are provided with sufficient practice in using them will learn more effectively than students who have had no experience with learning strategies.
3. Learning strategies transfer to new tasks. Once students have become accustomed to using learning strategies, they will use them on new tasks that are similar to the learning activities on which they were initially trained.
4. Academic language learning is more effective with learning strategies. Academic language learning among students of English as a second language is governed by some of the same principles that govern reading and problem solving among native English speakers.

Many older LEP students may have developed learning strategies attuned to educational experiences in their native countries. For example, in an educational system that places a high value on assimilation of facts, students might learn highly effective rote memorization strategies. Other strategies, however, are needed for integrative language tasks such as reading for information, explaining a process, or developing a report. Many students, whether LEP or English-proficient, need direct instruction and extensive teacher-supported practice or scaffolding in using learning strategies appropriate to different types of academic tasks. Because strategy transfer may be difficult, the teacher may need to provide extensive cued support with new or similar tasks. Classroom teachers who have used CALLA in classes with both English-speaking and LEP students report that instruction in learning strategies is as beneficial to native English speakers as it is to students learning English as a second language. Programs in which English-speaking students were taught to use learning strategies to improve their reading comprehension and their ability to solve problems in math and science demonstrated that instruction in learning strategies can be successful (Pressley et al. in press; Romberg and Carpenter 1986; Weinstein and Mayer 1986; White and Tisher 1986; Wittrock 1985). In extending this research to second language learners, we conclude that learning strategies seem to be as effective for learning a language as they are for learning in other areas. Good language learners use many different learning strategies, often in quite intricate ways, to help them understand and remember new information, whereas less effective learners have fewer strategies and apply them infrequently or inappropriately (Chamot et al. 1988a, b; Chamot and Küpper 1989; O'Malley et al. 1988).

As mentioned previously (see Chapter 2), learning strategies can be classified into three types (Chamot and O'Malley 1987; O'Malley et al. 1985b):

Metacognitive strategies, which involve executive processes in planning for learning, monitoring one's comprehension and production, and evaluating how well one has achieved a learning objective;

Cognitive strategies, in which the learner interacts with the material to be learned by manipulating it mentally (as in making mental images, or elaborating on previously acquired concepts or skills) or physically (as in grouping items to be learned in meaningful categories, or taking notes on important information to be remembered).

Social/affective strategies, in which the learner either interacts with another person in order to assist learning, as in cooperation or asking questions for clarification, or uses some kind of affective control to assist a learning task.

In studying learning strategies used in different contexts, we have come to the conclusion that a group of general learning strategies may be of particular use for LEP students who are learning both language and content (Chamot and O'Malley 1987). These can be thought of as core learning strategies, which are not only applicable to a variety of learning tasks but are also characteristic of highly effective second language learners (Chamot et al. 1988b; Chamot and Küpper 1989; O'Malley et al. 1988). Table 7.1 lists and defines this group of learning strategies.

Some of the learning strategies in Table 7.1 are often thought of as **study skills**. Study skills describe overt behavior, such as taking notes, writing summaries, or using reference materials, while learning strategies generally pertain to unobservable mental processes. Students need to learn study skills – the overt behavior associated with learning strategies – and they also need to learn to use nonobservable strategies such as monitoring for comprehension, elaboration of prior knowledge, and inferencing.

A number of the strategies described in Table 7.1 can assist in de-

TABLE 7.1. LEARNING STRATEGIES TAUGHT IN THE COGNITIVE ACADEMIC
LANGUAGE LEARNING APPROACH (CALLA)

Metacognitive strategies

Advance organization	Previewing the main ideas and concepts of the material to be learned, often by skimming the text for the organizing principle.
Advance preparation	Rehearsing the language needed for an oral or written task.
Organizational planning	Planning the parts, sequence, and main ideas to be expressed orally or in writing.
Selective attention	Attending to or scanning key words, phrases, linguistic markers, sentences, or types of information.
Self-monitoring	Checking one's comprehension during listening or reading, or checking one's oral or written production while it is taking place.
Self-evaluation	Judging how well one has accomplished a learning task.
Self-management	Seeking or arranging the conditions that help one learn, such as finding opportunities for additional language or content input and practice.

Cognitive strategies

Resourcing	Using reference materials such as dictionaries, encyclopedias, or textbooks.
Grouping	Classifying words, terminology, numbers, or concepts according to their attributes.
Note taking	Writing down key words and concepts in abbreviated verbal, graphic, or numerical form.
Summarizing	Making a mental or written summary of information gained through listening or reading.
Deduction	Applying rules to understand or produce language or solve problems.
Imagery	Using visual images (either mental or actual) to understand and remember new information or to make a mental representation of a problem.
Auditory representation	Playing in back of one's mind the sound of a word, phrase, or fact in order to assist comprehension and recall.

TABLE 7.1. (*continued*)

Elaboration	Relating new information to prior knowledge, relating different parts of new information to each other, or making meaningful personal associations with the new information.
Transfer	Using what is already known about language to assist comprehension or production.
Inferencing	Using information in the text to guess meanings of new items, predict outcomes, or complete missing parts.
Social and affective strategies	
Questioning for clarification	Eliciting from a teacher or peer additional explanation, rephrasing, examples, or verification.
Cooperation	Working together with peers to solve a problem, pool information, check a learning task, or get feedback on oral or written performance.
Self-talk	Reducing anxiety by using mental techniques that make one feel competent to do the learning task.

veloping motivation. For example, self-evaluation is an important key to increasing motivation, because students learn to attribute their level of achievement to their own efforts rather than to unchangeable innate ability. Other strategies that assist motivation are self-management, in which students set goals and arrange the conditions that help them learn, and self-talk, in which students learn how to control anxiety about a task.

General guidelines for learning strategy instruction were presented in Table 6.1 in Chapter 6. To summarize, CALLA teachers initiate learning strategy instruction by finding out what strategies students are already using for different learning activities. Teachers can interview students about ways they approach specific classroom tasks and can also have students think aloud as they take turns working on a task. These two activities help students become more aware of the mental processes they engage in when approaching and solving a problem and can help teachers diagnose learning strategy needs.

After identifying strategies students are already using, teachers can use the strategy list in Table 7.1 to select the new strategies to be taught.

In presenting a new strategy to students, CALLA teachers first explain the purpose and utility of learning strategies in general, name the strategy to be taught, and explain the benefits students will derive from using it. The names of strategies need not be the same as those in Table 7.1, but should be selected according to students' maturity level. Thus "selective attention" might be named "paying attention to big ideas," and "elaboration" might be named "thinking about what you know." The importance of giving strategies names is to heighten student awareness of cognitive processes and to facilitate instruction in strategy use. After naming and describing the strategy to be taught, the teacher then models the strategy by actually performing a task and thinking aloud about the mental processes comprising the strategy.

CALLA teachers provide students with repeated opportunities to practice the new strategies on a variety of tasks, so that eventually the strategy itself becomes part of students' procedural knowledge. Strategy practice can take place during all types of learning activities, in both large groups and cooperative learning teams. Students can also take turns thinking aloud as they solve problems and then discuss their strategies with other students. Those who have already developed effective strategies can provide to other students peer tutoring in how to use strategies. In the beginning of training, teachers remind students to use the strategies being taught, but later they remind students less frequently so that their pupils can begin to use the strategies independently.

Students also need to learn how to evaluate their own strategy use. To this end, CALLA strategy training includes activities such as writing down the strategies used immediately after completing a task, discussing and analyzing strategies used for different tasks, and keeping dialogue journals on strategy use in which each student writes down the conversation about their strategies with their teacher.

Finally, in order to help students expand their strategy use beyond the CALLA classroom, teachers initiate discussions on how students view themselves as learners and stress the utility of learning strategies as aids to motivation. Additional practice of strategies with academic tasks found in mainstream classrooms and reminders to students to use the strategies in other classes can also assist in the transfer of strategies to new tasks. Some of the new tasks on which strategies are used should be related to the cultural background of the students so that they can appreciate the usefulness of learning strategies in areas of their lives outside of school.

In summary, learning strategy instruction can play an important role in teaching LEP as well as native English-speaking students by showing them how to apply effective learning techniques to language and content learning.

CALLA lesson plan model

The CALLA lesson plan framework incorporates learning strategy instruction, content area topics, and language development activities. Learning strategy instruction is both direct and embedded. In CALLA lessons, new learning strategies are introduced and familiar ones are practiced, so that the use of learning strategies to approach all kinds of tasks becomes an integral part of the regular class routine instead of a supplementary activity. In this way, students have opportunities to practice the strategies on actual lessons, and use of the strategies becomes part of the class requirements and a daily topic for discussion.

CALLA lessons include both teacher-directed and learner-centered activities. They specify three types of objectives: content objectives, language objectives, and learning strategy objectives. Each CALLA lesson is divided into five phases: preparation, presentation, practice, evaluation, and expansion activities. These phases are often recursive in that the teacher may wish to go back to earlier phases in order to clarify or provide additional instruction. The following brief description of each phase indicates how content topics, academic language skills, and learning strategies can be developed in a CALLA lesson.

PREPARATION

In the preparation phase of the lesson, the teacher finds out, often through brainstorming or a concrete experience, what students already know about the concepts in the subject area to be presented and practiced, what gaps in prior knowledge need to be addressed, and how students have been taught to approach a particular type of learning activity or content area. The lesson's objectives are explained to students, and requisite new vocabulary is developed as an outgrowth of the initial prior knowledge activation activity. The learning strategies most commonly taught and practiced in the preparation phase are elaboration (students recall prior knowledge), advance organization (students preview the lesson), and selective attention (students focus on key vocabulary and concepts to be introduced in the lesson).

PRESENTATION

In the presentation phase of the lesson, new information is presented and explained to students in English that is supported by contextual clues such as demonstrations and visuals. Teachers make sure that students comprehend the new information so that they will be able to practice it meaningfully in the next phase of the lesson.

Some of the learning strategies taught and practiced in this phase are: selective attention while listening or reading (attending to or scanning for key ideas), self-monitoring (checking one's degree of comprehension), inferencing (guessing meaning from context), elaboration (relating new information to prior knowledge), note taking, imagery (imagining descriptions or events presented), and questioning for clarification.

PRACTICE

The practice phase of the lesson is learner-centered, as students engage in hands-on activities to practice the new information they were exposed to in the presentation phase. The teacher acts as facilitator in helping students assimilate the new information and use it in different ways. Cooperative learning in heterogeneous teams is particularly effective during the practice phase, as students can work together in small groups to clarify their understanding of the information previously presented. Where possible, LEP students can profit from working in small groups with native English speakers, who can serve both as language models and tutors. The learning strategies typically practiced in this phase of the CALLA lesson are: self-monitoring (students check their language production), organizational planning (planning how to develop an oral or written report or composition), resourcing (using reference materials), grouping (classifying concepts, events, and terminology), summarizing, deduction (using a rule to understand or produce language or to solve a problem), imagery (making sketches, diagrams, charts), auditory representation (playing back mentally information presented by the teacher), elaboration, inferencing, cooperation (working with peers), and questioning for clarification.

EVALUATION

In the evaluation phase of the lesson, students check the level of their performance so that they can gain an understanding of what they have learned and any areas they need to review. Evaluation activities can be individual, cooperative, or teacher-directed. Teachers can assess higher level comprehension by focusing on the meaning of student answers instead of on their grammatical correctness. Learning strategies practiced in the evaluation phase of a CALLA lesson are: self-evaluation, elaboration, questioning for clarification, cooperation, and self-talk (assuring oneself of one's ability to accomplish the task).

EXPANSION ACTIVITIES

In the expansion phase of the lesson, students are given a variety of opportunities to think about the new concepts and skills they have learned, integrate them into their existing knowledge frameworks, make real world applications, and continue to develop academic language. This phase also provides the opportunity to exercise higher order thinking skills such as inferring new applications of a concept, analyzing the components of a learning activity, drawing parallels with other concepts, and evaluating the importance of a concept or new skill. In the expansion activities of a CALLA lesson, any combination of learning strategies appropriate to the activities can be practiced.

The CALLA lesson plan model allows for flexibility and different types of activities. While lessons introducing new content topics should always begin with the preparation phase so that students' prior knowledge can be activated, the succeeding phases may be recursive, as students and teachers move backward and forward between phases in order to understand, practice, and consolidate new information and procedures. We recommend cooperative learning activities for part of each lesson, because cooperation not only improves student performance but also provides additional opportunities for students to use academic language skills for a learning task. The five phases of a CALLA lesson will vary in duration depending on the lesson topic and the extent of students' prior knowledge. In some cases, a CALLA "lesson" may extend to an entire thematic unit. The structure of the lesson plan model helps ensure that students have many opportunities to practice learning strategies and to use academic language skills as they work on grade-appropriate content.

In sum, the Cognitive Academic Language Learning Approach (CALLA) is an instructional program for LEP students who are preparing to participate in mainstream academic content instruction (Chamot and O'Malley 1986, 1987, in press; O'Malley 1988). CALLA provides transitional instruction for upper elementary and secondary students at intermediate and advanced ESL levels. This program furthers academic language development in English through content area instruction in science, mathematics, social studies, and literature and composition. In CALLA, students are taught to use learning strategies derived from a cognitive model of learning to assist their comprehension, retention, and use of the declarative and procedural knowledge underlying the academic school curriculum. The three components of CALLA have been integrated into an instructional sequence with five recursive phases of instruction that provide students with a variety of learning experiences to develop content knowledge and processes, academic language skills, and practice in using learning strategies to become self-regulated learners.

CALLA, in common with strategic teaching, requires a high level of teacher knowledge and skill. CALLA teachers need a solid understanding of the content areas of the mainstream curriculum as well as the ability to integrate language activities with the different subject areas. Most important, they need to be aware of their students' learning approaches and know how to show them additional approaches and strategies that can make them more effective learners.

In training workshops on CALLA, we have discovered that even teachers with quite different types of students find the model useful and applicable to their own situations. For example, ESL teachers seek ways to incorporate aspects of our model in a "Pre-CALLA" program for their beginning level students. Mainstream classroom teachers working with native English-speaking, educationally disadvantaged students have also indicated that CALLA teaching can provide their students with the additional support needed for greater school success; they see CALLA as a guide for implementing a whole-language or language-across-the-curriculum approach to instruction. Special education teachers, who are generally knowledgeable about the usefulness of learning strategy instruction, find that the integration of language and content development is valuable for their students. We believe that CALLA also has potential application in the foreign language classroom. Our current work with foreign language instructors on incorporating learning strategy instruction into foreign language classes, described in Chapter 6, indicates that by adding a focus on content, the CALLA model could be an effective approach to developing foreign language proficiency as well.

The applicability of CALLA to such different instructional settings is due, in our view, to its theoretical framework, which, in common with other current approaches to teaching, is grounded in cognitive learning theory.

Second language learning strategy training materials

In this section we will describe some recent instructional materials that have been developed to teach learning strategies to second language students. We also comment on their methodological approach and the specific learning strategies and other skills and content presented.

Learning strategy materials for adult language learners

Rubin and Thompson (1982) have developed a set of guidelines, suggestions, and explanations of the language learning process designed to assist foreign language students in becoming more successful language learners. Their objectives are to provide students with nontechnical explanations of the language learning process and the characteristics of good language learners, and to encourage them to try new language learning strategies. This approach is an example of separate and direct training, as the intention is for students themselves to use the information and suggestions instead of having teachers provide instruction as part of their foreign language class.

Rubin and Thompson (1982) provide practical suggestions for becoming a more successful language learner by describing the language learning process, recommending specific learning strategies, and suggesting helpful language learning resources. Information about the language learning process includes a comprehensive summary of major language acquisition issues. Individual attitudes and abilities, communicative competence, and the nature of language are discussed from the student's point of view.

They describe fourteen learning strategies that students can use to improve their foreign language acquisition. The strategies are not classified according to their characteristics (e.g., metacognitive, cognitive, or social and affective) but according to learning behaviors. Each strategy name is a phrase beginning with an imperative, such as, "Find Your Own Way," "Be Creative," "Make Your Own Opportunities," "Learn to Make Intelligent Guesses," and "Learn Production Techniques." These names focus attention on the overt behavior that students can use to improve their learning. For each strategy, suggestions are made for a variety of activities, which are sometimes specific behaviors and other times mental techniques or attitudinal approaches. In analyzing the many excellent suggestions for learning, we found that virtually all of the strategies we included in our classification system are represented. Some examples of specific applications of strategies identified in our research are:

Metacognitive strategies: Self-management is a key strategy recommended by Rubin and Thompson. Examples of applications of this strategy include identifying one's own successful learning experiences, organizing one's study approach, taking advantage of diverse learning opportunities, and interacting with native speakers of the language.

Planning strategies: These are also important in the Rubin and Thompson framework. For example, students are provided with suggestions on how to rehearse expected conversational exchanges, look at the major points of a story or conversation to get a general idea of the content, and plan to pay attention to major grammatical points explained by the teacher.

Monitoring strategies: Although these are not identified specifically, many of the suggestions for *self-evaluation* could also be applied on-line for self-monitoring. Students are advised to use their own errors in the second language to identify their areas of weakness, to understand why they are making certain types of errors, to make use of the teacher's corrections, and to evaluate the effectiveness of different kinds of practice on their learning. Thus self-evaluation is not only the evaluation of students' language production but includes evaluation of the learning strategies employed.

Cognitive strategies: A variety of cognitive strategies are suggested by Rubin and Thompson for different language tasks. Practice, or *rehearsal,* is recommended repeatedly, and suggestions are offered for silent rehearsal and learning formulaic and idiomatic language such as social conversational routines.

Deduction/induction and transfer strategies: These are illustrated by suggestions for applying grammar rules in language production and inducing rules from language input, using linguistic transfer to aid language learning.

The strategy identified by Rubin and Thompson as *mnemonics* includes practical techniques for memorizing language items, such as *grouping* words in various ways, using mental *images,* and using *context* to assist recall of specific words.

Elaboration, inferencing, and *substitution* are recommended throughout the book. Students are reminded to use what they already know to understand and produce the new language, to guess at unfamiliar items from the context (instead of overusing the dictionary), and to seek relationships and structure in language input in order to infer meaning. They are told to use paraphrases and synonyms as substitutes for language items that they do not know or cannot recall.

Social and affective strategies. Suggestions for using social and affective strategies are threaded throughout the fourteen strategy behaviors recommended by Rubin and Thompson. Students are reminded to ask *questions for clarification* not only in the classroom but also when interacting with native speakers of the target language so as to keep the conversation going. Students are encouraged to use *cooperation* in various ways, such as practicing with other students, playing games in the language, and sharing effective strategies with each other. *Affective* strategies designed to reduce students' anxiety are interwoven with many of the strategies described. Students are told not to be afraid to make errors, not to panic if they do not understand everything, and not to be discouraged if they make incorrect guesses.

Rubin and Thompson's (1982) practical suggestions for applying learning strategies in a variety of ways are particularly useful for the highly motivated and mature student who is already an autonomous learner. Teachers could use the suggestions for learning strategy applications to provide the scaffolding instruction needed by the less mature and motivated student. For teaching purposes, the strategies and activities suggested would need to be organized into an instructional sequence in which teachers ensure that students are aware of their own mental processes and existing strategies, perhaps model the strategies, and then provide ample practice and evaluation opportunities to develop procedural competence with the strategies. An adaptation of this nature presupposes a thorough understanding on the part of the teacher of the theoretical background and nature of learning strategies and cognitive processes in second language acquisition, as well as the ability to develop instructional materials based on the suggested activities.

Ellis and Sinclair (1989) have developed actual instructional materials to be used with intermediate-level EFL and ESL students in the language classroom. Their objectives are to help students become more effective and more responsible language learners, to provide the language teacher with a model for learner training, and to show the teacher how to integrate learner training with language instruction. Thus, this approach calls for integrated training of strategies and language, even though the materials themselves address strategy instruction only. These materials also provide direct training in learning strategy use, as students are made aware throughout of the value and purpose of strategy training.

A variety of classroom activities are suggested, including brief explanations of language learning processes, examples of strategy applications, quotes and photographs of other students telling about their strategies for various tasks, checklists, charts for students to complete of their own language learning progress, and pair and group activities. A teacher's guide provides an overview of the background knowledge teachers need in order to understand the rationale for instruction in learning strategies.

The model for strategy instruction consists of three phases. In the first phase students are introduced to language learning processes through discussions with the teacher, questionnaires about their learning approach, analysis of their language learning needs, and investigation of learning resources available outside the language class. The second phase, described more fully later, provides direct instruction and practice in learning strategies for particular skills. In the third phase of the model, students take charge of their own learning through activities that help them identify resources and plan realistically for continued language study as part of their overall schedule. These three phases follow a sequence similar to other learning strategy training approaches (e.g., Hosenfeld et al. 1981; Jones et al. 1987; O'Malley and Chamot 1988; Weinstein and Underwood 1985). Students are first made aware of their own mental processes, then they are provided with a rationale for strategy use and continued practice with strategies for different tasks, and finally the cues to use the strategies are reduced so that students can become autonomous strategy users.

The second phase of the Ellis and Sinclair model is the most extensive, as it integrates seven learning strategies and six areas of language focus within a matrix that provides forty-two different types of practice activities. The language areas addressed are vocabulary development, grammatical study, listening/viewing, speaking, reading, and writing. The first strategies to be presented are metacognitive ones, which provide a basis for the introduction of cognitive strategies.

The metacognitive strategies taught are:

— Self-awareness, in which students develop an understanding of themselves as learners and of their individual attitudes and motivation toward different aspects of the target language;
— Language awareness, in which students develop metalinguistic knowledge about language as an organized system. Such knowledge includes the ability to identify language register and functions, as well as strategies for different language skills, and the ability to make grammatical deduction and linguistic transfer;
— Self-assessment, in which students learn to monitor and evaluate their language learning progress; and
— Setting short-term aims, in which students identify goals and use self-management techniques to determine which are achievable in a realistic time frame.

The Ellis and Sinclair model identifies three cognitive strategies: (1) personal strategies, in which learners discover the different learning strategies that work for them; (2) risk taking, in which learners involve themselves actively in the language learning process; and (3) getting organized, in which learners organize their time and their materials. Upon close examination, each of these proves to be an extremely broad category that includes a cluster of metacognitive, cognitive, and social/affective strategies, as the following analysis demonstrates:

1. *Personal strategies*
   Vocabulary: Grouping words together by topic (grouping).
   Grammar: Collecting real world examples of grammar patterns (grouping and deduction).
   Listening: Using imagery while listening; planning to listen for selected information (selective attention); identifying prior knowledge before listening (elaboration).
   Speaking: Finding practice opportunities (self-management and cooperation); conducting imaginary mental conversations (auditory representation).
   Reading: Identifying a reason to read (problem identification); finding out about the topic before reading (planning, elaboration, resourcing); preliminary skimming to determine difficulty level (advance organization and self-evaluation); using L1 reading strategies (elaboration of prior strategy knowledge).
   Writing: Collecting models of different types of writing (grouping, elaboration of knowledge about discourse); keeping audience in mind (organizational planning).

2. *Risk taking*

Vocabulary: Using paraphrases, synonyms, inventions, and foreign words (substitution).

Grammar: Inventing personal rules from grammar examples (deduction/induction).

Listening and Reading: Predicting based on prior knowledge (elaboration and inferencing); using linguistic signals and paralinguistic cues (selective attention); guessing unknown words from context (inferencing).

Speaking: Using hesitation techniques to provide thinking time in a conversation (self-management and organizational planning); rehearsing (advance preparation); staying within one's own language repertoire (organizational planning and self-evaluation).

Writing: Using known vocabulary and structures (organizational planning and self-evaluation); composing directly in the target language (self-evaluation and substitution); revising (self-evaluation).

3. *Getting organized*

Organizing resources: Analyzing usefulness of available resources, including reference materials, media, and human resources (resourcing, selective attention, self-evaluation, cooperation).

Organizing materials: Collecting and classifying materials by topic, grammatical pattern, or language skill (self-management and grouping).

Organizing time: Scheduling regular practice for each language skill, both alone and with another person (self-management and cooperation).

This model reduces the number of learning strategy categories by describing a variety of examples of strategy use for each category. The descriptions of individual strategy use under the larger categories may be helpful to students in reducing the total number of distinct strategies to be learned. On the other hand, students may find it even easier to keep in mind three basic categories of strategies (metacognitive, cognitive, and social/affective) with subsets of strategies within each. This aspect of learning strategy training awaits investigation.

Although the teacher's manual provides detailed instructions for using the student workbook and cassette, extensive training would probably be necessary to familiarize teachers with this approach. In our own work with teacher training, we find that most teachers have difficulty initially with the distinction between learning strategies and teaching strategies, and that considerable discussion and practice activities are needed before they are able to begin thinking in terms of the learner's mental processes. The Ellis and Sinclair (1989) materials assume that teachers already have this understanding of language learning.

In sum, the Ellis and Sinclair (1989) ESL/EFL learning strategy training model provides a research-based approach to second language strategy training that can be applied in a number of second language learning contexts. For example, the activities in the students' workbooks could be adapted to ESL students at lower levels of language study, and college- and adult-level ESL and foreign language instructors could use most of the activities suggested to provide learning strategy instruction to their students. However, information about learning strategy instruction in the teacher's guide would probably need to be supplemented by staff development activities so that teachers unfamiliar with learning strategies use these materials successfully. A teacher would need to integrate these materials with their regular language materials and ensure that the strategies taught separately are transferred and practiced with other instructional materials and classes.

Learning strategy materials for content-based ESL

We have developed a set of instructional materials that teach learning strategies for both language and content (Chamot 1987a, b, c; Chamot and O'Malley 1988a, b, in press) to be used by upper elementary and secondary school ESL students at the intermediate level of English proficiency. The objectives of the materials are to develop academic English language skills through content-based instruction, to develop understanding and skills in content areas, and to teach students learning strategies that will help them become autonomous learners of both language and content. These materials are based on the CALLA model described earlier in this chapter and provide direct instruction in strategy use. The materials focus on the content areas of social studies and mathematics, where instruction is provided on learning strategies for developing procedural knowledge in all four language skills, and for understanding and recalling the declarative knowledge presented by the content topics.

Suggestions to the teacher for strategy instruction in social studies and mathematics activities include:

Previewing the book and new units. Advance organization is taught as students are shown how to use the table of contents, section headings, and questions to preview upcoming information. Elaboration is practiced as students engage in discussions of their prior knowledge about the social studies or mathematics topics to be presented.

Teaching vocabulary. Selective attention is taught as students identify unknown words, then use a variety of cognitive strategies to understand and remember them. Examples are transfer of cognates from the native language, making inferences by using context clues, grouping words according to function or semantic category, and elaboration by using the words in new sentences. Cooperative activities for vocabulary development include both pair and group work.

Teaching reading. A number of metacognitive, cognitive, and social and affective strategies are taught to develop reading comprehension in social studies. These include advance organization to skim a passage, selective attention to scan for specific information, evaluation of one's own comprehension, elaboration of prior knowledge, making inferences about meanings of new words, taking notes, producing oral and written summaries, and questioning for clarification and verification of meaning. Many of these activities are practiced in cooperative groups. In mathematics, strategies taught for oral reading of numbers and equations include attending to pronunciation of numbers (e.g., thirteen vs. thirty) and working in pairs to read and write down equations. Strategies for comprehension of word problems are taught concurrently with a five-step procedure for solving problems, which involves reading and discussing the problem before solving it. In this procedure, students use selective attention to linguistic clues that identify the question asked and the data needed, use inferencing and self-monitoring while reading the problem, use imagery, grouping, and selective attention as they discuss in cooperative groups how to set up a plan to solve the problem, and self-evaluation and imagery as they reread the problem to check the correctness of their solution.

Teaching listening. Strategies taught for listening comprehension include selective attention to main ideas, taking verbal notes in social studies, and writing numerical data while listening to mathematics problems. Students are taught to pay attention to linguistic markers that signal main ideas, details, and discourse structure in oral presentations on social studies topics. They practice note-taking skills using a *T* list, in which main ideas are written on the left side of a *T* and corresponding examples and details on the right. Following note taking, students work in cooperative groups to pool the information recorded, then develop summarizing skills by making oral or written summaries.

Teaching oral language. Discussion activities are integrated with the presentation and practice of content in both social studies and mathematics. Strategies taught for these activities include elaboration of prior knowledge, working cooperatively in pairs and groups, asking questions to increase comprehension, and using organizational planning to develop oral reports in social studies and explanations of problem solutions in mathematics.

Teaching writing. In addition to writing activities related to specific lesson topics, students also practice writing reports for social studies and writing word problems for mathematics. For both types of writing, the major strategy taught is organizational planning, in which students plan the parts and sequence to be produced. Other strategies practiced for writing include note taking, using resource materials in social studies, using imagery to illustrate word problems, and sharing written products during cooperative activities.

Teaching test-taking skills. Unit tests in both the social studies and mathematics materials are used to teach students strategies for taking tests as well as for evaluating their learning. Students are reminded to elaborate on their prior knowledge, make inferences, use self-talk to reduce test anxiety, and, most important, to evaluate their own performance.

Teaching content-specific concepts and skills. Learning strategies are taught to develop the declarative and procedural knowledge underlying the content topics presented in social studies and mathematics. Examples of these strategies are: creating imagery for map skills, graphing, measurement, and geometry; selective attention to words embodying key concepts and relationships; self-evaluation of one's level of understanding; elaboration of prior knowledge to relate to and understand new concepts presented; questioning when comprehension is incomplete; and working cooperatively with other students to develop and share both factual and process knowledge.

This model integrates content topics, language activities, and learning strategy instruction. Teachers can also develop their own CALLA instructional materials by adapting mainstream content materials and developing academic language activities and learning strategy instruction to accompany them. Although the teacher's guides present extensive information on how to teach the learning strategies included in the materials, our experience in staff development indicates that teachers still need a considerable amount of training before becoming adept at teaching learning strategies, as learning strategies are new to most language teachers and because new ways of teaching, in common with other types of procedural knowledge, take long periods of practice to perfect.

Conclusions

In this chapter we have described a few instructional models and materials that promote learning strategy instruction. The Strategic Teaching

Model (Jones et al. 1987) was developed for native English-speaking students in elementary and secondary schools and applies strategy instruction to the content areas of mathematics, science, social studies, and literature. The Cognitive Academic Language Learning Approach, or CALLA (Chamot and O'Malley 1986, 1987, in press; O'Malley 1988), was developed for students with limited English proficiency in upper elementary and secondary schools and includes strategy instruction in academic language skills and in the content areas of science, mathematics, social studies, and literature and composition. Both models are based on cognitive theory and research and therefore share a number of key elements. CALLA differs from strategic teaching mainly in its emphasis on developing academic language proficiency in all four language skills, its use of students' native language and culture as prior knowledge to be extended, and its use of cooperative learning techniques. Both models require extensive and ongoing teacher training for successful implementation.

Each set of instructional material described has a somewhat different approach toward instruction of learning strategies, but, more important, each addresses students directly in explaining the value and purpose of learning strategies. Learning strategies are defined and classified in somewhat different ways in these materials, and, although we are obviously proponents of our own classification scheme of metacognitive, cognitive, and social/affective strategies, there is as yet no evidence to show which scheme is easiest and most productive for teachers and students.

Continuing research is needed regarding classroom applications of learning strategies for second and foreign language students. Longitudinal studies of students instructed in learning strategies could investigate the long-term retention of strategies and their transfer to new tasks. Research is also needed on the most effective ways to motivate and train teachers in incorporating learning strategy instruction in their foreign and second language classrooms, and on the types of instructional materials that best facilitate this process.

8 *Summary and conclusions*

Our primary intent has been to establish a foundation for the application of learning strategies to theory, research, and practice in second language acquisition. We began by describing the state of knowledge on these issues at the beginning of our research. We then presented a rationale and approach in cognitive theory for discussing learning strategies in second language acquisition. In the process, we indicated the types of constructs in second language acquisition to which the cognitive theory can be applied and described contributions the theory makes to understanding second language phenomena. We then discussed specific studies of learning strategies in second language acquisition, including studies intended for strategy definition and classification, strategy description with different types of learners and tasks, and validation of strategy effectiveness, which included correlational studies and strategy training research. Finally, we presented some instructional models that draw specifically upon this work in learning strategies and discussed one model in particular that has applications for second language classrooms.

This chapter summarizes what is known in theory, research, and practice beyond what was known at the beginning of our work. We also indicate what is not known and what some of the limitations are of the work reviewed. Finally, we provide some direction for future theory development, research, and instructional modeling.

Theoretical developments

Where cognitive theory has succeeded is in drawing a picture of how information is stored in memory and what processes are entailed in learning. The theory suggests that information is stored as either declarative knowledge (what we know) or procedural knowledge (what we know how to do), which includes complex cognitive skills. Declarative knowledge is typically stored in terms of meaning-based propositions and schemata, while procedural knowledge is stored in terms of production systems or IF-THEN causal relationships. One of the advantages of this distinction lies in the suggestion that each type of knowledge is

214

learned most effectively in different ways. The processes entailed in learning procedural knowledge are of particular importance because language is represented within the theory as a complex cognitive skill. Consequently, learning a second language can be viewed as parallel to learning other complex cognitive skills. This has implications for research to clarify how a second language is learned and for instructional approaches in second language acquisition.

Because declarative knowledge is represented in long-term memory in terms of propositions and schemata, both of which are language based, the way in which information is stored in memory is inextricably related to language structure and meaning. Cognitive theory therefore has something to say about language and particularly about second language acquisition. Linguistic information is treated in memory just like other information when it is declarative knowledge, and it is best learned and retrieved by establishing linkages with related meaning-based concepts, propositions, or schemata. Using linguistic information that is stored as declarative knowledge in spontaneous language interactions would be burdensome, however, because: (1) retrieval of declarative knowledge is slow, (2) short-term memory has capacity limitations, and (3) rule-driven language production would require familiarity with an overwhelming number of and use of more rules simultaneously than could be maintained in short-term memory. Thus, it is important for language skills to become proceduralized through practice and to become automatic, thereby easing the burden on short-term memory.

Learning complex cognitive skills can be effective under either of two conditions: when there are repeated opportunities for practice with cued feedback (the low road to learning), and when the learner transfers an abstract principle from a similar task to guide in acquisition of the new skill (the high road). Perkins (1989) originally applied his description of the low and the high road only to metacognitive learning strategies, but in our discussion, we have indicated that language and learning strategies are both exemplars of complex cognitive skills. Consequently, the notion of a low and a high road to learning could apply to both.

In second language instruction, students may receive cued opportunities for practice with either the form of the language or the meaning expressed through the language. Thus, the theory can be used to examine various methods of instruction that have been of interest in second language acquisition, including the audio-lingual method (feedback on language forms), and communication-based methods (feedback on meaning). Perhaps more important, the theory can be used to examine the transfer of learning strategies used with tasks in the student's native language to similar tasks in the second language. What the theory suggests is that strategies learned with tasks in the student's first language may be transfered via the high road to similar tasks in the student's second language. That is, students who have had prior experience in using learning strategies in their first language may learn to apply them with second language tasks through extension of the principle guiding their use and not require extensive cued repetitions with the new task. However, even a straightforward extension of the principle governing use of a strategy might require some opportunities for cued practice with second language tasks.

There is a direct parallel between individual learning strategies and specific cognitive processes that give the strategies independent grounding in a theory-based analysis. The learning strategies include both metacognitive (e.g., planning, selective attention, monitoring, and advance organization) and cognitive strategies (e.g., inferencing, elaboration, grouping, imagery, and deduction). Learning strategies are represented in cognitive theory as complex cognitive skills that follow the same general rules as do other forms of procedural knowledge. Procedural knowledge has the capacity to transform declarative knowledge so that it is reorganized, summarized, or represented and linked to new information in memory. In effect, this is how learning strategies exert their influence on the acquisition process. Two of the more important characteristics of procedural knowledge are that it is difficult to learn and it is difficult to transfer to new situations. Thus, the acquisition of new learning strategies through training has been characterized as difficult for the learner unless opportunities for transfer become part of the instruction.

The cognitive theory described in this book is largely a theory of learning processes and not a theory that specifies precisely what is learned, what content will be easiest (or most difficult) to learn, or what learners will select to learn at different stages of development or levels of mastery of a complex skill. These factors depend on a variety of characteristics, including the previous exposure of the person to the subject matter (existing schematic linkages), the strategies used in learning, opportunities for learning, the nature of the task, and perhaps the unique characteristics of language as a subject matter for learning. This ambiguity with regard to the content of learning is the fundamental reason why the theory needs to be augmented with information from the field of linguistics before it has meaning in second language acquisition. In Chapter 3, we selected a number of constructs, such as common underlying proficiency, linguistic transfer, metalinguistic proficiency, and interlanguage, that had been discussed in the second language acquisition literature and examined them with the theory to determine if they could be explained adequately. The theory is unlikely to have predicted the existence of these constructs independently of linguistic analysis but is able to explain how information related to these constructs is learned, stored in memory, and retrieved. Furthermore, as with many other disparate phenomena, once the constructs have been identified, the theory may be able to predict experimental data on how students perform (Lehnert 1984). As Black and Lehnert (1984) note in reviewing one of Anderson's (1983) books in which the full theoretical model was presented, Anderson "provides the general mechanisms needed for cognition, but others (or perhaps Anderson himself) will have to determine the particular kinds of knowledge needed by these mechanisms" (p. 854).

Linguists have been quite demanding about what a theory should be able to supply. For example, Long (1985) notes that theories have dual roles of description and explanation in a causal sense. That is, theory should not only be able to make testable statements about what we understand about language but it should be able to predict when and why certain second language processes occur. Furthermore, the theory should bring together linguistic, cognitive, and social dimensions of second language acquisition. Larsen-Freeman (1985) suggests, after a review of extant theory, that it is probably premature to speak about theories of second language acquisition given either of these criteria.

We have not suggested that cognitive theory is able to explain all linguistic phenomena, since we examined only a subset of the full number of constructs that could have been discussed. Furthermore, there are psycholinguistic models encompassing second language acquisition that we have not even discussed (e.g., MacWhinney 1987). Thus, our purpose is not to be fully comprehensive but merely to illustrate potential applications of cognitive theory and to build a foundation for describing the influence of learning strategies on second language acquisition. For our immediate purposes, it is important that cognitive theory makes the following assertions:

– Learning is an active and dynamic process in which individuals make use of a variety of information and strategic modes of processing;
– Language is a complex cognitive skill that has properties in common with other complex skills in terms of how information is stored and learned;
– Learning a language entails a stagewise progression from initial awareness and active manipulation of information and learning processes to full automaticity in language use; and
– Learning strategies parallel theoretically derived cognitive processes and have the potential to influence learning outcomes in a positive manner.

Numerous unanswered questions remain about how a second language is learned, how the language is stored, and how the language is comprehended or retrieved for use. For example, the rules individuals use in parsing for language comprehension or language production are only partially understood and need to be examined in much greater detail (Howard 1985). Furthermore, the theoretical basis for describing language skills in terms of production systems needs greater elaboration and confirmation through research. Our own example (Chapter 3) and conclusions from our research (Chapter 5) are only a beginning in that direction.

In a general sense, the linkage between cognitive theory and second language acquisition needs to be drawn more closely through collaborative work between psychologists and linguists or others working in the field of second language acquisition. Interestingly, John Anderson has recently collaborated with a linguist in producing a theoretical work on the acquisition of grammar (McWhinney and Anderson 1986). There is considerable room for additional work, since much of the research underlying the theoretical developments we have discussed has been based on first language acquisition, and much of the work is based on comprehension of isolated sentences rather than extended texts. Furthermore, we noted earlier that theoretical models based on artificial intelligence have not taken into consideration important aspects of second language acquisition such as modeling and cooperative learning, which represent other areas for expansion of the theory. And finally, our description of cognitive theory is incomplete and should be augmented by a description of alternative views that have been reported in the literature (e.g., Rumelhart et al. 1986; Sternberg 1985).

More specific to the purposes of this book, however, there remain numerous theoretical questions about learning strategies in second language acquisition that need to be addressed. First, while we have suggested that learning strategies can be represented in cognitive theory as production systems, we have not attempted to build a theoretical rationale for indicating which strategies might be more effective with which types of language tasks. There is a strong precedent for this type of analysis emerging in cognitive psychology (Alexander and Judy 1989; Brandt 1989; Perkins and Salomon 1989). Gagné (1985) has indicated that declarative knowledge is more readily learned by building upon previous schemata, while procedural knowledge is more easily learned by using repetition with cued practice. We have added Perkins's (1989) suggestion that metacognition, an exemplar of procedural knowledge, can be learned through either a low road, as described by Gagné, or a high road, which entails transfer of a principle to guide learning with a similar task. If additional formulations delineate specific strategies that should be associated with specific language tasks, predictions could be made about learning that might be useful in instructional design. This suggests that cognitive theory needs to be linked more closely with instructional theory and our knowledge about language in order to generate predictions about second language learning in classrooms. The original theory was descriptive and focused primarily upon cognitive processing that occurs during learning instead of prescriptively indicating which processes should occur during instruction, although some of Anderson's other work has in fact been concerned with instructional systems (e.g., Anderson, Boyle, and Reiser 1985).

Second, the original theory did not isolate a special group of cognitive processes called learning strategies and made no distinction between metacognitive and cognitive processes. We have attempted to rectify this absence by showing how both metacognitive and cognitive strategies can be understood within the existing theory and by discussing the acquisition of strategies as complex cognitive skills. Strategy training should be most effective in enhancing learning outcomes and transfer when metacognitive and cognitive strategies are combined during instruction. A useful contribution to the theory would be to describe in greater detail if there are only some metacognitive strategies that will produce this effect with certain cognitive strategies and tasks.

Third, although we have indicated that much productive learning occurs through conscious and deliberate use of strategic processing, there have been doubts expressed by linguists about the effectiveness of control mechanisms as an aid to learning and about the accessibility of language learning to conscious introspection. There needs to be a more complete description of language learning within cognitive theory than we have been able to present. We have suggested that strategic learning processes may be conscious initially but become automatic with practice and consequently may be performed without awareness. A complementary view is that learning mechanisms that are performed without awareness cannot be referred to as strategic. But we also hold the view that mechanisms that have become automatic are accessible to on-line mental processing through spreading activation when a learning task is interrupted. Greater specificity is required to identify the types of tasks for which concurrent introspection will yield useful information about language learning processes.

And finally, the role of motivation in cognitive theory should be clarified. Motivation in cognitive theory is too often seen as an outgrowth of using strategic modes of learning successfully. With a classroom of unmotivated students, it seems too facile to indicate that if the students begin to use strategies they will become more motivated. A theoretical analysis is needed of the specific motivational attributes that are linked to cognitive theory and the ways in which these attributes can be called upon to facilitate learning. While a number of models of second language acquisition have already indicated the importance of social/motivational factors as accompaniments to cognitive and linguistic knowledge in learning (see Larsen-Freeman 1985), recent movement by cognitive theorists in this direction (e.g., McCombs 1988; Paris 1988a) need to be incorporated into this thinking.

Research

In Chapters 4 and 5, we classified the research on learning strategies into three general categories: studies to define and classify strategies, studies to describe strategies in greater detail and the types of tasks with which the strategies are effective, and studies to validate the influence of strategic processing on learning. We further divided the last category into correlational studies and experimental training studies. In the following section, this scheme is used to analyze the types of research needed to clarify the relationship between strategic modes of processing and second language acquisition.

Definitional/classification studies

Much of the early research on learning strategies in second language acquisition was concerned with definitions and classifications in which varied methodologies were used to identify strategies or to group strategies into common categories. The methodologies have included retrospective and concurrent (think-aloud) interviews, questionnaires, and observations. This focus reflects in part a degree of uncertainty about what learning strategies are, in part a reliance upon traditional modes of research in the field, and in part a certain hesitancy about moving too quickly toward training students to use the strategies since their effects with some students might prove to be detrimental to learning. Whatever the reason for this focus, the studies have been productive and have revealed important information about the definitions and classification of strategies. Representative findings are:

1. During small group interviews, provided that questions concerning the tasks are given sufficient structure, students can describe a wide variety of strategies used in learning English as a second language and in learning Spanish or Russian as a foreign language;
2. Strategies in second language acquisition can be classified in terms of three broad groupings that are commonly used in the literature on cognitive psychology (metacognitive, cognitive, and social/affective strategies); and
3. Individual learning strategies in second language acquisition that fall within these three broad groups do not appear to be any different from learning strategies involved in performing first language problem-solving tasks and receptive or productive language tasks.

It is quite conceivable that the debates about which specific definition of a particular strategy or which classification scheme is best could continue in the literature for some time. Our own definition and classification system underwent a series of minor adaptations (Chamot and O'Malley 1987; O'Malley et al. 1985b), and we continue to build upon the definition of specific strategies from our think-aloud studies (e.g., O'Malley et al. 1988). However, while these debates about definitions and classifications are productive, they should not occupy the exclusive attention of researchers. There are good reasons why differences might be expected in strategy definitions or classification schemes based on theory as opposed to definitions and classifications based on various methodologies of data collection. For example, a classification based on retrospective interviews could easily produce different results from one based on on-line processing studies, and these in turn could produce different classifications from results based on factor analysis of a lengthy questionnaire. Furthermore, classifications based on questionnaires could be susceptible to item sequence effects, since one item could easily elicit a strategy used in a context suggested by a previous item in the sequence. Few of the strategy questionnaires used in second language acquisition studies group questions about strategy use according to the context in which the strategy is used. Future research on questionnaire development should group items in terms of contexts such as the classroom or home and in terms of tasks such as reading or writing in order to clarify for respondents which context or task is being discussed.

Instrument development issues have not been totally resolved in our view despite the fact that a number of strategy self-report rating schemes have appeared in the literature. Messick's (1984) call for assessment instruments to go beyond the measurement of knowledge by measuring cognitive skills and the structuring and restructuring of knowledge is relevant here. Messick pointed out that cognitive constructs may vary depending on the level of achievement of the learner. For example, the acquisition of a critical mass of information is essential at the beginning stages of knowledge in an area, and the restructuring of knowledge is important at intermediate levels of knowledge. At expert levels of performance, the restructuring of knowledge and the flexible application of specialized schemata are appropriate cognitive skills. This analysis suggests that different strategies are appropriate at different levels of knowledge and that different forms of assessment may be appropriate to measure these varied types of strategies. Perkins and Linnville (1988) note that different cognitive constructs may emerge in second language acquisition during the accretion, tuning, and restructuring modes of learning suggested by Rumelhart and Norman (1978). Thus, there are numerous unanswered questions about strategy use at different stages of language acquisition that can be addressed through research in which new instrument development has a major role.

What seems to be more important than determining which classification scheme best represents a given set of data is to determine precisely what students do when using a strategy with a particular language learning task, to determine the relationship between the strategy use and learning outcomes, and to identify the impact of strategy use on second language acquisition. These topics occupy the remainder of the discussion.

Strategy description

Our initial research efforts to investigate students' retrospective strategy descriptions with different language tasks was followed by efforts using on-line processing studies to inquire about the precise ways in which students used a strategy and to identify in greater detail what students mean when they say that they use specific strategies. Another purpose of our on-line processing studies was to identify strategies that appear only for an instant in short-term memory because the strategic processing has long been automatic. These strategies may be performed with only marginal awareness and may not be recalled in retrospective reports. Some of these studies fall into the category of what Paris (1988b) refers to as comparative research, or studies designed to show how individuals who vary in certain characteristics such as age or intelligence use cognitive strategies. Some of the findings from these studies are:

– Students designated by teachers as more effective learners use strategies more frequently and use a greater variety of strategies than students designated as less effective learners;
– These differences between effective and less effective learners are consistent regardless of whether the students are learning English as a second language or learning a foreign language such as Spanish or Russian;
– Students use metacognitive and cognitive learning strategies with all four language skills (listening, speaking, reading, and writing);
– The specific strategies students select for a task often depend on the nature of the task demands, as when students select deduction and translation for classroom grammar tasks;
– One of the metacognitive strategies that differentiates effective from less effective learners is problem identification, which entails analyzing the task objective and one's own resources for accomplishing it;
– Among social/affective strategies, only questioning for clarification tends to be reported in concurrent introspection interviews, whereas instances of cooperation and self-talk are reported during retrospective interviews;
– The principal strategies that differentiate more effective from less effective learners on listening comprehension tasks are monitoring, elaboration, and inferencing;
– Certain strategies tend to occur together, such as elaboration, which co-occurred with inferencing, imagery, and transfer.

These retrospective and on-line processing studies are only a beginning of the data collection that needs to be performed in order to gain an understanding of the processes involved in using learning strategies. There are four fundamental limitations of on-line processing research, which suggest directions for further work. One limitation is that any single series of studies can only address a small number of questions due to the extensive planning and effort required to collect data from even a small number of students. The planning portion of the research requires that students understand what is expected of them and are able to generate usable protocols for later analysis. This is no small task, as anyone with experience in this type of data collection will testify. Furthermore, extensive effort is required because one hour of data collection is matched by numerous hours transcribing the taped interview, reviewing what the student said, training coders to an acceptable level of agreement, categorizing the student's narrative description as representing one strategic process rather than another, and deciding how or whether to represent the underlying data through statistical analysis.

A second limitation of on-line processing studies describing student strategy use with specific learning tasks is that the research tends to be atheoretical. For example, we may learn, from the research, that students use a particular strategy with a particular task but fail to learn how the strategy relates to a theoretical analysis of skilled performance on that task. We have tried to counteract this limitation in some of our own work. In our research on listening comprehension reported in Chapter 5, for example, we drew a theoretical model of the stages of listening comprehension and then showed the correspondence between strategy use and the stages we had identified. Far more work of this kind is necessary if we are to advance beyond the stage of simple replications of strategy reporting.

The third limitation of this type of research is of a more practical nature. Students often fail to return for repeat data collection sessions once they realize how much effort is involved in reporting their thought processes while learning. Unfortunately, this is particularly true of students rated by their teachers as among the less effective language learners. Consequently, data on an entire group of students can be jeopardized. Additional research could collect data during regular school hours instead of relying upon students volunteering for after-school scheduling.

A fourth limitation is that pretraining to think aloud while learning may change the ways in which students habitually respond to learning tasks. We discussed this difficulty in Chapter 4 and largely discounted it, but some possibility remains that student responses may be influenced by the data collection approach. The student could become sensitized to what the researcher is interested in hearing and begin to generate strategies where none otherwise would have been evident. The student's report of using a strategic mode of learning may therefore be more a product of the data collection procedures than of the student's response to the task demands. This limitation may not be as serious as it first seems, however, because students may not be able to generate approaches to learning that are not already part of their repertoire and because, at least in our studies, students seemed to use learning strategies that were so appropriate for the specific tasks we created that it is difficult to imagine their strategies as being artificial. Furthermore, we have experienced little change in reported strategy use over time by individual students, provided that the task and the method of strategy elicitation are constant.

What needs to be examined in far greater detail are the strategies associated with a theoretically derived understanding of language learning tasks. Topics of research should include the ways in which students use strategies with different language learning tasks and the sustained use or adaptation of strategies over time. There is also the question of the different types of strategies called forth in learning different languages. Some strategies may be more useful than others, depending on the language or the task. Not unimportant, different strategies may be evoked at different levels of proficiency in the language, particularly since language learning entails acquiring both declarative and procedural knowledge. Throughout all of this work, the influence of motivation on strategy use needs to be analyzed in greater detail both in theory and in research. And finally, descriptive work on strategy use in cooperative learning settings or in nonclassroom environments also needs attention.

Validation studies

By far the least satisfactory number of studies has been done on validation of learning strategies with second language acquisition tasks. For a variety of reasons, second language acquisition researchers have not conducted learning strategies training studies, and few have even conducted correlational studies associating strategy use with learning. So far only modest correlations have been shown between strategy use and learning outcomes. With the exception of a few training studies reported in Chapter 6, there has been little confirmation of the effectiveness of strategy training with second language tasks. The application of learning strategies to second language acquisition would rest on uncertain ground if there were not such a strong theoretical basis for their effects and if there were not so many extant training studies in educational psychology verifying strategy effectiveness with a variety of first language tasks. Some of the findings reported thus far in the second language research are:

1. There are modest correlations between self-reported strategy use and growth in language skills which occur during a course of instruction;

2. Students can learn to use strategies with both integrative and discrete language skills when the teacher provides direct training on strategy use;

3. Second language performance of students taught to use strategies is superior to the performance of students who received no such training, but the effects depend on the task, task difficulty, and the level of support for strategy transfer;

4. Strategy transfer requires extensive cued support for strategy use even with highly similar tasks presented in the same classroom where initial training occurred; and

5. Foreign language teachers will adopt strategies for use and instruct their students on how to use them in natural classroom environments for teaching Spanish at the high school level and Russian at the college level.

These modest findings in second language acquisition research leave a number of avenues open for further investigation. First, some of the correlational and training studies already performed in cognitive psychology should be replicated with students learning second languages. There are two possible approaches for exploration with the correlational work. The first is to correlate strategy use with language learning gains over time. These types of studies are not difficult to perform, since they require only a sound learning strategies questionnaire, of which there are at least a few examples available, and pre-posttest scores at selected intervals of students learning a second language, usually but not necessarily through instruction. The major difficulty in this research is to design reliable and valid instruments to assess language proficiency at different points in time for students at different levels of proficiency. Validity is especially important in studies analyzing learning from instruction, since the measures of language proficiency must reflect the objectives and content of the course. A second possible area for exploration is to determine the relationship between strategy use and performance on identical tasks in both the first and second language as in lexical access (e.g., Cascallar n.d.) or reading comprehension (e.g., McLaughlin 1987b). The expectation is that frequent strategy use would be associated with more rapid lexical access and higher performance on reading comprehension in both languages. However, strategies used on first language tasks may be more active and dynamic than strategies used in the second language on comparable tasks due to the higher level of proceduralization of first language skills. The need to improve student strategy use in learning a second language leads to the issue of strategy training.

Strategy validation through training research is far more complicated than in correlational studies because of the necessity of designing the training modules, randomly assigning students to treatment and comparison groups in field settings, implementing the training with fidelity to the original design, determining whether or not strategies transferred outside the training environment, and ensuring that there were increases in student use of strategies as well as attendant improvements in student performance. One way to guarantee adherence to the training design is to conduct it using the staff who designed the training modules. While there are advantages to this approach, the limitation is in the uncertainty of whether or not regular classroom teachers could or would be willing to implement the training. Despite the difficulty of performing this type of research, there are numerous advantages to using experimental designs, including the ability to test specific hypotheses about training, confirmation that the treatment was truly responsible for changes in student performance, and the ability to manipulate the training approach to maximize changes in student performance.

Previous work in educational psychology on strategy training provides a solid foundation on which these studies should be developed. The first general direction for studies on training is to analyze the results of training at different levels of second language proficiency with all four language skills. The training studies can build on the descriptive studies in which strategies of effective and ineffective language learners are analyzed at different stages of second language acquisition. This analysis is particularly important given that at some point in learning, language processes that occur with difficulty become automatic. Identifying strategies that assist in the proceduralization of language is an important area of inquiry. A second general direction for training studies is to determine the conditions that facilitate transfer of strategy use to similar tasks outside the context in which the learning occurred. These studies should explore the conditions and tasks for which both the low road and the high road to learning are most effective. The resistance of strategies to transfer is understandable theoretically given that other complex cognitive skills also have difficulty in transferring. A third direction for training is to combine strategies, as in the combination of metacognitive and cognitive or cognitive and social/affective strategies, with a single task. Combined strategy training is likely to result in discovering more quickly the most effective conditions for facilitating transfer, since metacognitive strategies give students more insight into the nature of the task demands. Other approaches that should be examined in the design of strategy instruction are direct instruction and modeling of the strategy by the teacher. A fourth direction for training is to analyze the procedures required to familiarize and support teachers in the use of learning strategies. Training strategies using regular teachers in natural classroom environments, while taxing in terms of planning and complexity, have potential for far greater results than more limited laboratory-type training studies. Among the models we discussed for supporting teachers in the familiarization and use of strategy training is staff development based on peer coaching.

We also have suggestions for specific strategy training studies that should be performed. One is to replicate successful strategy training studies, including studies of elaboration training, cooperative learning, and motivational skills training, using approaches drawn from the educational psychology literature. In reciprocal teaching, for example, studies should be conducted to determine if the procedures are adaptable to second language classrooms and have effects on reading comprehension in second language acquisition similar to those obtained for first language reading comprehension. A second type of training study is to teach strategies in the student's first language as a prelude to strategy training in the second language to see if this is more effective than training strategies in the student's second language alone. This study has particular significance given that students have difficulty transferring successful comprehension strategies from first to second language reading tasks. There is great potential for capitalizing on the high road to learning when transferring strategies from the first to the second language for the same task. A third type of training study is analyzing the influence of complete instructional models in which strategies are embedded, as was discussed in Chapter 7. These approaches address the need for what Derry and Murphy (1986) refer to as an "incidental learning model," which combines both detached training and cued support in the actual instructional environment. Instructional models such as strategic teaching (Jones et al. 1987) and the Cognitive Academic Language Learning Approach (Chamot and O'Malley 1987) have promise not only for understanding more about the effects of strategy training but for gaining knowledge about how learning strategies can be embedded in an instructional program.

Glossary

accretion   The gradual accumulation of new information by matching new data to existing schemata. See also *restructuring, tuning.*

advance organization   Previewing the main ideas and concepts of the material to be learned, often by skimming the text for the organizing principle.

auditory representation   Attending to and attempting to retain the sound of a word, phrase, or longer language sequence.

automatic processing   Performing a cognitive task rapidly and without awareness or without demands on short-term memory. See also *controlled processing.*

bottom-up processing   A special form of mental processing in which individuals attempt to derive meaning from novel textual information by analyzing individual word meanings or grammatical characteristics of the text. See also *top-down processing.*

cognitive strategy   One that involves mental manipulation or transformation of materials or tasks and is intended to enhance comprehension, acquisition, or retention.

controlled processing   Performing a cognitive task in which the learner's attention is required and demands are placed on short-term memory. See also *automatic processing.*

cooperation   Working together with one or more peers to solve a problem, pool information, check a learning task, model a language activity, or get feedback on oral or written performance.

declarative knowledge   A special type of information in long-term memory that consists of knowledge about the facts and things that we know. This type of information is stored in terms of propositions, schemata, and propositional networks. It may also be stored in terms of isolated pieces of information, temporal strings, and images.

deduction   The process of applying rules to understand or produce the second language or of making up rules based on language analysis.

directed attention   Deciding in advance to attend in general to a learning task and to ignore irrelevant distractors.

direct training   Learning strategy instruction in which students are informed about the value and purpose of learning strategies.

elaboration   The mental process of relating new knowledge to existing information in long-term memory. It has also been described as a process of making meaningful connections between different parts of new textual information.

embedded training   Guidance in the use of learning strategies that is embedded in the task materials but not explicitly defined to the learner as strategy instruction.

grouping   Classifying words, terminology, or concepts according to their attributes or meaning.

imagery   Using visual images (either mental or actual) to understand or remember new information.

inferencing   Using available information to guess meanings of new items, predict outcomes, or fill in missing information.

interlanguage   A linguistic system that results from a second language learner's attempt to produce the target language. It is considered to be a separate linguistic system from the native language and the target language.

keyword method   A mnemonic device in which individuals form a native-language homophone (the keyword) for the target word in the second language. The individual then imagines a scene in which the homophone and the referent object of the target word are interacting in some manner. Memory retrieval of the meaning of the target word consists of recalling the homophone, then recalling the imagined scene in which the homophone and the referent object are interacting.

knowledge compilation   A procedure involved in the acquisition of complex skills. The procedure consists of two components, proceduralization and composition. In proceduralization, the learner converts a sequence of actions into a propositional representation that is stored in long-term memory as a production system. Composition consists of combining several productions that have already become automatic into a single production.

lexical access   In language comprehension, the process of matching words in short-term memory with words and concepts in long-term memory in order to extract meaning.

long-term memory   The store of information in memory that is retained over a long period. The capacity of long-term memory to hold large amounts of information is probably unlimited. Information in long-term memory is considered to be inactive until it is activated and manipulated in either short-term or working memory. See also *short-term memory* and *working memory*.

metacognitive knowledge   Knowledge of one's cognitive processes related to learning and the cognitive processes of others.

metacognitive strategy   A learning strategy that involves thinking about or knowledge of the learning process, planning for learning, monitoring learning while it is taking place, or self-evaluation of learning after the task has been completed.

metalinguistic knowledge The ability to reflect on or analyze the forms and structures of a language independent of its informational or social functions.

organizational planning Generating a plan for the parts, sequence, main ideas, or language functions to be used in a language production task.

parsing In language comprehension, the construction of meaning-based representations of new information. Parsing is the second of three processes involved in language comprehension. See also *perceptual processing, utilization.*

perceptual processing In language comprehension, the retention of portions of a new text in short-term memory so that they can be processed for meaning. Perceptual processing is the first of three processes involved in language comprehension. See also *parsing, utilization.*

primary strategies Term used to describe strategies that operate directly on the material to be learned, such as comprehension and memory strategies. See also *support strategies.*

problem identification Explicitly identifying the central point needing resolution in a task, or identifying an aspect of the task that hinders its successful completion.

procedural knowledge Knowledge that consists of the things that we know how to do. It underlies the execution of all complex cognitive skills. Procedural knowledge is stored in long-term memory and is represented internally in terms of production systems. Procedural knowledge includes mental activities such as problem solving, language reception and production, and using learning strategies. It may also include physical activities such as driving a car and tying one's shoes. See also *production systems.*

production systems The processes by which procedural knowledge is stored in long-term memory. They consist of an interrelated chain of condition-action (IF-THEN) connections that underlie the execution of a complex skill. The conditions or the actions may be internal or external and, once learned, will tend to be executed rapidly and without awareness. See also *procedural knowledge.*

propositional representation A language-based mode of storing information in long-term memory. It consists of meaning-based abstractions of the original information, which may have been presented through auditory or visual text. Propositional representations are sometimes referred to as propositions.

questioning for clarification Eliciting from a teacher or peer additional explanations, rephrasing, examples, or verification for a learning task.

resourcing Using target language reference materials such as dictionaries, encyclopedias, or textbooks.

restructuring The development of novel knowledge structures for interpreting new information and for reorganizing existing knowledge. See also *accretion, tuning.*

schema Plural, *schemata*. One of the ways in which information is stored in long-term memory. Schemata are large information structures that are organized around a common topic or theme. They are considered to be larger in scope than propositional networks. Schemata are typically organized in hierarchies so that subsets of information are subsumed within larger or more inclusive concepts.

scripts Special schemata consisting of situation-specific knowledge about goals, participants, and procedures in real-life situations.

selective attention Deciding in advance to attend to specific aspects of input, often by scanning for key words, concepts, and/or linguistic markers.

self-evaluation Checking the outcomes of one's own language learning against a standard after the learning has been completed.

self-monitoring Checking one's comprehension during listening or reading, or checking the accuracy and/or appropriateness of one's oral or written production while it is taking place.

self-talk Reducing anxiety for learning by using mental techniques that make one feel competent to do the learning task.

short-term memory The store of information that a person is aware of at any moment. This type of memory holds modest amounts of information. New information that enters short-term memory easily replaces former information. Retention of new information can be aided by actively relating the new information to existing information in long-term memory.

social/affective strategy One of three general types of learning strategy. It may consist of using social interactions to assist in the comprehension, learning, or retention of information. It may also consist of using mental control over personal affect that interferes with learning. See also *cognitive strategy, metacognitive strategy.*

spreading activation The activation of one concept in long-term memory that activates other concepts to which it is connected by meaning or use. The spread of activation in long-term memory runs along the paths established by propositional networks and schemata. The availability of connections in long-term memory makes new information meaningful.

story grammar A special schema representing the discourse organization of fables, stories, and narratives.

study skills (Usually) overt behaviors, such as taking notes, writing summaries, and using reference materials, that are intended to enhance learning.

substitution Using a replacement target language word or phrase when the intended word or phrase is not available.

summarizing Making a mental, oral, or written synopsis of new information gained through listening or reading.

support strategies Term used to describe strategies that help maintain attention to materials and an appropriate attitude for learning. See also *primary strategies*.

T **list** A form of note taking in which the main ideas of a passage are noted on the left side of a page and the corresponding details are listed on the right. The designation of a "T" is derived from the fact that the learner makes a vertical line to separate the main ideas from the details and a crossing horizontal line at the top of the page on which to write the words "main ideas" and "details."

top-down processing A special form of mental processing in which individuals attempt to comprehend textual information by making use of schemata based on real-world knowledge or story grammars. See also *bottom-up processing*.

transfer Use of previous linguistic knowledge or prior skills to assist comprehension or production.

tuning The refinement of existing knowledge based on modifications of available knowledge structures. See also *accretion, restructuring*.

utilization In language comprehension, the process of relating a mental representation of a text to declarative information stored in long-term memory. Utilization is the third of three processes involved in language comprehension. See also *parsing, perceptual processing*.

working memory Term used to denote the active use of cognitive procedures with new information that is in the process of being stored. It may also denote the active use of cognitive procedures in which information drawn from long-term memory is associated with new information. Some theorists believe that working memory and short-term memory are identical.

References

Alexander, P. A., and Judy, J. E. 1989. The interaction of domain-specific and strategic knowledge in academic performance. *Review of Educational Research* 58:375–404.

Alvermann, D. 1987. Strategic teaching in social studies. In B. F. Jones, A. S. Palincsar, D. S. Ogle, and E. G. Carr (Eds.), *Strategic teaching and learning: cognitive instruction in the content areas* (pp. 92–110). Alexandria, Va.: Association for Supervision and Curriculum Development.

Anderson, C. W. 1987. Strategic teaching in science. In B. F. Jones, A. S. Palincsar, D. S. Ogle, and E. G. Carr (Eds.), *Strategic teaching and learning: cognitive instruction in the content areas* (pp. 73–91). Alexandria, Va.: Association for Supervision and Curriculum Development.

Anderson, J. R. 1976. *Language, memory, and thought.* Hillsdale, N.J.: Erlbaum.

1978. Arguments concerning representations for mental imagery. *Psychological Review*, 85:249–277.

1980. *Cognitive psychology and its implications.* San Francisco: Freeman.

1982. Acquisition of cognitive skills. *Psychological Review* 89:369–406.

1983. *The architecture of cognition.* Cambridge, Mass.: Harvard University Press.

1985. *Cognitive psychology and its implications.* 2nd ed. New York: Freeman.

Anderson, J. R. (Ed.) 1981. *Cognitive skills and their acquisition.* Hillsdale, N.J.: Erlbaum.

Anderson, J. R., Boyle, C. F., and Reiser, B. J. 1985. Intelligent tutoring systems. *Science* 228:456–462.

Anderson, R. C., and Pearson, P. D. 1984. A schema-theoretic view of basic processes in reading comprehension. In P. D. Pearson (Ed.), *Handbook of reading research* (pp. 225–291). New York: Longman.

Asher, J. J. 1969. The total physical response approach to second language learning. *Modern Language Journal* 53:3–17.

Atkinson, R. C., and Raugh, M. R. 1975. An application of the mnemonic keyword method to the acquisition of Russian vocabulary. *Journal of Experimental Psychology* 104:126–133.

Barnett, M. A. 1988. Teaching reading strategies: how methodology affects language course articulation. *Foreign Language Annals* 21(2):109–119.

Beach, R. 1987. Strategic teaching in literature. In B. F. Jones, A. S. Palincsar, D. S. Ogle, and E. G. Carr (Eds.), *Strategic teaching and learning: cognitive instruction in the content areas* (pp. 135–159). Alexandria, Va.: Association for Supervision and Curriculum Development.

Bialystok, E. 1978. A theoretical model of second language learning. *Language Learning* 28:69–83.

1980. On the relationship between formal proficiency and strategic ability. Paper presented at the annual meeting of TESOL, San Francisco, Calif., March 1980.

1981. The role of conscious strategies in second language proficiency. *Modern Language Journal* 65:24–35.

1986. Factors in the growth of linguistic awareness. *Child Development* 57:498–510.

Bialystok, E., and Kellerman, E. 1986. Language strategies in the classroom. Paper presented at the RELC Conference, Singapore, April 1986.

Bialystok, E., and Ryan, E. B. 1985. Toward a definition of metalinguistic skill. *Merrill-Palmer Quarterly* 31:229–51.

Black, J. B., and Lehnert, W. G. 1984. [Review of *The architecture of the mind.*] *Contemporary Psychology* 29:853–54.

Bobrow, D. G. 1968. Natural language input for a computer problem solving system. In M. Minsky (Ed.), *Semantic information processing.* Cambridge, Mass.: MIT Press.

Brandt, R. 1989. On learning research: A conversation with Lauren Resnick. *Educational Leadership* 46(4):12–16.

Brown, A. L., Armbruster, B. B., and Baker, L. 1986. The role of metacognition in reading and studying. In J. Orasanu (Ed.), *Reading comprehension: From research to practice* (pp. 49–75). Hillsdale, N.J.: Erlbaum.

Brown, A. L., Bransford, J. D., Ferrara, R. A., and Campione, J. C. 1983. Learning, remembering, and understanding. In J. H. Flavell and M. Markman (Eds.), *Carmichael's manual of child psychology* (Vol. 3, pp. 77–166). New York: Wiley.

Brown, A. L., and Palincsar, A. S. 1982. Inducing strategies learning from texts by means of informed, self-control training. *Topics in Learning and Learning Disabilities* 2(1):1–17.

Brown, H. D. 1984. The consensus: Another view. *Foreign Language Annals,* 17:277–280.

Brown, J. S., and Burton, R. 1978. Diagnostic models for procedural bugs in basic mathematical skills. *Cognitive Science* 2:155–92.

Byrnes, H. 1984. The role of listening comprehension: a theoretical base. *Foreign Language Annals* 17:317–29.

Calfee, R., and Drum, P. 1986. Research on teaching reading. In M. C. Wittrock (Ed.), *Handbook of research on teaching* (pp. 804–49). New York: Macmillan.

Call, M. E. 1985. Auditory short-term memory, listening comprehension, and the input hypothesis. *TESOL Quarterly* 19:765–81.

Campione, J. C., and Armbruster, B. B. 1985. Acquiring information from texts: an analysis of four approaches. In S. F. Chipman, J. W. Segal, and R. Glaser (Eds.), *Thinking and learning skills* (Vol. 1, pp. 297–317). Hillsdale, N.J.: Erlbaum.

Canale, M., and Swain, M. 1980. Theoretical bases of communicative approaches to second language teaching and testing. *Applied Linguistics* 1:1–47.

Carpenter, T. P., Fennema, E., Peterson, P. L., Chiang, C.-P., and Loef, M. 1988. Using knowledge of children's mathematics thinking in classroom teaching: an experimental study. Paper presented at the annual meetings of the American Educational Research Association, New Orleans, La., April 1988.

Carroll, J. B. 1981. Twenty-five years of research on foreign language aptitude. In K. C. Diller (Ed.), *Individual differences and universals in language learning aptitude* (pp. 83–118). Rowley, Mass.: Newbury House.

Cascallar, E. C. n.d. Syntactic and semantic processing in bilingual students and in second language learners: an information processing approach. manuscript. Technical Report Series. Los Angeles: Center for Language Education and Research.

Cazden, C. B. 1972. *Child language and education.* New York: Holt, Rinehart, & Winston.

Chamot, A. U. 1987a. *Language development through content: America: the early years.* Reading, Mass.: Addison-Wesley.

1987b. *Language development through content: America: after independence.* Reading, Mass.: Addison-Wesley.

1987c. *Language development through content: Teacher's Guide: America: the early years/America: after independence.* Reading, Mass.: Addison-Wesley.

Chamot, A. U., and Küpper, L. 1989. Learning strategies in foreign language instruction. *Foreign Language Annals, 22*(1):13–24.

Chamot, A. U., Küpper, L., and Impink-Hernandez, M. V. 1988a. *A study of learning strategies in foreign language instruction: findings of the longitudinal study.* McLean, Va.: Interstate Research Associates.

1988b. *A study of learning strategies in foreign language instruction: the third year and final report.* McLean, Va.: Interstate Research Associates.

Chamot, A. U., and O'Malley, J. M. 1986. *A cognitive academic language learning approach: an ESL content-based curriculum.* Wheaton, Md.: National Clearinghouse for Bilingual Education.

1987. The cognitive academic language learning approach: a bridge to the mainstream. *TESOL Quarterly, 21*(3):227–49.

1988a. *Language development through content: mathematics book A.* Reading, Mass.: Addison-Wesley.

1988b. *Language development through content: mathematics book A: Teacher's Guide.* Reading, Mass.: Addison-Wesley.

In press. *The Cognitive Academic Language Learning Approach: a resource guide for teachers.* Reading, Mass.: Addison-Wesley.

Chamot, A. U., O'Malley, J. M., Küpper, L., and Impink-Hernandez, M. V. 1987. *A study of learning strategies in foreign language instruction: first year report.* Rosslyn, Va.: Interstate Research Associates.

Chamot, A. U., and Stewner-Manzanares, G. 1985. *A summary of current literature on English as a second language.* Rosslyn, Va.: InterAmerica Research Associates.

Chase, W. G., and Simon, H. A. 1973. The mind's eye in chess. In W. G. Chase (Ed.), *Visual information processing.* New York: Academic Press.

Chesterfield, R., and Chesterfield, K. B. 1985. Natural order in children's use of second language learning strategies. *Applied Linguistics* 6(1):45–59.

Chi, M. T. H., Glaser, R., and Rees, E. 1982. Expertise in problem solving. In R. J. Sternberg (Ed.), *Advances in the psychology of human intelligence* (Vol. 1). Hillsdale, N.J.: Erlbaum.

Chipman, S. F., Segal, J. W., and Glaser, R. 1985. *Thinking and learning skills: research and open questions* (Vol. 2). Hillsdale, N.J.: Erlbaum.

Chomsky, N. 1980. Rules and representations. *Behavioral and Brain Sciences* 3:1–61.

Clark, H., and Clark, E. 1977. *The psychology of language: An introduction to psycholinguistics.* New York: Harcourt Brace Jovanovich.

Cohen, A. D. 1984. Studying second language learning strategies: How do we get the information? *Applied Linguistics* 5:101–11.

Cohen, A. D. and Aphek, E. 1980. Retention of second language vocabulary over time: investigating the role of mnemonic associations. *System* 8:221–35.

    1981. Easifying second language learning. *Studies in Second Language Acquisition* 3:221–36.

Cohen, A. D., and Hosenfeld, C. 1981. Some uses of mentalistic data in second language research. *Language Learning* 31:285–314.

Collier, V. P. 1987. Age and rate of acquisition of second language for academic purposes. *TESOL Quarterly* 21(4):617–41.

Craik, F. I. M., and Tulving, E. 1975. Depth of processing and the retention of words in episodic memory. *Journal of Experimental Psychology: General* 104:268–94.

Cummins, J. 1979. Linguistic interdependence and the educational development of bilingual children. *Review of Education Research* 49:222–51.

    1981. Empirical and theoretical underpinnings of bilingual education. *Journal of Education* 163:16–29.

    1982. Tests, achievement, and bilingual students (*Focus, 9*). Wheaton, Md.: National Clearinghouse for Bilingual Education.

    1983. Conceptual and linguistic foundations of language assessment. In S. S. Seidner (Ed.), *Issues of language assessment: Language assessment and curriculum planning.* Wheaton, Md.: National Clearinghouse for Bilingual Education.

    1984. *Bilingualism and special education: issues in assessment and pedagogy.* Clevedon, U.K.: Multilingual Matters.

    1986. Empowering minority students. *Harvard Education Review* 56:18–36.

Dansereau, D. F. 1978. The development of a learning strategies curriculum. In H. F. O'Neil, Jr. (Ed.), *Learning strategies* (pp. 1–29). New York: Academic Press.

    1985. Learning strategy research. In J. W. Segal, S. F. Chipman, and R. Glaser (Eds.), *Thinking and learning skills* (Vol. l, pp. 209–39). Hillsdale, N.J.: Erlbaum.

Dansereau, D. F., and Larson, C. O., Spurlin, J. E., Hythecker, V. I., Lambiotte, J., and Ackles, R. 1983. Cooperative learning: impact on acquisition of knowledge and skills. Paper presented at the annual meeting of the American Educational Research Association, Montreal, April 1983.

Dansereau, D. F., Rocklin, T. R., O'Donnell, A. M., Hythecker, V. I., Larson, C. O., Lambiotte, J. G., Young, M. D., and Flowers, L. E. 1984. *Development and evaluation of computer-based learning strategy training modules: final report.* Contract MDA 903-82-E-0169. U.S. Army Research Institute for the Behavioral and Social Sciences, Alexandria, Va.

Davidson, R. G., Kline, S. B., and Snow, C. E. 1986. Definitions and definite noun phrases: Indicators of children's decontextualized language skills. *Journal of Research in Childhood Education,* 1:37–48.

De Avila, E., and Duncan, S. E. 1979. The developmental assessment model. In H. T. Trueba (Ed.), *Futures of bilingual education: interdisciplinary perspectives*. Rowley, Mass.: Newbury House.

Derry, S. J. 1984. Strategy training: an incidental model for CAI. Paper presented at the annual meeting of the American Educational Research Association, New Orleans.

Derry. S. J., and Murphy, D. A. 1986. Designing systems that train learning ability: from theory to practice. *Review of Educational Research* 56:1–39.

Desrochers, A. 1980. *Effects of imagery mnemonic on acquisition and retention of French article-noun pairs*. Ph.D. dissertation, University of Western Ontario, London, Ont.

Ellis, G., and Sinclair, B. 1989. *Learning to learn English*. Cambridge: Cambridge University Press.

Ellis. R. 1986. *Understanding second language acquisition*. Oxford: Oxford University Press.

Ericsson, K. A., and Simon, H. A. 1980. Verbal reports on data. *Psychological Review* 87:215–51.

1987. Verbal reports on thinking. In C. Faerch and G. Kasper (Eds.), *Introspection in second language research* (pp. 24–53). Clevedon, U.K.: Multilingual Matters.

Faerch, C., and Kasper, G. 1984. Two ways of defining communication strategies. *Language Learning* 34:45–63.

1985. Procedural knowledge as a component of foreign language learners' communicative competence. In H. Boete and W. Herrlitz (Eds.), *Kommunikation im (Sprach-) Unterricht* (pp. 169–99). Utrecht: University of Utrecht.

1987. From product to process – introspective methods in second language research. In C. Faerch and G. Kasper (Eds.), *Introspection in second language research* (pp. 5–23). Philadelphia, Pa.: Multilingual Matters.

Feldman, C., and Shen, M. 1971. Some language related cognitive advantages of bilingual five-year-olds. *Journal of Genetic Psychology*, 118:235–44.

Feldman, U., and Stemmer, B. 1987. Thin _ _ _ _ aloud a _ _ retrospective da _ _ in C-te _ _ taking: diffe _ _ _ _ languages – diff _ _ _ _ _ learners – sa _ _ approaches? In C. Faerch and G. Kasper (Eds.), *Introspection in second language research*. Clevedon, U.K.: Multilingual Matters.

Flower, L. S., and Hayes, J. R. (1980). The dynamics of composing: Making plans and juggling constraints. In L. W. Gregg and E. R. Steinberg (Eds.), *Cognitive processes in writing*. Hillsdale, N.J.: Erlbaum.

Gagné, E. D. 1985. *The cognitive psychology of school learning*. Boston, Mass.: Little, Brown.

Gagné, R. M., and Paradise, N. E. 1961. Abilities and learning sets in knowledge acquisition. *Psychological Monographs: General and Applied* 75: Whole No. 518.

Gagné, R. M., and White, R. T. 1978. Memory structures and learning outcomes. *Review of Educational Research* 48:187–22.

Gardner, R. C. 1979. Social psychological aspects of second language acquisition. In H. Giles and R. St. Clair (Eds.), *Language and social psychology*. Oxford: Basil Blackwell.

Garner, R. 1986. Strategies for reading and studying expository text. Manuscript. Silver Spring, Md.: University of Maryland.

1988. Verbal-report data on cognitive and metacognitive strategies. In C. E.

Weinstein, E. T. Goetz, and P. A. Alexander (Eds.), *Learning and study strategies* (pp. 63–76). New York: Academic Press.

Gass, S. 1983. The development of L2 intuitions. *TESOL Quarterly* 17:273–91.

Graham, S., Harris, K. R., and Sawyer, R. 1987. Composition instruction with learning disabled students: self-instructional strategy training. *Focus on Exceptional Children* 20(4):1–11.

Grice, H. P. 1975. Logic and conversation. In P. Cole and J. J. Morgan (Eds.), *Syntax and semantics: Speech Acts* (vol. 3). New York: Academic Press.

Grotjahn, R. 1987. On the methodological basis of introspective methods. In C. Faerch and G. Kasper (Eds.), *Introspection in second language research.* Clevedon, U.K.: Multilingual Matters.

Guild, P. B., and Gerger, S. 1985. *Marching to different drummers.* Alexandria, Va.: Association for Supervision and Curriculum Development.

Hakuta, K. 1986. *Mirror of language.* New York: Basic Books.

Harris, K. R., and Graham, S. 1985. Improving learning disabled students' composition skills: self-control strategy training. *Learning Disability Quarterly* 8:27–36.

In press. Self-instructional strategy training: improving writing skills among educationally handicapped students. *Teaching Exceptional Students.*

Hayes, J. R., and Flower, L. S. 1980. Identifying the organization of writing processes. In L. W. Gregg and E. R. Steinberg (Eds.), *Cognitive processes in writing.* Hillsdale, N.J.: Erlbaum.

Hillocks, G., Jr. 1987. Synthesis of research on teaching writing. *Educational Leadership* 44(8):71–82.

Holec, H. 1987. The learner as manager: managing learning or managing to learn? In A. Wenden and J. Rubin (Eds.), *Learner strategies in language learning* (pp. 145–57). Englewood Cliffs, N.J.: Prentice-Hall.

Hosenfeld, C., Arnold, V., Kirchofer, J., Laciura, J., and Wilson. L. 1981. Second language reading: a curricular sequence for teaching reading strategies. *Foreign Language Annals* 14(5):415–22.

Howard, D. 1985. *Cognitive psychology.* New York: Macmillan.

Ianco-Worrall, A. 1972. Bilingualism and cognitive development. *Child Development* 43;1390–1400.

James, C. J. 1984. Are you listening? The practical components of listening comprehension. *Foreign Language Annals* 17:129–33.

Jones, B. F. 1983. Integrating learning strategies and text research to teach high order thinking skills in schools. Paper presented at the annual meeting of the American Educational Research Association, Montreal.

Jones, B. F., Amiran, M., and Katims, M. 1985. Teaching cognitive strategies and text structures within language arts programs. In J. W. Segal, S. F. Chipman, and R. Glaser (Eds.), *Thinking and learning skills* (Vol. 1, pp. 259–97). Hillsdale, N.J.: Erlbaum.

Jones, B. F., Palincsar, A. S., Ogle, D. S., and Carr, E. G. 1987. *Strategic teaching and learning: cognitive instruction in the content areas.* Alexandria, Va.: Association for Supervision and Curriculum Development.

Joyce, B. R., and Showers, B. 1987. *Student achievement through staff development.* White Plains, N.Y.: Longman.

Kagan, S. 1988. Cooperative group learning: theoretical and practical overview.

Paper presented at the annual convention of Teachers of English to Speakers of Other Languages, Chicago, Ill., March 1988.

Kintsch, W. 1974. *The representation of meaning in memory.* Hillsdale, N.J.: Erlbaum.

Kolb, D. 1984. *Experiential learning: experience as the source of learning and development.* Englewood Cliffs, N.J.: Prentice-Hall.

Krashen, S. D. 1977. The Monitor Model for second language performance. In M. Burt, H. Dulay, and M. Finocchiaro (Eds.), *Viewpoints on English as a second language.* New York: Regents.

1980. The input hypothesis. In J. E. Alatis (Ed.), *Current issues in bilingual education.* Washington, D.C.: Georgetown University Press.

1981. *Second language acquisition and second language learning.* Oxford: Pergamon Press.

1982. *Principles and practices in second language acquisition.* New York: Pergamon Institute for English.

Krashen, S. D., and Terrell, T. 1983. *The natural approach: Language acquisition in the classroom.* Hayward, Calif.: Alemany Press.

Krashen, S. D., Terrell, T. D., Ehrman, M. E., and Herzog, M. 1984. A theoretical base for teaching receptive skills. *Foreign Language Annals* 17:261–75.

Kulhavy, R. W., and Swenson, I. 1975. Imagery instructions and the comprehension of text. *British Journal of Educational Psychology* 45:47–51.

LaBerge, D., and Samuels, S. J. 1974. Toward a theory of automatic information processing in reading. *Cognitive Psychology* 6:293–323.

Lachman, R., Lachman, J. L., and Butterfield, E. C. 1979. *Cognitive psychology and information processing.* Hillsdale, N.J.: Erlbaum.

Lambert, R. D., and Moore, S. J. 1984. Recent research on language skill attrition. *ERIC/CLL News Bulletin* 8(1).

Lambert, W. E. 1981. Bilingualism and language acquisition. In H. Winitz (Ed.), *Native Language and Foreign Language Acquisition. Annals of the New York Academy of Sciences* 379:9–22.

Larkin, J. H., McDermott, J., Simon, D. P., and Simon, H. A. 1980. Expert and novice performance in solving physics problems. *Science* 208:1335–42.

Larsen-Freeman, D. 1985. Overview of theories of language learning and acquisition. In *Issues in English language development.* Rosslyn, Va.: National Clearinghouse for Bilingual Education.

Lehnert, W. G. 1984. [Review of *The architecture of the mind.*] *Contemporary Psychology* 29:854–55.

Levelt, W. J. M. 1978. Skill theory and language teaching. *Studies in Second Language Acquisition* 1:53–70.

Levin, J. R. 1981. The mnemonic '80s: Keywords in the classroom. *Educational Psychologist* 16:65–82.

1982. Pictures as prose-learning devices. In A. Flammer and W. Kintsch (Eds.), *Discourse processing.* New York: North-Holland.

Lindquist, M. M. 1987. Strategic teaching in mathematics. In B. F. Jones, A. S. Palincsar, D. S. Ogle, and E. G. Carr (Eds.), *Strategic teaching and learning: cognitive instruction in the content areas* (pp. 111–34). Alexandria, Va.: Association for Supervision and Curriculum Development.

Littlewood, W. 1979. Communicative performance in language developmental contexts. *International Review of Applied Linguistics* 17:123–28.

Long, M. H. 1985. Input and second language acquisition theory. In S. Gass and C. Madden (Eds.), *Input and second language acquisition* (pp. 377–93). Rowley, Mass.: Newbury House.

MacWhinney, B. 1987. Applying the competition model to bilingualism. *Applied Linguistics* 8:315–27.

MacWhinney, B., and Anderson, J. R. 1986. The acquisition of grammar. In I. Gopnik and M. Gopnik (Eds.), *From models to modules* (pp. 3–25). Norwood, N.J.: Ablex.

Markman, E. M. 1981. Comprehension monitoring. In W. P. Dickson (Ed.), *Children's oral communication skills*. New York: Academic Press.

Matsuyama, U. K. 1983. Can story grammar speak Japanese? *The Reading Teacher* 36:666–69.

Mayer, R. E. 1988. Learning strategies: an overview. In C. E. Weinstein, E. T. Goetz, and P. A. Alexander (Eds.), *Learning and study strategies* (pp. 11–22). New York: Academic Press.

McCarthy, B. 1987. The 4MAT system: teaching to learning styles with right/left mode techniques. Barrington, Ill.: Excel.

McClelland, J. L., and Rumelhart, D. E. 1986. *Parallel distributed processing* (Vol. 2). Cambridge, Mass.: MIT Press.

McCombs, B. L. 1988. Motivational skills training: combining metacognitive, cognitive, and affective learning strategies. In C. E. Weinstein, E. T. Goetz, and P. A. Alexander (Eds.), *Learning and study strategies* (pp. 141–69). New York: Academic Press.

McLaughlin, B. 1984. *Second-language acquisition in childhood*. Vol. 1, *Preschool children*. Hillsdale, N.J.: Erlbaum.

1987a. *Theories of second-language learning*. London: Edward Arnold.

1987b. Reading in a second language: studies with adult and child learners. In S. R. Goldman and H. T. Trueba (Eds.), *Becoming literate in English as a second language* (pp. 57–70). Norwood, N.J.: Ablex.

1987c. Restructuring. Paper presented at the Second Language Research Forum, Honolulu, Hawaii, March 1987.

1988. Restructuring. Paper presented at the Second Language Research Forum, Honolulu, Hawaii, March 1988.

McLaughlin, B., and Nayak, N. In press. Processing a new language: does knowing make a difference? In H. W. Dechert (Ed.), *Interlingual processes*. Tübingen: Narr.

McLaughlin, B., Rossman, T., and McLeod, B. 1983. Second language learning: an information processing perspective. *Language Learning* 33:135–58.

McLeod, B., and McLaughlin, B. 1986. Restructuring or automatization? Reading in a second language. *Language Learning*, 36:109–26.

Messick, S. 1984. The psychology of education measurement. *Journal of Educational Measurement* 21:215–37.

Moulden, H. 1978. Extending self-directed learning in an engineering college. Mélanges Pedagogiques, CRAPEL 81–102.

1980. Extending self-directed learning in an engineering college. Experiment 2. Mélanges Pedagogiques, CRAPEL 83–116.

Murphy, D. A., and Derry, S. J. 1984. Description of an introductory learning strategies course for the Job Skills Education Program. Paper presented at the annual meeting of the American Educational Research Association, New Orleans.

Nagle, S. J., and Sanders, S. L. 1986. Comprehension theory and second language pedagogy. *TESOL Quarterly* 20:9–26.

Naiman, N., Frohlich, M., Stern, H. H., and Todesco, A. 1978. *The good language learner.* Toronto: Ontario Institute for Studies in Education.

Newell, A., and Simon, H. 1972. *Human problem solving.* Englewood Cliffs, N.J.: Prentice-Hall.

Nisbet, J., and Shucksmith, J. 1986. *Learning strategies.* Boston: Routledge & Kegan Paul.

Ogle, D. S. 1987. K-W-L group instruction strategy. In A. S. Palincsar, D. S. Ogle, B. F. Jones, and E. G. Carr (Eds.), *Teaching reading as thinking.* Alexandria, Va.: Association for Supervision and Curriculum Development.

1988. Strategic instructional planning. Paper presented at the annual meeting of the American Educational Research Association, New Orleans, La., April 1988.

Oller, J. W., Jr. 1979. *Language tests at school.* London: Longman.

O'Malley, J. M. 1988. The cognitive academic language learning approach (CALLA). *Journal of Multilingual and Multicultural Development* 9(1&2):43–60.

O'Malley, J. M., and Chamot, A. U. 1988. How to teach learning strategies. In A. U. Chamot, J. M. O'Malley, and L. Küpper (Eds.), *The cognitive academic language learning approach (CALLA) Training Manual* (pp. 121–22). Arlington, Va.: Second Language Learning.

O'Malley, J. M., Chamot, A. U., and Küpper, L. 1989. Listening comprehension strategies in second language acquisition. *Applied Linguistics* 10(4).

O'Malley, J. M., Chamot, A. U., Stewner-Manzanares, G., Küpper, L., and Russo, R. 1985a. Learning strategies used by beginning and intermediate ESL students. *Language Learning* 35:21–46.

O'Malley, J. M., Chamot, A. U., Stewner-Manzanares, G., Russo, R., and Küpper, L. 1985b. Learning strategy applications with students of English as a second language. *TESOL Quarterly* 19:285–96.

O'Malley, J. M., Chamot, A. U., and Walker, C. 1987. Some applications of cognitive theory to second language acquisition. *Studies in Second Language Acquisition* 9:287–306.

O'Neil, H. F., Jr. (Ed.) 1978. *Learning strategies.* San Francisco, Calif.: Academic Press.

Oxford, R. L. 1982. Research on language loss: a review with implications for foreign language teaching. *Modern Language Journal* 66:160–69.

1985. A new taxonomy for second language learning strategies. Washington, D.C.: ERIC Clearinghouse on Languages and Linguistics.

1986. Development of the strategy inventory for language learning. Manuscript. Washington, D.C.: Center for Applied Linguistics.

Oxford, R. L., and Ehrman, M. 1987. Effects of sex differences, career choice, and psychological type on adults' language learning strategies. Manuscript. Washington, D.C.: Center for Applied Linguistics.

Oxford, R. L., Nyikos, M., and Crookall, D. 1987. Learning strategies of university foreign language students: A large-scale, factor analytic study. Paper presented at the annual convention of Teachers of English to Speakers of Other Languages, Miami, Fla., April 1987.

Oxford, R. L., Nyikos, M., and Ehrman, M. 1988. Vive la différence? Reflections on sex differences in use of language learning strategies. *Foreign Language Annals* 21(4):321–29.

Padron, Y. N., and Waxman, H. C. 1988. The effects of ESL students' perceptions of their cognitive strategies on reading achievement. *TESOL Quarterly* 22:146–50.

Paivio, A., and Desrochers, A. 1979. Effects of an imagery mnemonic on second language recall and comprehension. *Canadian Journal of Psychology* 73:780–95.

Palincsar, A. S., and Brown, A. L. 1984. Reciprocal teaching of comprehension-fostering and comprehension-monitoring activities. *Cognition and Instruction* 1:117–75.

1986. Interactive teaching to promote independent learning from text. *The Reading Teacher* 39(8):771–77.

Paris, S. G. 1988a. Fusing skill and will: the integration of cognitive and motivational psychology. Paper presented at the annual meeting of the American Educational Research Association, New Orleans, La., April 1988.

1988b. Models and metaphors of learning strategies. In C. E. Weinstein, E. T. Goetz, and P. A. Alexander (Eds.), *Learning and study strategies* (pp. 299–321). New York: Academic Press.

Pearson, P. D. 1985. Changing the face of reading comprehension instruction. *The Reading Teacher* 38:724–38.

Pearson, P. D., Barr, R., Kamil, M. L., and Mosenthal, P. (Eds.) 1984. *Handbook of reading research*. New York: Longman.

Pearson, P. D., and Dole, J. A. 1987. Explicit comprehension instruction: a review of research and a new conceptualization of learning. *Elementary School Journal* 88(2):151–65.

Perfetti, C. A., and Lesgold, A. M. 1979. Coding and comprehension in skilled reading and implications for reading instruction. In L. B. Resnick and P. A. Weaver (Eds.), *Theory and practice of early reading* (Vol. 1, pp. 57–84). Hillsdale, N.J.: Erlbaum.

Perkins, D. N. 1989. Teaching meta-cognitive strategies. Paper presented at the annual meetings of the American Educational Research Association, San Francisco, Calif., March 1989.

Perkins, D. N., and Salomon, G. 1989. Are cognitive skills context-bound? *Educational Researcher* 18:16–25.

Perkins, K., and Linnville, S. E. 1988. A construct definition study of a standardized ESL vocabulary test. *Language Testing* 4:125–141.

Politzer, R. L., and McGroarty, M. 1985. An exploratory study of learning behaviors and their relationship to gains in linguistic and communicative competence. *TESOL Quarterly* 19:103–23.

Posner, M. I., and Snyder, C. R. R. 1975. Attention and cognitive control. In R. L. Soslo (Ed.), *Information processing and cognition*. Hillsdale, N.J.: Erlbaum.

Pressley, M. 1988. Overview of cognitive and metacognitive theories as they relate to special education populations and findings of pertinent intervention research. Paper presented at Publishers' Workshop, Washington, D.C., June 1988. (Available from: Information Center for Special Education Media and Materials, LINC Resources, Inc., Columbus, Ohio)

Pressley, M., Johnson, C. J., Symons, S., McGoldrick, J. A., and Kurita, J. A.

In press. Strategies that improve children's memory and comprehension of what is read. *Elementary School Journal.*

Pressley, M., Levin, J. R., and Delaney, J. D. 1982. The mnemonic keyword method. *Review of Educational Research* 52:61–91.

Pressley, M., Levin, J. R., and Ghatala, E. S. 1984. Memory strategy monitoring in adults and children. *Journal of Verbal Learning and Verbal Behavior* 23:270–88.

Pressley, M., Levin, J. R., Nakamura, G. V., Hope, D. J., Bisbo, J. G., and Toye, A. R. 1980. The keyword method of foreign vocabulary learning: an investigation of its generalizability. *Journal of Applied Psychology* 65:635–42.

Pressley, M., Samuel, J., Hershey, M. M., Bishop, S. L., and Dickinson, D. 1981. Use of mnemonic techniques to teach young children foreign language vocabulary. *Contemporary Educational Psychology* 6:110–16.

Rabinowitz, M., and Chi, M. T. 1987. An interactive model of strategic processing. In S. J. Ceci (Ed.), *Handbook of cognitive, social, and neuropsychological aspects of learning disabilities* (pp. 83–102). Hillsdale, N.J.: Erlbaum.

Reder, L. M. 1980. The role of elaboration in the comprehension and retention of prose: A critical review. *Review of Educational Research* 50:5–53.

Richards, J. C. 1983. Listening comprehension: approach, design, procedure. *TESOL Quarterly* 17:219–39.

Rigney, J. W. 1978. Learning strategies: A theoretical perspective. In H. F. O'Neill (Ed.), *Learning strategies.* New York: Academic Press.

Romberg, T. A., and Carpenter, T. P. 1986. Research on teaching and learning mathematics: two disciplines of scientific inquiry. In M. C. Wittrock (Ed.), *Handbook of research on teaching* (pp. 850–73). New York: Macmillan.

Rubin, J. 1975. What the "good language learner" can teach us. *TESOL Quarterly* 9:41–51.

1981. Study of cognitive processes in second language learning. *Applied Linguistics* 11:117–31.

Rubin, J., and Thompson, I. 1982. *How to be a more successful language learner.* Boston, Mass.: Heinle & Heinle.

Rumelhart, D. E., McClelland, J. L. 1986. *Parallel distributed processing* (Vol. 1). Cambridge, Mass.: MIT Press.

Rumelhart, D. E., and Norman, D. A. 1978. Accretion, tuning, and restructuring: three modes of learning. In J. Cotton and R. Klatzky (Eds.), *Semantic factors in cognition* (pp. 37–53). Hillsdale, N.J.: Erlbaum.

Ryan, E. B. 1975. Metalinguistic development and bilingualism. Paper presented at the Summer Conference on Language Learning, Queens College, Flushing, N.Y. (ED 132842).

Samuels, S. J., and Kamil, M. L. 1984. Models of the reading process. In P. D. Pearson, R. Barr, M. L. Kamil, and P. Mosenthal (Eds.), *Handbook of reading research.* New York: Longman.

Saville-Troike, M. 1984. What really matters in second language learning for academic achievement? *TESOL Quarterly* 18:199–219.

Scardamalia, M., and Bereiter, C. 1986. Research on written composition. In M. C. Wittrock (Ed.), *Handbook of research on teaching.* 3rd ed. New York: Macmillan.

Schank, R. C. 1982. *Dynamic memory.* New York: Cambridge University Press.

Schank, R. C., and Abelson, R. 1977. *Scripts, plans, goals, and understanding.* Hillsdale, N.J.: Erlbaum.

Schneider, W., and Shiffrin, R. M. 1977. Controlled and automatic processing, I: Detection, search, and attention. *Psychological Review* 84:1–64.

Schumann, J. J. 1984. Acculturation model: the evidence. In *Current approaches to second language acquisition.* Symposium conducted at the University of Wisconsin-Milwaukee.

Segal, J. W., Chipman, S. F., and Glaser, R. 1985. *Thinking and learning skills: relating instruction to research* (Vol. 1). Hillsdale, N.J.: Erlbaum.

Seliger, H. W. 1983. The language learner as linguist: of metaphors and realities. *Applied Linguistics* 4:179–91.

Selinker. L. 1972. Interlanguage. *International Review of Applied Linguistics* 10:209–31.

Selinker. L., and Lamendella, J. 1976. Two perspectives on fossilization in interlanguage learning. *Interlanguage Studies Bulletin* 3:144–91.

Shiffrin, R. M., and Schneider, W. 1977. Controlled and automatic human information processing, II: Perceptual learning, automatic attending, and a general theory. *Psychological Review* 84:127–90.

1984. Automatic and controlled processing revisited. *Psychological Review* 91:269–76.

Showers, B., Joyce, B., and Bennett, B. 1987. Synthesis of research on staff development: a framework for future study and a state-of-the-art analysis. *Educational Leadership* 45(3):77–87.

Shuell, T. J. 1986. Cognitive conceptions of learning. *Review of Educational Research* 56:411–36.

Slavin, R. E. 1980. Cooperative learning. *Review of Educational Research* 50:315–42.

Spolsky, B. 1985. Formulating a theory of second language learning. *Studies in Second Language Acquisition* 7:269–88.

1988. Bridging the gap: a general theory of second language learning. *TESOL Quarterly* 22:377–96.

Stern, H. H. 1975. What can we learn from the good language learner? *Canadian Modern Language Review* 31:304–18.

Sternberg, R. J. 1985. *Beyond IQ: a triarchic theory of human intelligence.* Cambridge: Cambridge University Press.

Sternberg, R. J., Powell, J. S., and Kaye, D. B. 1982. Teaching vocabulary skills: a contextual approach. In A. C. Wilkinson (Ed.), *Classroom computers and cognitive science.* New York: Academic Press.

Tait, K., Hartley, J. R., and Anderson, R. C. 1973. Feedback procedures in computer-assisted arithmetic instruction. *British Journal of Educational Psychology* 13:161–71.

Tarone, E. 1981. Some thoughts on the notion of communication strategy. *TESOL Quarterly* 15:285–95.

Thibadeau, R., Just, M. A., and Carpenter, P. 1982. A model of the time course and content of reading. *Cognitive Science* 6:167–203.

Thompson, I. 1987. Memory in language learning. In A. Wenden and J. Rubin (Eds.), *Learner strategies in language learning* (pp. 43–56). Englewood Cliffs, N.J.: Prentice-Hall.

Tikunoff, W. 1985. *Applying significant bilingual instructional features in the classroom*. Rosslyn, Va.: National Clearinghouse for Bilingual Education.

Tulving, E. 1983. *Elements of episodic memory*. New York: Oxford University Press.

Tunmer, W. E., Pratt, C., and Herriman, M. L. 1984. *Metalinguistic awareness in children: theory, research, and implications*. New York: Springer-Verlag.

Tyler, R. W. 1934. *Constructing achievement tests*. Columbus: Ohio State University. Cited in Gage, N. L., and Berliner, D. C. 1984. *Educational psychology*. 3rd ed. Boston: Houghton Mifflin.

Ventriglia, L. 1982. *Conversations with Miguel and Maria: How children learn a second language*. Rowley, Mass.: Addison-Wesley.

Vollmer, H. J., and Sang, F. 1983. Competing hypotheses about second language ability: a plea for caution. In J. W. Oller, Jr. (Ed.), *Issues in language testing and research* (pp. 29–79). Rowley, Mass.: Newbury House.

Weinstein, C. E. 1978. Elaboration skills as a learning strategy. In H. F. O'Neill, Jr. (Ed.), *Learning strategies*. New York: Academic Press.

1982. Learning strategies: the metacurriculum in community college teaching. *Journal of Developmental and Remedial Education* 5(2):6–7, 10.

Weinstein, C. E., Butterfield, P. J., Schmidt, C. A., and Poythress, M. n.d. An experimental program for remediating learning strategies deficits in academically underprepared students. Report to Army Research Institute for Behavioral and Social Sciences.

Weinstein, C. E., and Mayer, R. E. 1986. The teaching of learning strategies. In M. C. Wittrock (Ed.), *Handbook of research on teaching* (pp. 315–27). 3rd ed. New York: Macmillan.

Weinstein, C. E., Schulte, A. C., and Cascallar, E. C. 1983. The Learning and Study Strategies Inventory (LASSI): initial design and development. Manuscript. Austin: University of Texas.

Weinstein, C. E., and Underwood, V. L. 1985. Learning strategies: the *how* of learning. In J. Segal, S. Chipman, and R. Glaser (Eds.), *Relating instruction to research*. Hillsdale, N.J.: Erlbaum.

Weltens, B. 1987. The attrition of foreign-language skills: A literature review. *Applied Linguistics* 8:22–38.

Wenden. A. 1983. Literature review: the process of intervention. *Language Learning* 33:103–21.

1987a. Metacognition: an expanded view on the cognitive abilities of L2 learners. *Language Learning* 37:573–97.

1987b. Incorporating learner training in the classroom. In A. Wenden and J. Rubin (Eds.), *Learner strategies in language learning* (pp. 159–68). Englewood Cliffs, N.J.: Prentice-Hall.

White, R. T., and Tisher, R. D. 1986. Research on natural sciences. In M. C. Wittrock (Ed.), *Handbook of research on teaching* (pp. 850–73). New York: Macmillan.

Wilson, J. E. 1988. Implications of learning strategy research and training: what it has to say to the practitioner. In C. E. Weinstein, E. T. Goetz, and P. A. Alexander (Eds.), *Learning and study strategies* (pp. 323–31). New York: Academic Press.

Winitz, H. 1978. Comprehension and language learning. In C. H. Blatchford and J. Schachter (Eds.), *On TESOL '78: EFL Policies, Programs, Practices* (pp. 49–56). Washington, D.C.: Teachers of English to Speakers of Other Languages.

Winograd, P., and Hare, V. C. 1988. Direct instruction of reading comprehension strategies: the nature of teacher explanation. In C. E. Weinstein, E. T. Goetz, and P. A. Alexander (Eds.), *Learning and study strategies* (pp. 121–39). New York: Academic Press.

Wipf, J. A. 1984. Strategies for teaching second language listening comprehension. *Foreign Language Annals* 17:345–48.

Wittrock, M. C. 1974. Learning as a generative process. *Educational Psychologist* 11:87–95.

1985. Cognitive processes in the learning and teaching of science. Paper presented at the annual meeting of the American Educational Research Association, Chicago, Ill., April 1985.

Wittrock, M. C., Marks, C. B., and Doctorow, M. J. 1975. Reading as a generative process. *Journal of Educational Psychology* 67:484–89.

Wong Fillmore, L. 1985. Second language learning in children: a proposed model. In *Issues in English language development*. Rosslyn, Va.: National Clearinghouse for Bilingual Education.

Wong Fillmore, L., and Swain, M. 1984. Child second language development: views from the field on theory and research. Paper presented at the TESOL convention, Houston, Texas.

Zimmerman, B. J., and Pons, M. M. 1986. Development of a structured interview for assessing student use of self-regulated learning strategies. *American Educational Research Journal* 23:614–28.

Author Index

Abelson, R., 39, 98
Alexander, P. A., 218
Alvermann, D., 190
Amiran, M., 157
Anderson, C. W., 190
Anderson, J. R., 17–18, 30, 32, 33–
  35, 37–44, 47–51, 53, 54–55,
  61–62, 68, 70–71, 76, 77–79,
  80, 82, 98, 136, 147, 148, 149,
  162–63, 192, 217, 218, 219
Anderson, R. C., 31, 34, 63
Aphek, E., 7, 101, 107, 112, 155,
  166
Armbruster, B. B., 152–54, 169
Asher, J. J., 129
Atkinson, R. C., 7, 49, 106, 115,
  163, 166

Baker, L., 153, 169
Barnett, M. A., 153
Beach, R., 190
Bennett, B., 155–56
Bereiter, C., 38, 39, 40, 151
Bialystok, E., 10, 17, 36–37, 59–63,
  66, 71, 80, 107–8, 109, 112,
  113, 148
Black, J. B., 217
Bobrow, D. G., 25
Boyle, C. F., 219
Brandt, R., 218
Brown, A. L., 7–8, 12, 36, 44, 54,
  91, 95, 97, 99, 101, 104–6,
  118, 139, 144, 153, 154, 169
Brown, H. D., 129
Brown, J. S., 18
Burton, R., 18
Byrnes, H., 33–34, 35, 130

Calfee, R., 54
Call, M. E., 34, 130
Campione, J. C., 7–8, 12, 44, 91,
  95, 97, 99, 104–6, 139, 144,
  152
Canale, M., 9, 73–75
Carpenter, P., 24–25
Carpenter, T. P., 164, 197
Carroll, J. B., 162–63
Cascallar, E. C., 93, 225
Cazden, C. B., 71
Chamot, A. U., 7, 15, 19, 31, 44,
  68, 70–71, 80, 99, 115, 120,
  123, 128, 133, 139, 152, 155,
  157–58, 160, 162, 163, 165,
  167–68, 169, 171, 175–76,
  182–83, 190–204, 207, 210–12,
  213
Chase, W. G., 99
Chesterfield, K. B., 164
Chesterfield, R., 164
Chi, M. T. H., 2, 18, 34, 52, 85, 148
Chipman, S. F., 7–8
Chomsky, N., 24, 98
Clark, E., 34, 41
Clark, H., 34, 41
Cohen, A. D., 7, 96–97, 101, 107,
  112, 155, 166
Collier, V. P., 192
Craik, F. I. M., 82
Crookall, D., 106–7
Cummins, J., 8–9, 17, 69, 72–73,
  129, 192, 195

Dansereau, D. F., 8, 100, 103, 152–
  53, 157
Davidson, R. G., 195
De Avila, E., 71

Delaney, J. D., 166
Derry, S. J., 53–54, 151, 152–5, 157, 167, 227
Desrochers, A., 166
Doctorow, M. J., 99
Dole, J. A., 151, 157, 184–85
Drum, P., 54
Duncan, S. E., 71

Ehrman, M. E., 106, 164
Ellis, G., 207–10
Ellis, R., 33, 41–42
Ericsson, K. A., 87, 91–92, 96, 97, 129

Faerch, C., 32–33, 43–44, 55, 58–59, 62, 68, 80, 82, 85–86, 90, 148
Feldman, C., 71
Feldman, U., 90
Ferrara, R. A., 95
Flower, L. S., 38, 40–41
Frohlich, M., 3, 5, 6–7, 14, 45, 89, 95, 98, 101, 109

Gagné, E. D., 19, 30–31, 32–36, 39–41, 50, 79, 87, 148–49, 164, 168, 218
Gagné, R. M., 18, 20
Gardner, R. C., 17
Garner, R., 2, 17, 129
Gass, S., 121
Gerger, S., 163
Ghatala, E. S., 164
Glaser, R., 8, 148
Graham, S., 151, 157, 170
Grice, H. P., 40
Grotjahn, R., 90, 94
Guild, P. B., 163

Hare, V. C., 154
Harris, K. R., 151, 157, 170
Hartley, J. R., 31
Hayes, J. R., 38, 40–41
Herriman, M. L., 71
Hillocks, G., 151
Holec, H., 155, 166–67
Hosenfeld, C., 96, 155, 157, 159, 166, 182, 207
Howard, D., 34, 36–37, 217

Ianco-Worrall, A., 71
Impink-Hernandez, M. V., 123, 139

James, C. J., 129
Jones, B. F., 152–53, 156, 157–58, 160–61, 187–90, 207, 213, 227
Joyce, B., 155–56, 184
Judy, J. E., 218
Just, M. A., 24–25

Kagan, S., 169
Kamil, M. L., 65
Kasper, G., 32–33, 43–44, 55, 58–59, 62, 68, 80, 82, 85–86, 90, 148
Katims, M., 157
Kaye, D. B., 51
Kellerman, E., 17
Kintsch, W., 20
Kline, S. B., 195
Krashen, S. D., 10, 58, 78, 79, 80–81, 115, 129
Kulhavy, R. W., 50
Küpper, L., 7, 120, 128, 139, 197

LaBerge, D., 27, 98
Lachman, J. L., 17, 47
Lachman, R., 17, 47
Lambert, R. D., 82
Lambert, W. E., 71
Lamendella, J., 58
Larkin, J. H., 99
Larsen-Freeman, D., 217, 219
Lehnert, W. G., 217
Lesgold, A. M., 31
Levelt, W. J. M., 66–67
Levin, J. R., 7, 50, 106, 163, 164, 166
Lindquist, M. M., 190
Linnville, S. E., 221
Littlewood, W., 41–42
Long, M. H., 129

MacWhinney, B., 217–18
Markman, E. M., 7, 48
Marks, C. B., 99
Matsuyama, U. K., 70
Mayer, R. E., 2, 17–18, 43–44, 49, 154
McCarthy, B., 164

McClelland, J. L., 55, 218
McCombs, B. L., 219
McGroarty, M., 93, 95, 108–09,
  113, 114
McLaughlin, B., 11, 17, 19, 57–58,
  63–69, 72, 79, 80, 89, 110,
  146, 148, 150, 192, 225
McLeod, B., 11, 17, 58, 63, 66
Messick, S., 221
Moore, S. J., 82
Moulden, H., 167
Murphy, D. A., 53–54, 151–52,
  154–55, 157, 167, 227

Nagle, S. J., 17
Naiman, N., 3, 5–7, 14, 45, 89, 95,
  98, 101, 109
Nayak, N., 146
Newell, A., 25
Nisbet, J., 44, 48–49, 53
Norman, D. A., 29–30, 66, 72, 79,
  98, 145, 221
Nyikos, M., 106–7, 164

Ogle, D. S., 152, 156–58, 160–61,
  169, 187–90, 207, 213, 227
Oller, J. W., 148
O'Malley, J. M., 7, 15, 44, 68, 70,
  71, 80, 99, 115, 120, 123, 128,
  152, 155, 157–58, 160, 162,
  165, 167–68, 169, 171, 182–83,
  221, 227
O'Neil, H. F., Jr., 98
Oxford, R. L., 7, 82, 93, 103–4,
  106–7, 114, 164

Padron, Y. N., 109–10, 114, 164
Palincsar, A. S., 8, 36, 54, 99, 101,
  118, 152–54, 156–58, 160–61,
  169, 187–90, 207, 213, 227
Paradise, N. E., 18
Paris, S. G., 161, 184–85, 219, 222
Pearson, P. D., 34, 62–63, 151, 157,
  184–85
Perfetti, C. A., 31
Perkins, D. N., 53, 215, 218
Perkins, K., 221
Politzer, R. L., 93, 95, 108–9, 113–
  14
Pons, M. M., 93, 95, 110–12, 114

Posner, M. I., 27
Powell, J. S., 51
Pratt, C., 71
Pressley, M., 7, 49, 115, 163–64,
  166, 197

Rabinowitz, M., 2, 18, 29, 34, 52,
  62, 85, 145
Raugh, M. R., 7, 49, 106, 115, 163,
  166
Reder, L. M., 36
Rees, E., 148
Reiser, B. J., 219
Richards, J. C., 34–36, 129–30
Rigney, J. W., 99
Romberg, T. A., 197
Rossman, T., 11, 17, 63
Rubin, J., 2–4, 7, 14, 45, 94, 98,
  100–1, 103, 109, 204–7
Rumelhart, D. E., 29–30, 55, 66, 72,
  79, 98, 145, 218, 221
Russo, R., 7, 120
Ryan, E. B., 36–37, 59–63, 66, 71,
  80, 121, 148

Salomon, G., 218
Samuels, S. J., 27, 65, 98
Sanders, S. L., 17
Sang, F., 37–38
Saville-Troike, M., 12
Sawyer, R., 157
Scardamalia, M., 38–40, 151
Schank, R. C., 39, 55, 98
Schneider, W., 27, 80
Schulte, A. C., 93
Schumann, J. J., 17
Segal, J. W., 7–8
Seliger, H. W., 96–97
Selinker, L., 58, 78, 79, 147
Shen, M., 71
Shiffrin, R. M., 27, 80
Showers, B., 155–56, 184
Shucksmith, J., 44, 48–49, 53
Shuell, T. J., 1, 17
Simon, D. P., 99
Simon, H. A., 25, 87, 91–92, 96–97,
  99, 129
Sinclair, B., 207–10
Slavin, R., 8, 169
Snow, C. E., 195

Snyder, C. R. R., 27
Spolsky, B., 11–12, 16, 17, 150
Stemmer, B., 90
Stern, H. H., 2–3, 5–7, 14, 45, 89, 95, 98, 101, 109
Sternberg, R. J., 51, 218
Stewner-Manzanares, G., 7, 19, 31, 120
Swain, M., 9–11, 16–17, 73–75
Swenson, I., 50

Tait, K., 31
Tarone, E., 10, 43–44
Terrell, T. D., 58, 129
Thibadeau, R., 24–25
Thompson, I., 165–66, 204–7
Tikunoff, W., 9
Tisher, R. D., 197
Tulving, E., 20, 82
Tunmer, W. E., 71
Tyler, R. W., 83

Underwood, V. L., 153, 155, 157, 159, 168, 207

Ventriglia, L., 78
Vollmer, H. J., 37–38

Walker, C., 68
Waxman, H. C., 109–10, 114, 164
Weinstein, C. E., 17–18, 43–44, 49, 93, 153–55, 157, 159, 164, 168, 197, 207
Weltens, B., 82–83
Wenden, A., 14, 88, 93, 101–3, 152, 154, 160–62, 166
White, R. T., 20, 197
Wilson, J. E., 155
Wilson, L., 155, 157, 159, 166, 182, 207
Winitz, H., 129
Winograd, P., 154
Wipf, J. A., 129
Wittrock, M. C., 99, 197
Wong Fillmore, L., 10–11, 16–17

Zimmerman, B. J., 93, 95, 110–12, 114

Subject Index

Page numbers in italics indicate material in tables or figures.

academic language development, CALLA and, 194–204
accretion, 29, 30, 80
affective strategies, 8, 45, *46*, 118, 121, *126*, 127, *139*, 197, *199*, 206
American Language Program, 161
artificial intelligence, 24
associations, 21, 163, 167
  learning and linking of, 7
  learning vocabulary lists and, 107, 166
attentional processes, 48
attrition and retention of language, 81–83
audiolingual instruction approach, 31
  see also instruction
aural texts, language comprehension and, 33–34
automatic processing (skill acquisition), 27, 78–79, 80

bottom-up processing, 36, 47, 48

classification scheme; *see* learning strategy classification scheme
classroom instruction
  study of English as second language and, 170–75
  see also instruction
classroom observation, 101, 117, 124
Cognitive Academic Language Learning Approach (CALLA), 157, 210, 212, 213
second language context and instructional model and, 190–204
cognitive strategies, 10–11, 44–45, 49–52, 118, *119–120*, *126*, 127, *138–39*, 171–72, 197, 206, 208
cognitive theory
  developments in, 214–20
  fundamental principles of, 1
  learning strategies and, 1–2, 7–8
  second language acquisition and, 8–13, 18–19, 57–68, 83–84
cognitive theory of learning
  adult language learning materials and, 205, 206, 208
  CALLA and, 193, 194
  competence in performance of complex cognitive skills and, 18–19
  instructional approaches and, 30–33
  language as cognitive skill and, 19–42
  language comprehension and, 33–37
  language production and, 37–42
  learning by formal rules and, 27–28
  learning strategies as cognitive skills and, 42–54
  learning strategies and information acquisition and, 17–18
  learning strategy model and, 195, 197
  learning strategy studies and, 115, 121, 125, 134, 144–45, 153, 162, 171–72, *173*, 183
  linguistic theories and, 16–17
  memory and, 18, 20–25

cognitive theory of learning (*cont.*)
  new information and encoding process and, 17–18
  second language acquisition and, 18–19
  skill acquisition stages and, 25–27
  theoretical developments and, 214–20
  unitary process concept and, 28–30
communication
  language production and, 39
  learning strategies and strategies for, 43–44
  procedural knowledge and competence in, 73–77
  teacher-student, 32
communicative competence, 73, 127
complex cognitive skill, 1, 16, 18–19, 24, 42–43, 54, 63, 214
comprehensible input, 129
Computer-Assisted Cooperative Learning (CACL) Program, 152
computer use, 170
conscious awareness of learning, 79–81
conscious processing, 129
construction (language production stage), 38–40
content-specific concepts and skills (teaching), 212
controlled processing (skill acquisition), 27, 71, 80
conversation
  general model of, 76
  IF-THEN production system example and, 67, 74–75, 76, 77
cooperation (student), 179, 181, 200
  learning strategy, 169
cooperative learning, 161, 169
CRAPEL (Centre de Recherches et d'Applications Pédagogiques en Langues), 166–67
cultural background, 164–65
curriculum, CALLA and, 194
curriculum development (instruction), 157–60

data collection
  classification scheme (Rubin) and, 3

elicitation procedures and, 92–94
  individual versus group, 95
  informant training and, 91–92
  interrater reliability, 117, 125, 131, 135–36, 174
  language task and, 88–90
  learning strategy studies and, 116–17, 128, 131, 141, 144
  multiple approaches to, 95–96
  objective of, 86–88
  research and, 221
  self-report data and, 96–97, 112
  students and, 223
  temporal relationship and, 90–91
declarative knowledge, 20–24, 36, 58–62, 68–73
  transfer of, 70–71
  versus procedural knowledge, 13, 24, 58–62, 73, 87, 145, 214–15
decoding, 34
deduction, 140, 164, 178
deduction strategies, 206
development (literature on), 105, 106
  learning and, 188
differentiation of language input, 35
direct explanation (teacher demonstration), 161
discourse competence, 74, 75
discourse markers, 76
discourse knowledge, 38–39

elaboration, 35, 51, 139, 142, 167–69, 178–79, 183, 192, 206
English proficiency levels, ESL student study and, 116, 130
ESL instruction model, 190–204
ESL students (English as a second language)
  attitude and motivation and, 161–62
  learning strategy study and, 14–23, 170–75, 209, 210
  listening strategies and, 128–33
  reading comprehension and reading errors and, 66
  see also learners; students
execution (language production stage), 38, 40

Foreign Language Course Development Study, 175–76
foreign language students, 133–44
see also learners; students
formal practicing, 10, 108, 115
formal rules (learning by), 27–28
see also rules
French, 154, 157, 166
functional communication, 116, 122, 124
see also operational communication
functional practicing, 10, 107, 108, 115

gender, 106, 112, 164
gradient condition (for learning to occur), 12
grammar, 26, 140
communicative competence and, 75
technique for second language learning and, 6
grammatical aptitude, 162–63
grouping, 163–64

Hebrew, 166
hypothesis formation, 33
hypothesis testing, 33

IF-THEN production system, 67, 74–75, 76, 77, 145, 146, 214
imagery, 139
images, theoretical description of, 49–50
imitation, learning through, 32–33
Individual Learning Skills program, 168
induction strategies, 206
inductive language learning ability, 163
inferencing, 10, 50–51, 108, 139, 140, 164, 178, 182, 206
information processing, 2, 11, 19
information transfer, 68–69
instruction, 84
cognitive theory of learning and language as cognitive skill and, 30–33
complex skills and, 79

direct versus embedded, 153–54, 184
English as second language and, 170–75
first language context and, 167–70
foreign language instructors and, 175–84
language proficiency and, 160–65
materials and curriculum development and, 157–60, 184
procedural knowledge and, 73
second language context and, 165–67
separate versus integrated, 152–53
teacher training and, 154–57
theoretical development and, 215
see also learning strategies; learning strategy studies
instructional models; *see* models (teaching)
interlanguage concept, 58–59, 67, 78

knowledge
analyzed and linguistic, 59–63
bilingual and academic, 69
cognition and declarative, 84
cognition and procedural, 47
cognitive skill and linguistic, 36–37
cognitive theory and factual, 18, 19
communicative competence and procedural, 73–77
data collection and declarative versus procedural, 87
elaboration and, 51
instruction and declarative, 151
language aptitude and, 163
language production and, 38–40
language proficiency and, 191–92
language retention and attrition and, 82–83
learning by formal rules and, 27–28
learning and prior, 187
learning strategy studies and, 145–46
memory and declarative, 20–24
memory and procedural, 24
metacognitive, 105, 106

knowledge (*cont.*)
  prior linguistic, 33
  proceduralization of, 77
  propositions and declarative, 36
  research premise and declarative,
    85
  second language acquisition and
    declarative and procedural, 58–
    59
  theoretical developments and,
    214–15
  transfer of, 70–72, 168, 192
  unitary process for learning con-
    cept and, 29
knowledge compilation (skill acquisition), 26–27
K-W-L (Know-Want-Learned) program, 169–70

language
  as cognitive skill, 19–42
  cognitive theory and, 1
  memory and, 20–25
  second language acquisition and,
    19–20
language aptitude, 162–63
language attrition, 81–83
language competence, 8, 9–10
language comprehension
  CALLA and, 192
  cognitive theory of learning and,
    33–37, 55
  second language acquisition and, 1
language production, 78
  CALLA and, 192, 193
  cognitive theory of learning and,
    37–42, 55
language proficiency, 8–9, 160–65,
  191
language retention, 81–83, 84, 107
  see also language attrition
language transfer, 148, 192
learners
  CALLA and, 196
  characteristics of effective, 3
  conceptual processing and, 81
  conscious awareness and, 79–80
  experts versus novices and, 149
  good language, 2, 3, 100, 101,
    128, 169, 188

instruction analysis and, 30–3
learning from, 98, 101
learning strategy goals and, 43
retention and, 83
skills acquisition analysis and, 77–
  79
use of learning strategies and, 7
see also students
learning
  cognitive theory and, 217
  instructional model and, 187–88
  learners and instructors and, 98,
    101
learning disabled, 170
learning strategies
  application of, 52–53
  cognition in second language
    learning and, 10–11
  cognitive, 44–45, 49–52
  cognitive skill learning and, 19–20
  cognitive theory and, 1–2, 7–8
  cognitive theory and instruction,
    30–33
  conscious awareness of learning
    and, 79–81
  data collection and, 86–97
  defining, 99–103, 112, 113, 136–
    40, 220–22
  developmental delay and, 105
  developmental literature and, 105,
    106
  gender and, 106
  information acquisition and, 17–
    18
  metacognitive strategies and, 44,
    46, 47–49
  primary and support, 100
  research on, 3–8
  research on description of, 222–24
  research on applications of, 98–
    112
  research base for, 85
  skill acquisition and second lan-
    guage, 77–79
  social/affective, 45, 46
  strategy transfer and, 53
  study research and, 2
  task differences, 122, 127, 133,
    140, *142*, 143
  training program and, 53–54

validation and training and, 224–27

learning strategy classification scheme, 3, 4–5, 6, 7, 12, 42, 43–47, 103–104, 112, 113, 193, 197

learning strategy study (ESL student) and, 114–23

research and, 220–22

learning strategy studies
beginning and intermediate ESL students and, 114–23
declarative and procedural knowledge and, 145–46
experts versus novices and, 149
foreign language students and, 123–28
listening strategies and ESL students and, 128–33
longitudinal study of foreign language students and, 133–43
metacognitive and cognitive strategies and, 144–45
skill acquisition and, 147–49

LEP students
CALLA and, 190–204
see also learners; students

letter-deletion task (syntatic processing analysis), 64

lexical access, 34, 36

lexical retrieval, 63–64

linguistic knowledge
analyzed knowledge and cognitive control (Bialystok and Ryan) and, 59–63
cognitive skill and, 36–37
prior, 33
see also knowledge

listening
ESL study and, 173, 174
learning strategy model and, 208, 209
teaching, 211

listening comprehension, 47, 108, 163
foreign language instructor study and, 178, 179, 180, 185
learning strategy study and, 128–33
perceptual processing and, 34

technique for second language learning and, 6

materials for learning strategy training, adult language learners and, 204–10, 213

materials development (instruction), 157–60

memory
automatic processes and, 63
cognitive theory and, 18
complex cognitive skills and, 24–25
data collection and, 87
declaration knowledge and, 20–24, 68–73, 215
elaborated, 51
learning disabled program and vocabulary study and, 170
lexical access and, 34, 36
linguistic information and, 215
modeling and, 33
oral or written texts and, 34
procedural knowledge and, 24
recall of word lists and, 107
rote learning and, 163
second language learning and, 67, 165–66
storage of images in, 49, 50
word retrieval and, 82

metacognitive strategies, 11, 44, 45, 46, 47–49, 118–19, 120, 121, 126, 127, 137–38, 139, 144–45, 171–72, 197–98, 205

metalinguistic awareness, 71–73, 121, 162

metalinguistic skills, 59–61, 62

modeling (teacher demonstration), 161

models (teaching)
first language context of instructional, 187–90
learning style, 163
learning through, 32, 33
second language context of instructional, 190–204
staff development, 155–56

monitoring, 10, 106, 108
megacognitive strategies and, 48–49

monitoring (*cont.*)
    see also self-monitoring
monitoring strategies, 205
motivation (student), 160–61, 182,
    183–84, 185, 219
MURDER (learning strategy system),
    152–53

necessary conditions for learning to
    occur, 11–12

operational communication, 116,
    122, 124
    see also functional communication
oral language (teaching), 211
organizational strategy, advance
    planning and, 136

parsing, 34, 35, 50, 79, 162, 193
    listening comprehension and, 130,
    132
perceptual processing, 34, 162
    listening comprehension and, 130
phonetic coding ability, 162
planning, 106, 170
    activity (instructional), 157
    language production and, 41
    learning strategy studies and, 121,
    125–26, 127
    metacognitive learning strategies
    and, 47
    organizational, 135, 146
    research, 223
    strategies for, 205
preference rules (second language ac-
    quisition model), 11–12
problem identification, 139
problem-solving tasks, 18, 71, 97,
    106
    strategic training and, 7
procedural knowledge, 24–26, 58,
    145
production systems, 24–25
    see also IF-THEN production
    system
proposition, 34–35
propositional networks, 20–24, 69,
    84

reading, 31
    cognitive theory and, 65–66
    developmental literature and, 106
    elaboration and, 35
    learning model and, *208, 209*
    perceptual processing and, 34
    second language learning and
    learning of, 6, 166
    teaching, 211
    validation and, 109–11
reading comprehension, 18, 109,
    110, 157
    cognitive framework of language
    abilities and, 61–62
    first language learning strategies
    and, 167
    foreign language instructor study
    and, 178, *179*, 180–81, 183
    strategy training and, 7, 154
recall (word list), 107
Reciprocal Teaching program, 169
rehearsal, 105, 127
research
    background on second language
    acquisition, 57–68, 185–86
    base for learning strategy, 85
    bilingual students and, 164
    classifying language, 86
    curriculum, 159–60
    data collection analysis and, 86–
    97
    definitional and classification,
    220–22
    direct versus embedded instruc-
    tion, 153
    directions for, 83–84
    grouping, 163
    language aptitude, 162
    learning and, 187–88
    learning strategies and, 3–8, 151,
    170–71
    listening comprehension and, 129–
    30
    staff development, 155
    strategy application descriptions
    and, 104–107
    strategy definition and classifica-
    tion and, 99–104
    strategy description, 222–24

study and, 1, 2
transfer and, 192
validation of strategy, effectiveness
and, 107–12, 224–27
restructuring, 80
reading comprehension and, 66,
67
unitary process for learning concept and, 29, 30
retention and attrition of language,
81–83
rote learning ability, 163
rote recall, 106
rules
communicative competence and
grammatical, 75
deduction and language, 164
learning by formal, 27–28
learning second language and complexity of, 30–31
linguistic, 129
students and, 147
Russian, 123, 124, 125, 126, 127,
134, 135, 140, 141, 148, 176,
177

scaffolding instruction, 161
see also instruction
schema (schemata), 163, 167
declarative knowledge in memory
as, 70
language retention and, 84
propositional networks requirement for, 23–24, 69, 84
restructuring and metacognitive,
67
schema induction, 72
second language acquisition
analyzed knowledge and cognitive
control and, 59–63
attrition and, 81–82, 83
cognitive theory and, 1, 18–19,
54–55, 214–20
communicative competence and
procedural knowledge and, 73–
77
conscious awareness of learning
and, 79–81
data collection objectives and, 86

declarative knowledge and, 85
declarative knowledge in memory
and, 68–73
declarative and procedural knowledge and interlanguage concept
and, 58–59
domain-specific capabilities and,
69
formal rules and, 27–28
inductive and deductive theories
and, 57–58
information processing theory and
cognitive theory and, 63–67
instruction and cognitive theory
and, 30–33
language production and, 38, 41–
42
language retention and, 81–83
learning strategy research and, 3–
8, 43
linguistic theories and, 16–17
rate and type of language skills
and, 81
research in psychology and, 2
research literature and, 57–68
skill acquisition and, 25, 26, 77–
83
"techniques" for, 6–7
theoretical background on, 8–11
segmentation, 35
selective attention, 136, 178, 200
self-evaluation (student), 179, 181
self-monitoring, 103, 136, 142, 180,
182
see also monitoring
skill acquisition
CALLA and, 192
learning strategy studies and, 147–
49
second language acquisition and,
77–83, 84
stages of, 25–27
unitary process concept and complex, 28–30
social strategies, 8, 45, 46, 118, *120*,
121, *126*, 127, *139*, 197, *199*,
206
socioeconomic status (SES), 112
sociolinguistic competence, 74, 75

Spanish, 116, 117, 121, 123, 124, 126, 127, 130, 131, 134, 135, 140, 141, 142, 148, 165, 176, 177
speaking skills, 66–67, 167
  ESL study and, 173–74
  of foreign language students, 178, 179, 181–82, 183
  learning model and, 208, 209
spreading activation, 35
staff development, 155, 156
story grammars, 36
strategic competence, 74, 75
Strategic Teaching Model, 187–90
  see also models (teaching)
strategy classification; see learning strategy classification scheme
Strategy Inventory for Language Learning (SILL), 103–4, 106
strategy transfer, 8, 53–54, 153–54
students
  CALLA and LEP, 190–94
  foreign language, 133–43
  instruction and characteristics of, 160–65, 185
  learning strategy study and ESL, 114–23, 170–75
  learning strategy study and foreign language, 123–28
  listening strategies and ESL, 128–33
  reading comprehension and ESL, 66
  see also learners
studies; see learning strategy studies; research
substitution, 140, 179, 181, 206
summarization, 105, 127
syntactic processing, 64–65
syntax, language production and, 37–38, 41–42

teachers
  cognitive theory of learning analysis and, 31, 32
  learners and, 78
  learning strategies taught by foreign language, 175–84

student's strategy use and, 115, 118, 122
teacher training, 154–57
  see also models (teaching)
teaching; see instruction; models (teaching)
test-taking skills (teaching), 212
top-down processing, 36, 47, 48, 167
transfer strategy, 139, 148, 179, 182–83, 192, 206
  second language learning and, 216
transformation (language production stage), 38, 40, 41
translation, writing and language production and, 40
tuning, 80
  unitary process for learning concept and, 29, 30
typicality conditions for learning to occur, 12

utilization, 35, 193

validation, 107–12
  studies of, 224–27
videotaping, teacher training and, 156
vocabulary, 18, 25, 78, 107, 163, 181
  acquiring (in specific domains), 69
  Asian students and, 165
  ESL study and, 171-73, 175, 185
  learning of, 49–50
  learning disabled and, 170
  learning model and, 208, 209
  memory training and, 165–66
  teaching, 210–11
  technique for second language learning and, 6, 7

writing, 31
  language production and, 40–41
  learning model and, 208, 209
  second language learning and learning of, 6
  teaching of, 212
written texts, language comprehension and, 33–34

Printed in the United States
66243LVS00006B/31-69